FIVE AND A HALF
TIMES THREE

FIVE AND A HALF TIMES THREE

The Short Life and Death of Joe Buffalo Stuart

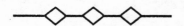

ALEXANDER STUART AND
ANN TOTTERDELL

HAMISH HAMILTON
LONDON

HAMISH HAMILTON LTD
Published by the Penguin Group
27 Wrights Lane, London W8 5TZ, England
Viking Penguin Inc., 40 West 23rd Street, New York, New York 10010, USA
Penguin Books Australia Ltd, Ringwood, Victoria, Australia
Penguin Books Canada Ltd, 2801 John Street, Markham, Ontario, Canada L3R 1B4
Penguin Books (NZ) Ltd, 182–190 Wairau Road, Auckland 10, New Zealand

Penguin Books Ltd, Registered Offices: Harmondsworth, Middlesex, England

First published in Great Britain by Hamish Hamilton Ltd 1990
1 3 5 7 9 10 8 6 4 2

Copyright © Alexander Stuart & Ann Totterdell, 1990

The moral rights of the authors has been asserted

Acknowledgement is made for permission to quote excerpts from
Amos and Boris by William Steig (Copyright © 1971 by William
Steig. Reprinted by permission of Farrar, Straus and Giroux, Inc.);
from *The House at Pooh Corner* by A. A. Milne (Copyright 1928 by A. A.
Milne. Reprinted by permission of Methuen Children's Books); and to United Media
Licensing for permission to reprint from the *Peanuts* booklet GB900-4

Printed in Great Britain by Richard Clay Ltd, Bungay, Suffolk

A CIP catalogue record for this book is available from the British Library

ISBN 0-241-12889-7

This book is for our parents,
Alice McCarthy
and
Eileen and Fred Stuart,
whose loss is as great as ours

Contents

List of Illustrations

Preface

This book is about five and a half years shared by three people, our son and us.

For almost two of those years, we knew that he had a rare form of cancer, yet despite that – perhaps even because of it – we look back on the entire period of Joe's life as one filled with immense happiness, hope and enthusiasm for living.

Without question, Joe's birth was the most thrilling event in our lives. He is – was – an only child; there may not be others. That we had to share in his death seems unbelievably cruel and unjust. Yet Joe's death was beautiful in its own way. Like his birth, like his life, like the incredibly powerful and entertaining character he became, it gave us courage and cut a clear line through so much of the rubbish with which we clutter and distort our lives.

Joseph Buffalo Stuart was our friend as well as our son. He taught us probably a great deal more than we taught him. If this book serves as the kind of handbook we hope it might – offering, simply as a guide, our responses to the shock of childhood cancer and charting the ups and downs of dealing with hospitals without being crushed by them – then it is also a testament to Joe himself, for he held us together when we were worn down, he made us smile when we wanted to scream.

We have chosen to use individual voices in our writing, rather than fuse together our experiences into an agreed 'we'. The three of us were very much a family throughout Joe's illness – for much of the time we felt like parts of a single, organic whole, each balancing the other – but childhood cancer places great strains upon the parents' relationship and many break up. For that reason, we feel that our individual insights might be more helpful than a joint statement.

There are a few, too few, books available to help when you are faced with the sort of experience we went through. No book, no amount of support from family and friends, no amount of counselling, no matter how good, can deliver what you really want at the time: for the facts to be changed, for the clock to be turned back, for the cancer – or whatever it is – not to exist.

This book is offered in that knowledge, but also in the belief that great sadness opens the doors to good things as well, and that if we can learn anything from being forced to confront our fear of death, it is that life deserves a whole lot more than many of us put into it. And our children deserve everything – love, trust, time – we can give them.

Alexander Stuart and Ann Totterdell
1 May 1989

A Note to Parents of Children with Cancer

If you are the parent of a child with cancer, especially one recently diagnosed, please know that Joe was unlucky in having a rare and particularly aggressive tumour type, which was not even the normal form of Wilms tumour, rare enough in itself.

With many types of childhood cancer there is an excellent chance of full recovery – although, of course, statistics are of no real value to you whatsoever: all you are interested in is your child's individual case.

We have met a number of children who have survived cancer and now lead full, healthy lives. We know of many others. May your child be one of them.

The Naming of Friends

Extracted from a taped conversation with Joe Buffalo, aged four and a half, remembering the names of his soft-toy and glove-puppet animals for a friend in America; March 1988:

ALEX: You could tell Cherie about your friends. Who's this?
JOE: Ralph Stuart.
ALEX: Ralph Stuart, the hedgehog. And who's that?
JOE: Melissa.
ALEX: What's Melissa?
JOE: A raccoon.
ALEX: [gruff voice] Hey, Joe, what about me? Coooookies!
JOE: Cookie Monster. And Parrot.
ALEX: Parrot – good name for a parrot. And what about downstairs, what other friends have you got? You've got friends like . . .
JOE: Snoopy, Snoopy. Two Snoopies!
ALEX: Two Snoopies. And . . .
JOE: A dolphin.
ALEX: Called . . .
JOE: Clarabel. And a rhinoceros called Jackie.
ALEX: A rhinoceros called Jackie. And there must be two buffaloes. What are they called?
JOE: Buffalo, Buffalo.
ALEX: Buffalo, Buffalo!
JOE: Two buffaloes!
ALEX: Two buffaloes. And what are you called?
JOE: Joe!
ALEX: And then what?
JOE: Buffalo!
ALEX: And then what?
JOE: Stuart!

ALEX: Joe Buffalo Stuart! But we also call you 'Trouble' for short, don't we?

JOE: [laughing] You're Trouble!

ALEX: I'm Trouble? No, you're Trouble!

JOE: No – I'm not a toy.

ALEX: [laughing] You're not a toy, but we love you.

1 *The Diagnosis*

'A whale sailing along in the water with stars' by Joe Buffalo,
aged four and a half, 1988

ANN I have a fantasy. In my fantasy Joe wakes one night
with a tummy-ache. I cuddle him and he settles down again.
The ache has passed. In the morning I take him to the doctor.
'Joe has a tummy-ache,' I tell him. 'It must be a tumour in his
kidney.'

Without argument our doctor sends us straight to hospital for
tests. He is operated on immediately, the cancer is contained, no
secondaries. There is, of course, a long period of uncertainty
after such a discovery, but Joe remains well, the threat recedes.
We all live happily ever after.

The reality was different. Joe did wake one night complaining of a tummy-ache. He did settle immediately he'd had a
cuddle. The pain must have been slight and he didn't mention

it again for a couple of days. Two or three nights later he again woke. Again the discomfort seemed minor and he settled immediately.

The next day I took him to the doctor. Joe had been to see our GP quite a bit in the past couple of months because he had been plagued with a series of colds and bugs. I had had great difficulty persuading him to take antibiotics which were of doubtful benefit – Joe had a normal three-year-old's dislike of medicines – and we had decided to let the bug run its course. Our doctor examined Joe thoroughly, including a great deal of prodding of Joe's tummy, which inspired a lot of giggling but no discomfort. My greatest fear had been appendicitis. I could think of nothing worse. The doctor explained that the glands in Joe's neck were enlarged as a result of his earlier ailments and that this had caused an enlargement in corresponding glands in his tummy. This was a common condition in children, could go on for some time and was nothing to worry about. No need for conflict over nasty medicines, the problem would sort itself out.

That evening a friend called to invite Joe to a last-minute party she was giving for her son's fourth birthday. I remember being glad that I had taken Joe to the doctor. If I hadn't reassured myself I would have hesitated to let him mix with other children just in case he had something infectious.

For the next week or so Joe seemed fine, he didn't mention the tummy-ache. And then it started again. He would tell me that his tummy ached; the attacks seemed very brief, maybe ten minutes, never prolonged, a hot water bottle seemed to help. I took Joe back to the doctor. Again Joe was given a thorough examination – the routine and diagnosis were the same, right down to the giggles. We went home but the tummy-aches continued. Joe seemed in lower spirits now and his appetite, never brilliant, was not quite so good. I phoned our health visitor to ask if she thought I should get a second opinion. She confirmed what my doctor had said – that the glandular condition was quite common among children. She thought that it was lasting rather longer than usual. 'Give it till next week,' she suggested. 'If he isn't better, then he could see a doctor at the clinic.' She was sympathetic about my concern. Joe was a bit ratty and low on energy: very typical, she said; he doesn't have anything very wrong with him but he is a little run-down, just treat him a bit like an invalid. A little extra babying.

The thing about children is that, when they are ill, the most minor ailments can seem very dramatic, very scary. Usually their recovery is equally dramatic in its swiftness. I wanted to hear that Joe had nothing wrong with him. He didn't really behave as if he had anything dreadfully wrong with him. He was a bit tired – but even that had a logical explanation. One day on the five-minute walk to nursery school, he had complained of tiredness. I had offered him a piggyback, something he wasn't used to and greatly enjoyed. It seemed that after that he always wanted a piggyback and we became quite a feature for a week or so on that walk across the Brompton Road through Montpelier Street and Trevor Place up to Hyde Park Barracks, which housed his nursery school. I thought then that he wanted the rides because they were fun – now I think his energy really was running out. But all that had been explained away.

Some days I have another version of my fantasy. The doctor diagnoses Joe's cancer on our first visit, but in spite of prompt surgery there are already secondaries. This time, the outcome of his illness matches reality, except that we spend an extra month tied to the hospital – an extra month of fear and lost normality.

A kinder fantasy not because Joe still dies, but because it removes the guilt, the appalling possibility that he might have been saved if I'd made more fuss, if I hadn't accepted so readily that he was all right, that it was something that would pass. If he'd been diagnosed faster. If I'd been psychic.

The reality is that I did what was reasonable at the time. When I took him to the doctor the first time, I thought I would seem over-fussy: children do get tummy-aches sometimes, with no dramatic consequences. I had no reason not to accept his opinion. Joe's colds had run him down quite a lot and I had almost got used to him not being on top form. Mixed up in this was a growing concern that he wasn't happy at nursery school any more. Around the time he was three, Joe had started asking for friends; he had a number, all children of our own friends, but none who lived close enough for regular play. Going to nursery school four afternoons a week proved a good compromise, and when Alex started working outside our home and had to cut down on his weekday outings with Joe, I found I appreciated the break. Then, just after Christmas, I discovered from Joe's teacher that he was being bullied by another child whose *modus operandi* was to scratch and run away. A complication was that the other child was a full year younger than Joe, and considerably smaller. I don't think he had any special grudge against Joe, it was just that Joe was the only one who didn't know how to deal with him. The teacher had promised to tackle the situation and as far as I could tell she did, because the scratching stopped, but the incident had been enough to disturb Joe's sense of security and our confidence in his happiness at the school.

So, mixed up with the concern about his health was the worry that it could all be psychosomatic. Part of me wanted to remove him from the nursery school, but my feelings were tempered by the fact that it was a very nice school and the worry that if I simply solved Joe's problem for him by removing him from the school, he would never be able to confront greater problems he might find in the future.

Sometimes I have the feeling that we loved Joe far more than other parents love their children. Common sense tells me that every parent feels this way. Another voice says perhaps it was true, perhaps some subconscious part of me knew it had to be more concentrated than most loves, that we were running out of time. Joe wanted to do everything with us, get up when we did, go to bed when we did – we both hated leaving him with babysitters and did it as little as possible. Joe went to dinner parties and restaurants with us; other guests who'd left their children with sitters thought we were mad, but we were happier that way. Alex and I had very little time alone, but we regarded it as a temporary, not unpleasant situation that would automatically adjust itself when Joe started full-time school. Even his four afternoons at nursery school had put bedtime forward to nine o'clock. We thought of it as a period of our lives which we might think of nostalgically when he adopted a more conventional timetable. We made no real efforts to change his habits. Then, I thought it was partly laziness on my part. It was easier to let him keep to the cycle that was natural to him, and created no problem since school didn't start till 1.15 p.m., than to struggle to make him conform to another schedule.

Now I wonder if some subconscious voice was telling me to let him get away with his possessiveness, telling me to make the most of the time we had with him. Now he isn't here any more, I'm glad. Glad I didn't work, glad I let him stay up, glad I did so much with him. Comparing my life with Joe to the lives of our friends who've opted to be working mothers and use nannies or minders, I probably spent as much time with Joe in his five and a half years as they will with their kids by the time they are leaving school.

I don't mean that to sound especially virtuous or judgemental. I considered working after Joe was born, but I am so bad at organizing myself that I knew I would never cope, that I'd end up failing in both areas. Also, I had what then seemed the advantage of being an older mother (I was thirty-nine when Joe was born). I'd had a good shot at working, I was ready for a break and was prepared to adjust my pace to a child's for a while.

ALEX For the first time in Joe's life, I was seeing less of him than I had. The five or six months before Joe's diagnosis were completely unlike any other period we had known as a family, and yet, perhaps for precisely that reason, came as close as we would get to what other families might call 'normality'.

I was miserable about seeing so little of Joe. As a writer, I had always worked at home, apart from brief periods of involvement with making films. Since Joe's birth, I had greatly enjoyed the freedom to share in his world, to break off from work to play with him if he wanted my attention. He would often sit on my lap while I made telephone calls. Even when he was a baby, I would take him out with me if I went to get pages photocopied and we might combine this with a trip to Hyde Park to feed the ducks or, once he was walking, to kick a football around or take a skiff out on the Serpentine.

Other fathers said to me, 'Don't you need space? Don't you need to escape?' But I didn't, particularly. I would get up early in the morning, to work before Joe woke up (he was always a late sleeper), or I would simply shut myself away, shut myself off to outside interference. My escape was in my head – I liked the physical proximity of Joe, the fact that if the day's writing went off course and started driving me crazy, I could stop and turn to him.

But for the months preceding what was to be the most horrific turning point in our lives, I had been working away from home, at an office in Covent Garden. I was also working on a novel, *Mackerel Sky* (later retitled *The War Zone*), which Hamish Hamilton had commissioned. This meant getting up at 5.30 or 6.00 a.m. to write, then leaving for the office by about 9.00, often while Joe was still asleep. In the evenings, work might delay me until 7.00 p.m. or later – and, most unusually for Joe, he was frequently sleepy now by 9.00 p.m., so that on weekdays I might hardly see him at all.

I knew that Joe had not been feeling at his best for some time, but now I discovered how difficult it can be for a father – or any working parent – to judge just what is going on in his child's life. We had all enjoyed a last-minute weekend break in Rome in December 1986, when a friend had offered us cheap tickets. We had all come back with colds, but while Ann's and mine had cleared up before Christmas, Joe had never been entirely well since. It was now April 1987.

In January, when Joe had been feverish with no obvious symptoms, we had taken him one evening to our local casualty department, at St Stephen's Hospital in Fulham Road. The doctor there could find nothing to worry about, suggested that Joe was perhaps just a little run-down, and told us simply to keep an eye on him.

Now, in early April, Joe had had a succession of colds and for two or three weeks had mentioned several times that he had a stomach-ache. Most of this I knew from Ann, but I also knew that when I saw him in the evenings and at weekends, he was not as lively as he had been.

Of course, with hindsight, I wish I had been working at home as usual; perhaps then, with both Ann and me to observe him, we might have been jointly more concerned. But would we? Ann had taken him to our GP's surgery twice and had followed that up with a phone call to the health visitor. What difference would I have made? Perhaps two worried parents might have achieved more than one, but perhaps not. Neither of us had the faintest idea Joe had anything seriously wrong with him, and one of the most difficult lines to tread as a parent is that between showing adequate concern and being vastly over-anxious.

On the weekend he was diagnosed, I had promised to take him swimming on Saturday afternoon. Joe and I had been going swimming each week since he was about two and it was something we loved doing together. That Saturday, I was perhaps a little concerned at the thought of taking him to a public pool when he had been complaining of stomach pains – both from the point of view of possibly infecting other children and of Joe's own immunities being low. In any case, my anxiety over the slow progress of my novel (due at the end of August) got the better of me and I told Joe I would take him on Sunday instead.

This change of plan troubled me. I hated breaking any bond with Joe, and the fact that I had told him we would go swimming that afternoon and then didn't left me feeling guilty. Ann and I had tried from the start to be honest with Joe and to treat him as we tried, mostly, to treat each other. A commitment was a commitment, no matter how small, and we hoped this was something Joe would learn.

While I was writing, Joe's stomach pains must have got worse because, by mid-afternoon, Ann and I had decided to call Great Ormond Street Children's Hospital to find out if they had a casualty department we could take Joe to for an examination. They didn't, and anyway, by 6.00 p.m., Joe was well enough again to want to go out on his bicycle, so he and I went round the block, his trainer wheels rattling along the pavement as we went past Harrods – which Joe had nicknamed 'The Train Shop', as a result of all the time he spent playing (rather than buying) in the toy department.

This swift recovery says something about how difficult it was to know how ill Joe was. The stomach-aches would come and go. Joe had always been a healthy child and not the sort to exaggerate anything. Ironically, his resilience may have made his cancer harder to spot – although, possibly not. Cancer, we would learn, is notoriously hard to diagnose early, because the tumour cells themselves don't hurt until they start to cause damage to or create pressure on healthy tissue.

That evening, Saturday 11 April 1987, we had one of our twice-weekly treats: a sandwich dinner in bed, watching television, with Joe snuggled between us. God knows what he made of it, but he enjoyed watching the Channel 4 comedy show, *Saturday Live* – especially Rik Mayall and Ade Edmondson's decidedly anarchic act, the 'Dangerous Brothers'. In fact, Ann and I were fairly careful about what we would let him watch, but Joe liked the energy of *Saturday Live* and it seemed a good deal less worrying than much of the children's programming. We were looking forward to seeing the sort of adult Joe would become; as it happened, we weren't to have the chance.

ANN The Sunday after my conversation with the health visitor, Joe's tummy-ache got worse. As usual it came on after a long spell of feeling all right. But he seemed more distressed than before and the pain didn't pass in the usual ten minutes or so. Alex had planned to take Joe swimming – a favourite outing – before we went to Alex's sister for dinner that evening. 'Joe, what would you rather do?' Alex asked him. 'Go swimming or see a doctor?' 'See a doctor,' Joe said.

The reply was so out of character that we leapt into action. Grabbing a quilt, his hot water bottle and a couple of toys, we got him into the car and headed for St Stephen's.

On the weekends, we learnt in due course, there is only one doctor on duty on the children's ward – a house officer who will have started her shift on Friday morning and will finish it on Monday evening. During the weekend she will sleep when she can and be available twenty-four hours a day for casualty patients and any children needing attention on the ward.

I doubt whether Lucy Moore had been lucky enough to be sleeping on a Sunday afternoon when she came to see Joe after an eighty-minute wait in Casualty. In situations like ours the wait seems unbearable, frustrating, unnecessary. After a few weeks of hospital life, you take a more enlightened view of the problems.

Immediately Lucy started examining Joe, she pointed out how swollen his tummy was on one side. It had not been like that when I dressed him only a couple of hours before. You couldn't miss a swelling like that. That must have been the moment when

we began to feel really afraid. Before, there had been the element
of raising a problem that had already been seen by our own
doctor – now something completely alien and frightening was
happening. Within moments of entering the examination room,
Lucy was telling us that she thought the problem was in Joe's
left kidney. She wanted him to have some X-rays right away.

There are times in all parents' lives when they have to hide
their fear from their child – when the stomach is dropping away,
the head spinning in panic, the scream starting, and you hear
yourself telling your child in a calm, cheerful voice that everything is OK, the hospital doctor is going to take some special
pictures to see what's wrong with his tummy.

We knew nothing about kidneys. Were we facing surgery,
dialysis, a condition easily dealt with or a lifetime of delicate
health? It had not occurred to me yet that whatever we were
dealing with could be fatal.

Later, we are taken up to the ward. There is no question of us
going home and coming back the next day. Already Joe has had
X-rays, the ward's consultant (who is officially on sick leave) has
said he'll be in first thing the next morning to see Joe, and more
tests are being organized.

The staff nurse who shows us our room is called Sharon. The
room is large, perhaps 28 × 10 feet, not what we expect; already
a few toys have been put on the bed. Sharon is friendly, sympathetic, concerned for our comfort; she brings cups of tea. Earlier
experiences with hospitals come back to me. The more the staff
pamper the patient's family, the more serious his condition.

Another doctor appears. Later we learn that she is Lilias
Lamont, the registrar on call that weekend, and that she has
come in after Lucy has telephoned her at home.

She too examines Joe. Alex and I are sitting close together on
straight-backed chairs; Lilias sits with us. Joe is sitting on my
lap, turned away from us, more interested in looking around the
room and out of the window. 'I expect you've already considered
that it might be cancer,' Lilias starts.

We haven't considered it, it has never crossed our minds. The
terror is a numbness of body and brain. I can barely think, I
daren't look at Alex, I have to keep control. Joe is still sitting on

my lap. From behind me Alex gives a single sob. It is enough to
unlock me, and I feel silent tears rolling down my face. Joe is
looking at us.

How quickly we rally for our children. 'Don't worry, darling,' I
say. 'Mummy and Daddy are just upset because we've got to stay
in hospital for a while and we'd rather go home.'

ALEX Your whole life can change in so few seconds. The
whole of Sunday evening became like a dream – too numbing to call a nightmare – but two particular moments stand out
as the points at which our lives shifted from what had seemed
like normality into a world of extremes: extreme love and extreme fear.

The first was when Lucy Moore pointed out Joe's swollen left
kidney. My immediate thought was, 'Dialysis!' In a fraction of a
second, my son, whom I loved more than anything in the world,
went from being a healthy child to someone who might have to
spend the rest of his life taking extra care and making regular
visits to hospitals.

But more than this, I was thrown back to a memory from my
childhood: a school-friend's father had died from kidney failure.
Already, before the word 'cancer' had been mentioned by anyone,
I was scared enough about the prospects for Joe if he were to be
left with only one kidney.

The other moment, of course, which changed everything was
when Lilias Lamont told us, with a degree of certainty which
unnerved me, that she thought it might be cancer.

We had just met her. I had no clear idea what a registrar was;
only later did I learn that she was senior to the house officers
and, in fact, next in line under the consultant. I remember her
manner at that moment, which was a mixture of cautious and
direct. If she was fairly sure of the diagnosis, she was less than
certain how to tell us. I remember her hair, which fell forward
on to her face at the sides. I remember her glasses, the unhappy
line of her mouth as she tried to make her words matter-of-fact
rather than alarming: 'I expect you've already thought about the
possibility that it might be cancer.'

To say that we hadn't would be a massive understatement. Of

all the fears we might have had as parents – busy roads being the worst, with perhaps child abduction the second – cancer had certainly never entered my mind. I know that I looked at Joe and at Ann and could almost see our lives together dropping away, literally sliding into some sort of shapeless, gaping hole. I cried, then tried to stop because I didn't want to frighten Joe. I felt sick, I wanted to vomit, and I think I may have rushed outside the room for a moment to catch my breath and try and stop the retching in my stomach and throat.

Back in the room, I looked at Joe and Ann and saw the best and most beautiful part of my life ending there. The most powerful sense was of denial, of not wanting to believe what I had just heard. This must be unreal, this must be a dream, this is something you read about, something from other people's lives, not ours – something so terrible it can only happen to those poor children you see on television, not our beautiful, wonderful son.

Cancer meant death to me. The only possible outcome in my mind at that moment was death. I thought Joe might be dead within the week, I literally thought that it might all be over within a matter of days, and yet, only two and a half or three hours ago, we had brought Joe to the hospital with what we thought was a bad stomach-ache. We were meant to be at my sister's soon for dinner.

In this sense, I think we were lucky to be told so quickly. You hear so often of bad diagnoses, of long periods of doubt and uncertainty when doctors aren't sure or simply make mistakes. Of course, a mistake might have been made here, and despite the hell it put us through, we would gladly have heard that it wasn't cancer after all. But we were grateful for how promptly and straightforwardly we were told, and if Lilias's choice of words hardly seemed adequate, I don't envy her the fact that she had to tell us at all. How do you tell anyone that their child has cancer? I would far rather have heard that I had it myself.

I know now that Ann's immediate reaction was different from mine, in terms of the shape of her fear. Her first husband had died of lung cancer; her father had also died of cancer. She knew the pattern it could follow, the months of treatment, the slow and possibly painful decline. She was afraid of a long, drawn-out period of suffering for Joe. I was afraid that I would lose him within a week.

ANN I can't remember exactly what was said in that conversation with Lilias. I do remember her being taken aback when she realized how unprepared we were for what she was saying to us. If I'd had any emotion to spare, I would have felt sorry for her.

She must have told us that Joe would have an operation to remove the diseased kidney; she may even have told us that the Wilms tumour they suspected had a very high survival rate. Whatever she said would have been expressed in a way not to frighten Joe, who was still sitting on my lap.

I can't remember, either, what Alex and I said to each other. Not very much, I think. We would each have known how the other was feeling, though not, as it turned out, what the other was thinking.

If we were to spend the next few days in hospital, one of us would have to go home and get a change of clothes for all of us. I was very eager to go, even though it wasn't very practical. We had come to the hospital by car, but I didn't drive, so it would mean a bus or taxi back to the flat, a short, straightforward journey. One reason I wanted to go myself was that I was convinced Alex would never find the things Joe and I needed; I doubt if I could have even decided then and there which clothes I wanted. I needed to be alone quite badly, too. I wanted to sag, to stop smiling, to think about what was happening. Alex must have been feeling the reverse because he agreed quite readily: he must have wanted to cling to Joe, liked the idea of having him to himself for a little while. And Joe can't have been feeling too bad, or he wouldn't have wanted me to go.

I explained to Joe that I had to get clothes and his pyjamas and toothbrushes. I asked him what toys he wanted me to bring back. The only thing he asked for was his Snoopy doll; I think he had already learnt that the ward had a playroom full of interesting toys, and wanted to keep his options open.

ALEX After Lilias leaves, the three of us are alone in the room for a while. We barely speak. I just want to hold Joe; I am terrified of losing him. The one thing that keeps going through my mind is that, if Joe dies, I won't hear him saying

'Daddy!' all the time. I love that one word, I love hearing his voice as he says it, sometimes playfully, sometimes crossly, but always reminding me that there is someone whose life, for the moment, is my total responsibility.

I sit in a hospital armchair with Joe on my lap, my arms round him. Part of how terrible I feel is because I have seen so little of him lately. This isn't so much guilt as a fear of losing him when, for the past five or six months, I have lost him a little already. I want to be with him; of course, Ann does too, but she offers to go back to our flat to get some clothes and things for Joe. This is also a conscious decision on our part: we know the hospital will let Ann stay tonight, but will they let a father stay as well? I just don't intend moving – they will have to make me go.

Before Ann leaves, I telephone my sister. It is now about 7.30 p.m. During our long wait in Casualty, before we saw Lucy Moore and everything changed, I had called Lynne to tell her we had brought Joe to hospital because of his stomach-ache and that we might be late for dinner. I am worried now about telling her that Joe might have cancer. Lynne herself has suffered for ten years from multiple sclerosis and the last thing she needs is bad news about Joe.

I use the pay phone on the ward and can't remember Lynne's number at first. Finally, I get through to her. I try to be strong but end up crying. I tell her that I can't face calling our parents tonight, but that I feel I should tell them rather than her. I ask if she's all right, then tell her I love her and ring off.

Ann goes home. I am worried about the state she is in – we're both in shock and I worry that she might just walk into the road in front of a car. I sit in the hospital room with Joe on my lap, quietly rocking him as he sleeps. My mind is not functioning in any normal way: I feel outside time, floating in a large room in which, an hour before, someone told me my son had cancer and which, twenty minutes before that, I had walked into for the first time in my life.

It is Sunday evening. Sunday evenings have a mood of their own and this one seems to take me back to my childhood. One of the nurses wheels a television set in on a trolley for me to watch. A fuzzy black and white picture comes on – a variety show. It is only when Jimmy Tarbuck appears that I realize it must be

Sunday Night at the London Palladium. I didn't know the show
was back on the air: strangely, it is something I remember (and
remember not liking) from childhood.

Now I watch it, hearing the bad jokes as if they were in a
foreign language. I would like to switch it off, but can't get up
without disturbing Joe, who is still asleep in my arms. Howard
Keel comes on and performs songs from *Oklahoma*. It depresses
me, yet also it makes me think about the millions of people
watching at this moment – all the families at home with children
who don't have cancer.

I sit, rocking back and forth with Joe, holding him, thinking
he might be dead before next weekend, and humming to him, for
some reason, the tune of Simon and Garfunkel's *The Boxer*. It is
not the kind of music I listen to any more, but it is a song from
my childhood, perhaps from other Sunday evenings when I would
listen to the chart show on the radio and mourn the loss of the
weekend. I hum it endlessly, almost numbing my brain with it,
but not escaping the thoughts everyone must have in this situation: 'Why did it have to be Joe? This can't be happening to us.'

ANN At home, I collapsed on the sofa for a few minutes. I had
had a bad headache all day and the events of the afternoon had
aggravated it to the point where I felt queasy and disorientated.
I was exhausted and confused, I couldn't put my mind to what I
should be packing. Underwear, socks, day clothes, night clothes,
toothbrushes, contact lens equipment – I knew I was going to
forget something. I made sandwiches and packed tea-bags, some
knitting, found Snoopy and a couple of other toys and books for
Joe, a book for Alex, a book for me. I was reading *A Maggot* by
John Fowles, and though Fowles's title referred to an archaic
use of the word, meaning a whim, I must have found the connection very disturbing, because I have never finished the book.

I know I was at home for hours, feeling leaden and indecisive;
I must have gone to the loo at least five times. My panic was
manifesting itself in a very physical way while my mind was
staying positive. On the way back to the hospital, carrying an
overstuffed holdall and with Snoopy under one arm, I went via
the postbox before hailing a taxi.

The letter I posted was our acceptance of an invitation to a friend's wedding reception a couple of weeks ahead. I figured that if Joe made a good recovery from his operation he would be well enough to leave for a couple of hours, with his grandparents as hospital babysitters. When the time came, Joe was indeed in good enough form to be left, but we didn't go: we would have felt too much like the Ancient Mariner.

ALEX After what seems like an eternity, Ann returns. We haven't eaten; she has made sandwiches, but each mouthful is hard to swallow. Joe stirs and seems quite comfortable with the idea of spending the night in hospital with us, even if it means sleeping in a large, metal-framed cot.

Ann has brought several of his favourite toys to help him feel more at home. Among them is a glove puppet of Cookie Monster from *Sesame Street*; this has never held any particular significance for Joe, but it will become Joe's constant friend and interpreter in hospital – in fact, Cookie Monster will become one of the family.

Without discussion, it is accepted by the staff that I am staying, too. Two somewhat battered zed-beds are brought into the room and made up. Ann's is placed next to the cot; mine, a little further away. We use the parents' toilet, which is outside our room on the ward, and clean our teeth at the basin by Joe's cot, barely aware of our surroundings.

I literally fall into sleep, exhausted by shock and glad to escape the day. At some point in the night, around 3.00 or 4.00 a.m., I wake up disorientated and look at Ann and Joe sleeping. I pull on my jeans to go out on to the ward to the loo. The night staff are on: different faces. One of them, a young staff nurse named Lyn Martin, whom we will get to know well, asks if I'm all right, if I would like a cup of tea. I say yes and sit at the desk while she makes it. She comes back and sits next to me. 'Are there any questions you want to ask?' she says. 'Everything,' I reply. 'I can't bear the thought of losing him. I love him more than anything or anyone. He is my life. Is there any chance at all that he might live?'

She is wonderful. While admitting that no one can know for

sure, she tells me that many childhood cancers are very treatable. She explains in basic terms the difference between radiotherapy, which uses radiation to treat specific areas of the body, and chemotherapy, which uses drugs to treat different or more widespread tumours. She tells me that Joe will probably have a plastic tube called a Hickman line implanted into him, to administer the chemotherapy drugs, and draws a simple diagram to explain how it works. Children, she says, have a remarkable ability to accept these things; at least the cancer has been diagnosed now and can be treated.

I return to bed feeling calmer and more hopeful, thankful that the staff seem so friendly and sympathetic, but most importantly that they are prepared to answer questions in a straightforward manner.

I manage to sleep for another couple of hours. It is only when I wake at 6.30 a.m. that I lose all sense, for a few moments, of what has happened. Briefly, marvellously, I believe that nothing is wrong. I have been in a deep sleep. My life seems to shift around me as I try to pinpoint where I am. There is some small sense of an horrific dream, something involving Joe, but it is just that: a dream.

Then the hospital room takes shape. I see Joe asleep in the cot, Ann on the bed beside him. The horror is a reality. My son has cancer.

2 Birth

Joe's birth announcement card, by Gray Jolliffe

*A*LEX The period leading up to Joe's birth was the most remarkable time of my life. I was very excited about becoming a father and accompanied Ann to the various clinics for check-ups and tests. The extraordinary sense of a new life developing inside her made the world seem somehow different and us feel very close – like every prospective father, I used to lie with my head on her belly, listening for sounds of movement, waiting for the magic of the first kicks.

At the ante-natal clinic we both watched with fascination on the ultrasound screen the little, peanut-shaped blip which would become our child. The sight of its tiny heart beating was almost too miraculous to comprehend, but there is an irony now in thinking about those pre-birth scans, since the last nineteen months of Joe's life involved a quite different relationship with ultrasound equipment to check for developing tumours.

Ann's pregnancy was exceptionally trouble-free, but as an 'older mother' (she was thirty-nine when Joe was born; I was twenty-eight) she agreed to have an amniocentesis, to test for Down's syndrome. We were both in a highly emotional state by the time the results came through, because we already felt so totally in love with the idea of our baby. We were absolutely convinced that we were going to have a daughter and had already chosen 'China' as her name, thinking it both delicate and strong. The amniocentesis revealed that we were going to have a son – so that, in addition to an overwhelming sense of relief that our child was apparently healthy, or at least free of one of the worst risks of disability, we had a large mental and emotional adjustment to make with regard to our whole picture of the future. We also had to find a new name.

ANN I'm not sure why the name Joseph appealed to me so much, but it had been in my thoughts for some time as seeming pleasant and elegant and solid all at once. When we found out that we would have a son, the name came immediately to mind.

We spent a great deal of time trying to think of a Scottish name we both liked, to perpetuate Alexander's family links, but none seemed quite right and finally Alex agreed that Joseph was the best choice. We knew that, whichever name we chose, we would have to like its diminutive, since there was no way of controlling what other people would call him. Until we decided upon Buffalo as a middle name, I had intended to use the full form, Joseph, but Joe Buffalo sounded so eminently right that he immediately became Joe.

The choice of a middle name had not been so easy. For a long time, Alex had been keen on Hunter (after Hunter S. Thompson), which I instantly disliked. As I had chosen the first name, it was tacitly agreed that Alex would choose the second, but I still had to approve it. When he started talking about choosing an animal name I wasn't too happy, especially when he started scouring *The Jungle Book* for inspiration. Ballou and Baghira did not appeal to me; nor did his next line of thought that, as Japanese culture was becoming so influential, a name like Takedo or Koji might be a good idea. Secretly, I thought this was all a cunning ruse to make Hunter seem more acceptable, and when Alex first suggested Buffalo, I didn't take it seriously, though it seemed more dignified than Ballou.

About a month before Joe's birth, Alex was invited to a film workshop in America and while he was away I thought a bit more about Joe Buffalo, and it began to sound rather nice. I thought too about how vehemently some people would say they hated their middle name and then, when pressed, admit to Robert or Charles or Andrew. If such reserved names caused so much dissatisfaction, why bother to be safe? I began to see that a child would probably love being called Buffalo and that, as an adult, he could drop it if he preferred. By the time Alexander came back from Rockport, he was committed to the name and I was quite happy to agree.

ALEX The choice of the name in itself is linked in my mind to the connection Joe's birth drew for me between life and death. During the two weeks I spent in Rockport, everybody I spoke to loved the name Joe Buffalo, which up till then had been only an idea Ann and I were toying with.

It was certainly an unusual name to think about for a British child, but buffaloes seemed to speak of freedom, of broad expanses of earth and sky, of a fierce yet non-aggressive independence. (Perhaps we should have dwelt more on the fact that buffaloes were slaughtered almost to extinction?) When Ann heard how enthusiastic everyone had been, we decided we would risk incurring Joe's later wrath and take a chance.

I had been elated throughout my stay at Rockport by the prospect of Joe's arrival sometime in August, and as Peter Werner, the director teaching the directing workshop, had with him his wife and their own thirteen-week-old baby, birth and life seemed very much in the air. Rockport itself is a very life-affirming place, a beautiful fishing town on the Maine coast, backed by hills and woods and lakes, and it was while swimming in a lake there one evening that I know I first accepted, completely, tangibly, the idea of my own death.

Part-way out in the lake, surrounded by trees and hills, with birds calling, a motorboat some distance off, the water warm and somehow reassuring, I thought about stopping – simply letting go. If death had come at that moment, if the motorboat had churned me up or it had happened some other way, I would have submitted to it willingly, happily. My son was not yet born, everything seemed possible; I was only twenty-eight, yet I think I could have embraced dying without complaint, I felt so much a part of some larger cycle.

Written down it seems a banal moment, yet I know that whereas I had thought often about death in the past, and had enjoyed predictable, adolescent suicidal fantasies while at school, I had never before felt physically comfortable with the idea of my body, and whatever it contains, ceasing to exist – at least as any coherent whole.

When Joe was born, that feeling was magnified. I watched him emerge from Ann, bloody and messy like an animal, and I felt my cells resound with the knowledge that we come out of something – not simply our mothers; something more fundamental, some collective pool of life or being – and when our particular part of the cycle is complete, we go back into it. I knew, at that moment, standing in the hospital room with Joe's mucous-smeared eyes and mouth peeling open for the first time outside the womb, that I would die one day, and so would she, and so would he – though I don't believe that I had any sense that he would die first.

I formed then a very loose and all-encompassing conception of continuity which helped me greatly when, five and a half years later, I had to come to terms with Joe's death. The concept of reincarnation as it is usually understood seemed too clumsy to me, too rooted in the persistence of individual souls or personalities. The feeling Joe's birth induced was of our indivisibility from nature, from the planet, from the cosmos. Whatever is constant is constant, but I don't believe it includes individuality. We are all a part of each other, and we are most alive at those moments when we discover that.

*A*NN The weekend Joe was due to be born, shooting stars were predicted. On the Saturday night, we went up on to the flat roof of the building in Soho where we lived. The sky was hazy, the stars barely visible. You never get a good night sky in the city – there is far too much reflected light.

We stood on the roof, looking at the sky and wishing we could be transported to some spot in the country where the night would appear truly black and the stars would be bright. The sky here was soft and mysterious, but it didn't give us the sign we were looking for. I wanted to see a shooting star and go into labour right away! I wanted Joe to be born on a night when there was magic in the sky.

We were in the middle of a heatwave: as I got heavier, I got hotter. I spent the weekend lying about hoping something would happen. Joe had actually been due on the Thursday, but I had known he would be a bit late. I thought of friends whose babies had been two or even three weeks late, but I didn't believe Joe would keep us waiting that long. I wasn't worried about the birth. I felt confident that it would go well, and I had decided that even if it were painful or difficult, I would be able to keep it in perspective. A few hours of discomfort in exchange for a lifetime with your child didn't seem a bad deal to me.

So as I waited for Joe, I felt calm and happy. I was looking forward to seeing him at last; I already felt as if I knew him. On Sunday afternoon my waters broke, and I waited for labour to start. I should have called the hospital right away, but I didn't, I had a horror of having the labour induced. Later the midwife was very annoyed with me about this, but, surprisingly, the male registrar who delivered Joe defended me, telling her I had the right to manage my labour as I wished.

One of the things I remember about the birth was that I had prepared sandwiches for Alex. I had a marvellous and endlessly practical (if not exactly feminist) ante-natal teacher who had said that if you expected your partner to sustain you during labour, you must sustain him. Her theory was that if a father fainted in the delivery room, it was more likely to be from hunger than shock. We arrived at the hospital around four in the morning, and I have a feeling that Alex devoured his snack right away, like a child eating the picnic before he'd arrived at the site.

It doesn't seem quite fair that the father gets a better view of the delivery than the mother. It wouldn't involve a great deal of trouble or expense for hospitals to place strategic mirrors over the delivery beds. Perhaps some do, but the Middlesex didn't, so that it was Alex who had the excitement of the first glimpse of Joe's head. I didn't see him until he had almost completely emerged, but I certainly heard him yell, even before he was out of me. Maybe he knew something we didn't, or maybe it was, more prosaically, a response to the misplaced forceps gripping him across his right eye. Whatever the reason, he was handed to me looking like a disgruntled little boxer, one eye screwed up in pain. His face was fine and pixie-like, his look was challenging.

It was only when a paediatrician had taken him back to examine him that I thought to ask: 'Has anyone checked that he really is a boy?' They had. He was.

During labour, a junior doctor had been eager for a forceps delivery, and had been overruled by the registrar. But when my temperature had suddenly shot up, the risk of Joe getting an infection made the registrar change his mind, even though the labour was proceeding well, if slowly. The slight concern about Joe meant now that he would be kept in a special unit for the first twenty-four hours or so, for observation.

Though this sounded rather daunting at first, it proved to be an extremely informal arrangement, and in practice I was able to have Joe beside me most of the time, returning him for brief spells during the day and at night so they could keep a constant eye on him. He was a perfectly healthy full-term baby in a tiny ward with very premature babies, a baby with a heart defect, babies with real problems. Seeing them and their mothers made me very grateful for my own sound child.

3 *Life before Cancer*

'A little sun creature' by Joe Buffalo, aged three years three
months, 1 November 1986

ALEX Sadness needs a perspective. I think it's very import-ant, even for us, to remember that before the diagnosis, Joe appeared to be a totally healthy child. There was some debate among the consultants over how quickly the cancer might have developed – the general feeling was that it was such an aggres-sive type, it might have taken hold in as little as a month – but Ann and I feel, with hindsight, that Joe may have been sick for perhaps the previous six months. In some photographs of that period he has a haunted look, and – again with hindsight – seemed to be getting thinner and looking flushed. But at the time, the thought of Joe having cancer would have seemed ridiculous, for he had lived his first three years avoiding almost all of the common childhood ailments.

My memories of those healthy years seem to run backwards. I can picture him in Hyde Park very easily; we spent a lot of time there. There was a section known to us as 'Daddy's Park' – around the road bridge over the Serpentine – and another which of course was 'Mummy's Park' – an area including a playground and part of Rotten Row and within sight of the Hyde Park Barracks nursery school, which Joe would briefly attend.

In summer, especially, Joe and I would go to Hyde Park virtually every afternoon. We loved taking a boat out on the water and often, even when he was quite small, Joe would sit in my lap so that we could row together. At the water's edge we had a favourite tree, a willow, which Joe liked me to row under so that he could grab hold of the overhanging branches, as if we were in a jungle.

If this sounds almost too gloriously innocent, let me add that Joe's other favourite position was sitting in the prow of the skiff, swigging from the can of lager I usually took along with us. He had developed a taste for beer – particularly American beer – at a decidedly early age and would not countenance alcohol-free lager.

He was good with a football and could perform a better drop-kick at three than I can now. Often the 'bigger boys', as Joe called them, would ask to borrow Joe's ball if we weren't playing with it for a moment, and I was always impressed by how twelve-or sixteen-year-olds would involve Joe in their games, and how well he would fit in, returning the ball when it was passed to him and running after them.

We played cricket once, with a junior cricket set some friends had given Joe for his third birthday, but he was frustrated by even the most basic rules and didn't really enjoy it. We often made friends with other children and parents in the park, and I remember one game of tennis, in particular, involving plastic rackets and a sponge ball, which Joe then wanted us to buy for him.

I also recall that he used to love to sit on my lap and steer the car round the car park while I had my foot lightly on the accelerator or brake – he did this from about eighteen months and could navigate the parked cars well by the time he was two and a half. He was adept at spotting a parking space: we often drove to Hyde Park, taking his bike or the ball with us in the car, so as to maximize the time on the grass.

ANN I always thought it was very important that Joe and Alex should do things together away from me. Not only did it give me a break, but it gave them a chance to know each other. Joe was very lucky to have a father who had the time to take him swimming and boating, to play ball games with him. I was lucky, too, to have these more physical aspects of Joe's life taken care of. I'm not especially fond of swimming or boats, and though I went with them from time to time, in order to admire new accomplishments or share a new pleasure, it left me free to get on with more domestic mothering, the feeding and washing and quiet cuddles.

We played cars, and laid out wooden train tracks, or got out the paints, but the truth is that I wasn't very good at playing, it was the companionship I liked. Before Joe was born, my picture of motherhood had always been the two of us sitting on a sofa reading a story. But for a long time Joe wasn't very interested in books. He owned a great many of varying kinds, all bought to try to capture his elusive interest, but few appealed to him.

I remember Alex reading to him when he was only a few weeks old. I was captivated by *Winnie-the-Pooh*; Joe, of course, just slept. He did have a few favourites – that Sunday, when I grabbed a few toys to take to the hospital, I must have packed some of his *Thomas the Tank Engine* books, probably *Where the Wild Things Are*, and definitely the superb *Amos and Boris*. Maybe it was because Joe was entering a more confined period of his life, or maybe he was simply getting older and more sophisticated, but we were heading for a new phase in which books finally played an important part.

When we first moved to Knightsbridge, Joe was nearly eighteen months old, and in far greater need of space to play and the company of other children. Eventually I found a playgroup that met three times a week in a local church hall and Joe and I started going there.

It took him a few sessions to adjust to the hurly-burly of being in a crowd. For our first few visits Joe took refuge in the Wendy house and insisted that I sat in there with him. One of the other mothers came to rescue me from our 'tea parties', so that I could have a real cup of tea, but this phase only lasted a short while. Joe was soon enchanted by the space outside the Wendy house, and since the group was run by mothers who all stayed with their children, he felt very secure.

It amused me that, although the group owned a good selection of toys, those he chose to play with almost always duplicated ones he already had at home. One exception to this was a toy garage, owned by the group, which he liked so much that I made sure he was given his own that Christmas. He still continued playing with the garage on our visits, and it was nice to see him rattling around, quite serene, not taking too much notice of anyone else. Some of the children were aggressive and snatched toys or pushed. I was pleased that Joe was neither an aggressor nor, at this time, at the receiving end of such treatment.

We went for just over a year, spasmodically at first, then more and more frequently as Joe became increasingly enthusiastic. We kept to traditional school terms and during the second summer, when he was nearly three, the June weather was so good that there was a marked falling off in attendance of children, who were taken to the park instead.

I felt that Joe had sufficient visits to the park already, and that the companionship of the group was equally important to him. One afternoon, only two parents turned up: Joe and me, and the organizer, Elizabeth, and her two sons. Elizabeth felt that she had no choice but to close early for the summer when support was so poor, and I sadly agreed with her.

One of the rituals of the playgroup was that we finished with a session of nursery rhymes and dances such as 'Here we go round the mulberry bush'. Elizabeth suggested that we did a couple of verses of the 'hokey-cokey' and called it a day. I danced in that strange state between laughing and crying. We must have looked quite absurd, two women and three little boys in the middle of a large hall, but it was touching too: the solemnity of our dancing, none of us entirely sure of the words.

I was sorry that the summer break had been brought forward; Joe needed those visits. It was around this time that he started asking for friends and we found him a nursery school which, because it was designed primarily for working mothers, did not keep conventional holidays.

ALEX It was some small consolation, during the months we spent with Joe in hospital wondering whether he would live or die, to think about all the things he had done in his life already. Not that lives can be measured by 'things done', but we knew how much we loved him and the fact that he had also enjoyed a range of experiences counted for something.

He travelled quite a bit in his first three and a half years, which was good since, once chemotherapy began and his immune system was knocked down, we never felt confident enough or had a sufficient interval between treatments to travel with him again. Our trips with Joe were always the more rewarding for having him along – and we wouldn't have dreamt of going without him. He was a good traveller and seemed to enjoy himself, but I wonder whether, ultimately, a foreign country is any more alien to a young child than his own?

When Joe was eight months old we went to the Caribbean. On Barbados, Joe drove around with us through cane fields, sat in the shade on his first sandy beach, and was happily pushed in his buggy most evenings to a restaurant called the Witchdoctor, where, being Joe, he seemed to enjoy tasting the rum punch and daiquiris as much as we did.

On an island called Bequia, Joe stayed in a cabana surrounded by banana palms, sailed on a marvellous old ferryboat complete with pigs and a goat, went in his first swimming pool, and was carried daily through the waves, across sand and over rocks and walls along the seafront, to the town of Port Elizabeth and its supplies of fruit and mineral water. The people of Bequia clearly loved children, and we were very struck by how keenly even the men offered to entertain Joe and push him around in his buggy.

Shortly after Joe's first birthday we spent two months in America, in Rochester, New Hampshire and Provincetown, Massachusetts. Part of that time we stayed up at 'camp' – a wonderful summer house belonging to friends, in the middle of a pine forest and about ten feet from the shore of the Great East Lake. There, in a setting right out of *On Golden Pond*, Joe saw and heard loons (the extraordinary birds whose cry is such an unforgettable part of that film), helped gather firewood (it was October), watched chipmunks run under the porch and rowed out with Ann and me on the lake to share the stillness and beauty of the sunsets.

ANN When Joe was three and a quarter we spent a weekend in Rome. Joe greatly enjoyed the flight and it seemed that, for the first time, he was really aware that he was in another country. The buses were yellow and the taxis were orange, a fact he never forgot. In all future games which involved travel – flying a plane was a popular one – he would always be going 'a Rome'. (For a long time he used 'a' instead of 'to', though this had no basis in a knowledge of French or Italian.)

Of course, we visited the Vatican and though we weren't able to see the Sistine Chapel, which was being renovated, we did see St Peter's. Joe was not at all daunted by the awesome vastness of the building or the astonishing pieces of sculpture. 'What do you think of it, Joe? Would you like it for your bedroom?' Alex joked. 'It's quite a nice room,' Joe conceded.

It was very like Joe not to be impressed. He was a child who liked to be in control. Later, in hospital, it was amusing to see how he would take charge of a situation, even when surrounded by doctors. He'd certainly had us under control since the day he was born!

ALEX There is a powerful element, in thinking about Joe's life before the cancer was diagnosed, of what might have been: other lives we might have lived.

When he was two and a half, for example, and our finances were in a disastrous state, we decided we would sell our London home and move to southern Spain, where we convinced ourselves life would be cheaper. I had failed, after *Insignificance*, to set up a series of film projects, and the plan was that I would now concentrate on writing, while we all enjoyed the sunshine and healthier environment and Joe learnt Spanish and English side by side.

Thus, Joe spent ten days touring round various Spanish properties, greatly enjoying, I think, the contact this afforded with Spanish children and the opportunities to play or to watch snatches of cartoons on TV or, an old favourite, *Sesame Street* – with the regulars, Kermit, Cookie Monster, Bert and Ernie, suddenly speaking in a language he couldn't understand but might one day.

We found one house, our dream house, in the hills behind a town called San Pedro de Alcantara, a little along the coast from Marbella. After endless inspections of new villas with their gleaming marble floors and manicured estates, this *finca* was a revelation. Perched on a rock ledge in a quiet, overgrown valley, with an orange tree growing right on the patio, it wasn't even officially on the market. It had been empty for seven years, its floors were cracked and crumbling, but the moment we saw it, we loved it.

We could picture Joe Buffalo growing up there, driving us crazy as he disappeared amongst the undergrowth (we had thoughts of equipping him with a walkie-talkie when he was a little older), enjoying the proximity of the sea – only a ten-minute drive or perhaps bicycle ride away – and generally having the kind of childhood that's alive to all the possibilities of the world.

It didn't happen. We could not sell our Knightsbridge flat and the Spanish house was, somewhat suddenly and mysteriously after seven years, sold. A year later, to the week, we were all spending the first of many nights in St Stephen's.

It is tempting to see this as some sort of intervention by fate. If we had moved to Spain, would Joe's cancer have been spotted? Or would it, we asked when we still thought he might live, have been spotted in time to save him? Of course, you might also ask, if we had moved to Spain, would Joe have got cancer at all? But that is in another realm of questioning altogether.

4 *St Stephen's*

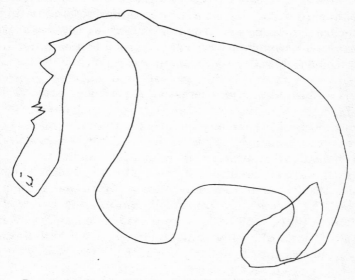

Dragon by Joe Buffalo, aged three years three months, 30 October 1986

MONDAY, 13 APRIL 1987

ANN When Joe woke that first morning in St Stephen's he had the air of someone with important news. 'I'm better now, let's go home,' he told me urgently. I pointed out that he had felt all right most of the time before, but that didn't mean the pain had gone for ever. He started gathering up his things. 'Let's go,' he repeated.

When the staff nurse, Sharon, came on duty she told me it was a common reaction, this need to escape. Or maybe Joe was convinced that the magic of a night on hospital premises was enough to cure him.

ALEX We were in a continual state of shock, certainly for the first week, probably for the first two or three. On the Monday morning I ventured outside at some point, around midday, to buy Joe a present. As I was about to cross Fulham Road, a friend approached, beaming, and said, 'Alexander! How are you?' I burst into tears and explained, shaking, about Joe. I then crossed the road to a gift shop, chose a soft-toy rhinoceros and returned just in time to find Joe with Ann in X-ray, crying because he was about to have a hypodermic syringe plunged into him.

The whole of Monday was a mixture of confusion, fear and a barrage of new faces. Finding yourself in an alien environment such as a hospital is a disorientating experience. You feel displaced, unsure of the ground rules, your position, your 'rights'. I remember using the parents' kitchen for the first time, which was reached through the playroom, and making Ann and myself a cup of tea in rather dismal institutional surroundings.

As with every children's ward, great efforts had been made to disguise the fact that Kenneth Grahame Ward was part of a hospital. There were large, framed oil paintings inspired by *The Wind in the Willows*. Children's drawings and paintings covered the walls. The ward itself was in a relatively newly-built section of St Stephen's (since completely demolished to make way for an unpopular mega-hospital), boxy but bright, with large windows and a view of trees and the skyline of Fulham and Chelsea.

The playroom was filled with toys and pictures, but the parents' kitchen attempted a slightly more serious vein, with posters advising mothers on breast-feeding and the importance to children of parental contact in hospital. Boiling a kettle and rinsing cups at the coffee-stained sink, I think a new realization struck me of what lay ahead.

It was partly a social awareness – that our lives would now be lived in something of a fishbowl, with the glass-partitioned plan of the ward affording little privacy even in our spacious double room. But it was also a huge uncertainty on my part of how much of a role I, as a father, would be allowed to play – having stayed one night, would I be allowed to stay every night? – and an anxiety about how much control over our own lives we would have while living in hospital, especially given the rather unorthodox timetable Ann, Joe and I were used to keeping.

Another question in my mind – though hardly a major one, compared to my fears for Joe's life – concerned work. I was due in the office, but had already phoned to explain what was happening. I was working for a friend, Mozafar Aminian, trying to establish a film and theatre production company and, still more ambitiously, to set up The One World Festival, a series of international charity concerts on a scale similar to Live Aid.

My wages were helping to rescue us as a family from a huge overdraft and mortgage, but I knew that money within the company was tight and that it could not afford to pay me if I did not work. So, already, even on the first day, the only solution that presented itself, if I were to stay constantly with Joe as I wished, was to sell our flat (which, a year earlier, we had been unable to sell), repay the mortgage and try to find somewhere to live with what was left.

We had no clear idea of how long we might be in hospital, but I know I was in no hurry to leave: given my perhaps unreasonable dread that Joe might die within days, the hospital provided a sense of security. Already, from the first ward rounds by Professor Wastell and his team of surgeons, and Dr Sinclair, the consultant paediatrician, we felt that Joe was going to get excellent treatment. There had been talk of operating that morning to remove the left kidney, but more extensive tests were required to check for cancer elsewhere, and surgery had been set for Wednesday.

At this stage everyone was unfamiliar to us, and it was an effort simply to put names to faces. I had spent little time in hospitals since childhood and was encouraged to find that many of the staff were my age or younger, but still the sense of anonymity – of isolation – remained. This, I suspect, is a major source of discomfort for most people: the monolithic force of any hospital suddenly bearing down upon your life, reducing you to a problem to be diagnosed, a condition to be treated, a file number. We were fortunate in that St Stephen's had a particularly relaxed approach to administration and presented a truly human face, but nothing alters the fact that you are in their hands – and any hospital, public or private, large or small, is bigger than you are.

Everyone on Kenneth Grahame Ward, however, seemed remarkably approachable and concerned for our welfare – not
simply Joe's treatment, but our well-being as a family. Joe's
middle name, Buffalo, amused people and I suppose Ann's involvement in journalism and mine in films gave us a certain novelty
value, although the ward's nurses and doctors had cared for the
children of well-known television celebrities, and I doubt that
they were particularly impressed. In any case, their treatment of
other parents, as we were to observe in coming months, was
uniformly sensitive and intelligent, and in no way obscured
their main concern – the children who were their patients.

In spite of this, we appreciated almost immediately – perhaps
without consciously recognizing the fact at first – that there is a
sort of inescapable class system on any ward which has to do
both with the hierarchy of doctors and nurses and with how
articulate you are. In the case of a children's ward, this affects
you as parents in terms of how much information you are given
and, ultimately, the choices you may have to make.

We asked endless questions and probed and pushed, but it was
not difficult, because the staff were enormously sympathetic and
quickly became our friends. I am sure they would have done
their utmost to inform us clearly, whatever questions we had
asked, but we soon learnt, as a generalization, that house
officers and experienced nurses often provide much fuller and
more comprehensible information than consultants. It may
simply be a matter of time – consultants tend to make ward
rounds whereas junior doctors and nurses spend whole days and
nights on the ward and can form closer relationships with long-
term patients and their parents – or it may be that they are
better listeners, in that they are less absolute in their opinions,
more open to challenge, more prepared to consider your un-
informed, perhaps intuitive feelings about your child's condition.

Much depends, of course, upon the individual, and we were to
encounter house officers, in particular, who were far better than
others – we were particularly lucky that the three on duty
during the first four months of Joe's illness were outstanding.
We came to depend on them for an interpretation in plain
English of some of the choices we faced, and felt reassured by
the fact that, from day one, we established – or were allowed to

think that we had established – an active role in deciding the course of Joe's treatment.

*A*NN The most immediate problem after the diagnosis was, what were we going to tell Joe? He was about to have a major operation, something completely outside his experience. The tangible parts would be the pre-med, the anaesthetic, bandages and, most in need of explanation, a lot of pain afterwards. Somehow we had to justify all this to him, and give him a picture of what was going to happen, as simply as possible and without frightening him. The concept of a bug was one he was familiar with from various minor ailments, so we told him that there was a bug in his tummy that was making it hurt, and that the doctors were going to get rid of it with what was called an operation.

The playroom staff were extremely helpful here and provided several aids – a couple of books about staying in hospital, including a scrapbook of photographs taken on the ward showing all the stages of preparing for an operation, and a cleverly constructed learning aid which allowed the child to uncover layer after layer of a cross section of the body to discover veins and arteries, the vital organs and the structure of the skeleton. Joe especially enjoyed looking at this and trying out a toy doctor's kit – stethoscope, blood pressure equipment, etc – on us.

We decided to avoid the fact that he would be cut open until later – the concept seemed too frightening for him at three and a half, expecially as he was not particularly articulate for his age, though I might have attempted an explanation if he had been older. Luckily Joe didn't ask exactly how they would get the bug out. We told him it would involve going to sleep for a while and that when he woke up his tummy would still hurt but in a different way, and that there would be special medicine to help stop the pain. It was hard to put it to him that the treatment would hurt more than the illness, but we did tell him that the pain after the operation would go away and then he would feel much better.

I felt comfortable about telling him this because, as far as the surgery was concerned, it was true. A more complicated outcome was still hypothetical. It's hard now to think that though our imaginations turned this into a threatening period, it was also the time when we were being reassured that the survival rate from a Wilms was over 90 per cent. Our favourite house officer described it to us as 'a lazy old tumour' which rarely had secondaries.

TUESDAY, 14 APRIL 1987

ALEX Tuesday, the day before Joe's nephrectomy (surgery to remove the diseased kidney), was exceptionally tense. In part, I was responsible for the tension: realistically or not, I thought it possible that Joe might die during surgery.

With such a thought in mind, Joe provided a remarkably poignant start to the day when, having been given sheets of paper and felt pens to draw with, he announced, 'When I grow up, I want to be a man who draws cartoons.'

He had never before offered any hint of what he might like to do as an adult – Ann and I had never prompted him on the subject – yet suddenly here he was, perhaps sensing our anxiety about the future, telling us of his newly-discovered ambition.

One of the nurses suggested that perhaps we should all leave the hospital and go out for the afternoon, take Joe to the zoo maybe, and I interpreted this as possibly a last outing. I don't think I voiced my fears to Ann, and certainly I tried to be relaxed around Joe, but my behaviour was quite manic.

I called some theatrical contacts and arranged tickets to *Starlight Express*, which was sold out. This put pressure on our trip to London Zoo, which was a favourite of Joe's, and meant that we dashed around, wheeling him in his buggy through the elephant house, past the monkeys and flamingoes and penguins, stopping only to push him back and forth on a tyre swing (he looks quite happy in photographs of this and I'm smiling). Then I drove, doubtless with enormous aggression, to the theatre in Victoria where the musical was playing, the consequence being that Joe fell asleep in the first half – which seemed disturbingly noisy, given our state of mind – and we left during the interval.

ANN Though the afternoon exhausted Joe, he brightened up enough to eat a good supper when we got back to the flat and be lively when Alex's parents (known to Joe as 'Gran and Fred') and my mother ('Nana') first arrived. The plan was that they would all come to St Stephen's with Joe and leave us there.

Joe was not so keen to go back, having made his getaway. He got his old cot quilt and a pillow, made himself comfortable on the floor, and ostentatiously settled down. His assumption that we couldn't take him anywhere while he was asleep was thwarted when Alex picked him up and carried him out to the car.

Back in his hospital room, both grandmothers produced presents they had saved till the last minute: a plane from Alex's mother and a Spiderman helicopter from mine. There was also a parcel waiting for him from Alex's work colleagues. The sudden holiday mood of gifts and family made the return more bearable and Joe said goodbye to his grandparents quite cheerfully.

Looking at our photographs of that afternoon, days later, was especially sad. The film had been started before we knew how ill Joe was, and the pictures were a link between an innocent time and the period of fear we had entered. There were shots of Joe in Harrod's ball pool, looking bouncy and happy, which were probably only taken a week or so earlier, then Joe in his hospital room and at the zoo.

Alex was upset that I had taken so few pictures of Joe. I remember Joe wanted me to photograph lots of animals to show his rhinoceros – it was a project to stop him minding that the new toy he'd wanted to bring with him had been left behind.

I didn't have the same sense as Alex that it might be our last family outing. I had forced myself to think that everything would be all right because cancer had become so much more treatable. Even my doubts didn't create any feeling of finality, because experience had taught me that death would probably not come quickly – that whatever the outcome, we still had time together.

WEDNESDAY, 15 APRIL 1987

ALEX The only way I could deal with my fears surrounding Joe's operation on Wednesday was by forcing myself into a mood of enormous fatalism. I don't believe in simply letting life happen, but, as far as surgery was concerned, there was nothing I could do. Joe would either die or live; it was not in my hands.

ANN We had promised Joe that we would all be together during his illness, that he would never be left alone in hospital. He was not a very independent child, and he needed the security of having us with him, but I think the promise was as much for our sake as his. We couldn't bear to let him out of our sight, and were concerned that something that frightened or worried him might happen while we weren't there to give him moral support. Even routine observations like taking his blood pressure or temperature were disturbing at first. Children who are old enough to have settled into full-time school may take these things in their stride more readily, but Joe had not reached that level of self-assurance.

The marvellous thing about St Stephen's was the effort staff made to make things easy for Joe. Not just on the children's ward, where a sensitive approach might be expected, but in departments more used to dealing with adults who understood what was happening than with the nebulous fears of small children. Later, when I'd experienced more hospitals, I began to wonder if staff who rarely encountered very sick children actually had a heightened level of consideration – people who routinely dealt with children sometimes seemed comparatively desensitized.

We were allowed to accompany Joe for X-rays, scans and consultations without question. The first big concern was how would he get through the operation? Would he have to part with us on the ward, or could we go with him to the operating theatre? We were impressed and reassured that Joe was to have all the top people for the nephrectomy. Not only was Professor Wastell himself going to perform the operation, but Joe was to have the senior anaesthetist, Dr Plumbley.

When Dr Plumbley had come to see us on Tuesday, he had told us that Joe would have a pre-med on the ward. This would be a mild sedative to calm him down, and might well mean Joe was unconscious before he left his room. But what if he wasn't? Miraculously, Dr Plumbley asked if I would like to go with Joe to the operating theatre. It seemed an unbelievable piece of luck that he should volunteer this. He must have decided I would behave reasonably, because he added that he didn't always allow it. Later, he told me that while some parents had a calming influence and helped his job go smoothly, some had the opposite effect.

The pre-med was going to be an injection, and I made a mistake that I would never repeat. When the time came for it, early on the morning of the operation, Joe was fast asleep. I suggested the injection be given while he slept. My logic was that though it would wake Joe, it would be over before he was properly conscious, it would hurt less because he'd be completely relaxed, and he would be spared the anticipation which is usually the worst part of having an injection. Unfortunately he was very distressed at being woken up so unpleasantly, and I was consumed with guilt. In future I made sure he was woken for injections, even though it then involved a period of coaxing him to have what he called 'a neegle'.

He was very drowsy when the time came to take him downstairs to surgery. Alex and I both went with him, squeezing into the lift with the two orderlies in charge of the large trolley Joe lay on. Alex waited with Joe while I hurriedly prepared to go into the sterile area – changing all my everyday clothes for a gown, cap and sandals.

There were a lot of people crammed into the little ante-room where he was prepared for the operating theatre, and their faces were all hidden behind masks. Gradually I began to recognize the ones who had visited Joe on the ward. I talked to Joe soothingly, explaining that we would be waiting for him when he woke up, and when he was clearly unconscious I slipped away.

It is an extraordinary feeling to leave your child in the hands of people who are going to cut him open. Joe looked so small and defenceless, but I feared the cancer inside him more than I feared what the surgeons might do. I didn't doubt that he would survive the actual operation, my fear was that the tumour might not be completely removed, or that there were already secondaries. I'd always felt that the immediate danger during an operation was a mishap with the anaesthetic, but our contact with Dr Plumbley had left me completely confident in him.

Alex and I sat in Joe's hospital room feeling totally at a loss. I think that at some point we went to the canteen, the first time we'd been there together. And we drank a lot of tea. I have some memory of washing cups in the kitchen and a sympathetic sister asking me if I was trying to keep busy. We'd been told that it would take about an hour and a half and we were watching the clock all the time. Did we have time to go for breakfast? Go to the loo? Have a shower? We wanted to be ready the moment Joe was out of the operating theatre. I hoped he would still be unconscious when they brought him back. I didn't want him awake and confused in a strange place.

For the projected ninety minutes of the operation we felt reasonably calm, just wanting it to be over, to have Joe back in the room. When that time was up and there was no news, our anxiety became more concrete. The sister on duty called the theatre and came in to tell us that they were still operating. This seemed terribly ominous, but she explained that because children's bodies are smaller the work is more intricate and can take much longer. Even the most experienced surgeon might underestimate how long an operation would take unless he was used to operating on children.

With the call to say that Joe was in the recovery room came the offer that one of us could be with him until he regained consciousness. Until the doctor was sure he was coming round from the anaesthetic satisfactorily, Joe couldn't come back to the ward.

We raced to Recovery – I to put on sterile clothing again, and Alex to wait outside. Joe was drowsy when I saw him, too sleepy to be intimidated by the large room he was in, lined with trolleys bearing other patients in various stages of consciousness. He had a drip attached to his left arm, and a drip in his nose. He looked pale and fragile, but he was alive, the hateful tumour, the thing, was out of him.

A nurse was with him, checking his vital signs, waiting for an indication of alertness so that Joe could be allowed back to the ward. A doctor came and injected a top-up of pain-killer which would also help Joe sleep through the first, and worst, part of the discomfort. It seemed paradoxical to give him something to make him sleep when we were waiting for him to come round, but controlling the pain was more important than getting him out of Recovery. In the interval before the new injection took hold, Joe stirred and recognized me. It was enough. When we wheeled him out, Alex was waiting for us, and we returned thankfully to Kenneth Grahame Ward, all together again.

ALEX When it was over, when we brought him back to the ward, I simply felt relief. The wait, while he was operated on, had seemed interminable. Now that he was back with us, I wanted to think that the cancer had gone, we were through the worst part, but the sight of him – a scraggly little boy with a naso-gastric drain in his nose and an intravenous drip in the back of his hand – somehow didn't permit such optimism. He had survived the first round, that was the main thing. I felt we were all living from moment to moment.

THURSDAY, 16 APRIL 1987

ALEX Joe seemed to recover well from the nephrectomy and by Thursday afternoon the naso-gastric drain had been removed from his nose, though the drip was still attached to his hand. We were told that the operation was considered a success, that his left kidney had been removed 'cleanly', along with the adrenal gland and a lymph node which had appeared enlarged, and that hopefully no tumour cells remained.

Now we were to wait for the histology – the analysis of the tumour – which would tell us more about the type of cancer Joe had. Tomorrow was Good Friday; Ann and I were anxious because the pathology laboratory was closed for all but emergency work over the Easter weekend and so the histology would be delayed. We were told that it would take some days in any case, but the wait seemed unbearable. We had to keep reminding ourselves that what we knew didn't necessarily alter reality – if Joe was free of cancer, our knowing or not knowing for a few

more days made no difference except to our emotional stability.
If, on the other hand, the cancer had somehow spread, we
wanted (and we didn't) to know as soon as possible, so that some
kind of treatment might be started.

*A*NN As Joe spent more time awake, not very comfortable at
first and in need of soothing, I discovered a problem I had
not anticipated.

Joe had actually been observed sucking his thumb in my
womb, and had been a dedicated thumb-sucker since birth. As he
got older it had phased out until he only sucked his thumb if he
was very sleepy or upset; during his time in hospital it had
naturally increased. Though I thought of myself as an attentive
mother, I had never noticed that Joe only used his left thumb.
And the drip, complete with an inhibiting splint, was on his left
arm. Joe was very upset at not being able to get at his thumb,
and adamant that the right one was no substitute. Fortunately
the drip was taken down after about thirty-six hours, but I was
very sad that I hadn't had the foresight to protect this important
comfort habit.

Because making phone calls from a hospital public phone is
complicated and time-consuming, Alex asked his father to call
a number of our friends with the news that Joe was recovering
from the operation. In one or two cases, because everything
had happened so fast, people were not even aware that he was
ill. The tension of making the calls, with the necessary explanations, had obviously been quite an emotional strain. Alex's
mother, Eileen, told us how distressing the calls had been for
Fred, and we became aware of how careful we had to be with
our immediate family. Protecting Joe's physical and mental
well-being had been our priority, but there were so many other
people to consider. Joe was not just an only child, but an only
grandchild; our parents needed to be kept informed and
involved.

When friends got in touch they wanted to know the whole
story; going over and over how it had all happened was indeed
exhausting. We also had to be careful what we said in Joe's

hearing, as we wanted him to maintain a positive attitude. We felt as if we had to take care of everyone – but how could anyone take care of us?

*A*LEX I was worried about the strain Joe's illness was placing on all our immediate family – I think the frequent visits were as much to comfort them as to entertain Joe Buffalo – but I was particularly troubled by the effect on my sister, Lynne.

I felt the sight of him on a drip and looking rather weak saddened her not simply because she loved Joe, but because she knew how treacherous and fragile life could be. She had been struck by multiple sclerosis shortly before her twenty-first birthday, but on top of that had suffered a massive (and apparently unrelated) stroke three years later, which had placed her in a coma for three weeks, after which she virtually had to learn how to walk and talk again. I think as much as anything she survived as a result of her husband Peter's love for her, together with her own strength of will and the decidedly black sense of humour she developed about life. Joe's condition now perhaps made it more difficult for her to find any humour in her own situation or in his.

On Thursday night, Ann was extremely tired. Joe was now in a small observation cubicle opposite the nurses' station, with barely enough room for his cot, let alone two zed-beds, though we managed to squeeze them all in. One of the nurses, Stephanie, suggested that Ann should move to an adjoining room, where she could have at least one night's sleep undisturbed by regular checks and changing the bag on Joe's drip. Ann was reluctant to go at first, but I encouraged it, since she did look very ragged and because I felt it would give my continuing presence on the ward at nights greater legitimacy.

Paramount in our concern over Joe was that all of us should be allowed to stay together on the ward as a family. We realized that this sometimes made life more difficult for the staff, simply in terms of having access to Joe's bed, or, for example, for the domestics cleaning the floor, so we did everything we could to ease the situation. We made our beds and folded them up as quickly as we could in the mornings and generally tried to keep

'Two wonderful birds' drawn by Joe Buffalo, aged three years
eight months, at St Stephen's, 22 April 1987

out of everyone's way. Later, when Joe's empire of toys and ours
of clothes and books had grown, we even began washing the
floor ourselves, often with Joe's help – though this was perhaps equally motivated by our minimal confidence in the
thoroughness of the cleaning. In any event, by the end of the first
week or so, my fears of being told I could no longer stay all the
time were finally overcome. I seemed to be accepted as a
permanent fixture.

FRIDAY, 17 APRIL – MONDAY, 20 APRIL 1987

ALEX I have always hated Easter, and this certainly wasn't
one of my favourites. Joe seemed very perky again and the
weather was sunny and somehow hopeful, but the Easter weekend stretched before us as a dead period, delaying everything we
thought so vital.

The ward was fairly quiet, yet had a festive air. Joe received quite a few Easter cards, which we stuck up on the walls and on the locker next to his bed, along with the numerous Get Well cards which friends were sending. The nurses seemed stunned by the number of cards he got, and we, in turn, were surprised that they thought this out of the ordinary – we would have expected even a child with something as straightforward as a broken leg to be deluged with cards, but apparently most children were lucky to get one or two.

Joe was fortunate, too, in having many visitors, and we were relieved that the ward placed no restrictions on when people could visit or how many could come at one time. The visitors helped reduce the strain of spending day after day in the same room, though I think the three of us were so happy to be together that this was not as great as it might have been.

We tried not to overwhelm Joe with presents, but inevitably our family and friends brought him gifts and we found ourselves using particularly the bookshop just across Fulham Road to find things to keep Joe occupied. I have in front of me as I write this a photograph of Joe in his hospital bed 'boxing' with a pop-out prize fighter from a marvellous Jan Pienkowski book bought around this time, *Little Monsters*.

*A*NN An aspect of post-operation life that I hadn't considered was that Joe was much too vulnerable to be cuddled. He had a long incision from his chest to below his navel which was very sore at first. It was hard that, at a time when I most longed to have him close, I had to content myself with touching him very carefully when I kissed him. There is something very special about the warmth and touch and smell of your own child. It was wonderful when his pain had receded enough for me to have him on my lap and give him the first big hug.

When the dressing was removed from Joe's chest and he saw his scar for the first time, he seemed quite shocked. I wondered if I should have tried to discuss it earlier, but telling him about it when he could actually see what I was talking about seemed less disturbing. I said that the doctors had had to cut him to get at the bug, but that they had sewn him up again and that was why he'd had the bandages.

He seemed quite satisfied with this explanation, particularly when I showed him the scar I had across my midriff from an earlier gall-bladder operation. I would have been happy enough with his adjustment, a couple of days later, when he started showing off his scar to visitors, were it not for the fact that he thought it would be a good idea if I showed people mine at the same time. As Lilias, the registrar, observed, my surgeon's work wasn't as impeccable as Professor Wastell's, and my stomach wasn't too streamlined either.

We had asked very early on if we could talk to the family psychiatrist attached to the hospital. We wanted advice on how to approach this sort of situation, as well as how to deal with the question of the cancer itself, but by the time we met her we had had to decide for ourselves. Maybe she would have suggested different tactics, but probably our knowledge of how Joe would react to the information he needed was the most important element.

ALEX I kept telling myself that the one good thing about Joe's illness was that it had freed me from the office – that, despite our continuing financial problems, I could be back with Joe Buffalo, spending whole days with him as I'd used to. Of course, the threat of losing him forever destroyed any real comfort I might take from this, but at least the past two years of lack of income and ever-increasing bank debts were put firmly into perspective. Nothing mattered now except whether Joe lived or died.

After the tension and activity of the first few days in hospital, the Easter weekend was at least a chance to enjoy being with him. We did a lot of drawing together and played with his new toys, inventing games with the Spiderman helicopter and his plane that could be played on the bedcovers. We had brought Joe's own child-size duvet on to the ward, with his favourite aeroplane and Snoopy duvet covers, and together with familiar toys and books, we managed to pretend that the hospital room was simply an extension of home. Long hours of sitting by the bed prompted new ideas and one morning Joe and I cut up several small, one-serving breakfast cereal boxes to make a cardboard sculpture of Frosties and Rice Crispies characters which I still have.

My own state of mind over the weekend was brought home to me when I was stopped by the Regent's Park police for speeding after taking Ann's mother home. I had had no idea how fast I was going, but my general anxiety must have been apparent because I had barely even begun to explain why I was so upset when the police practically apologized for stopping me.

TUESDAY, 21 APRIL 1987

ANN On the Tuesday after Easter, Alex went to the office to find out how everything was going. While he was out Dr Sinclair appeared with Anna, the playworker, and asked if we could talk. Anna amused Joe while we went into the tiny doctors' office. He told me that a test taken during Joe's operation had shown that there were microscopic tumour cells in his bone marrow. Tension is such a physical thing, a stiffness, a heaviness. I felt cold, rigid. I wished that Alex were with me, I wished we could have heard it together. I didn't know what to ask, I'm not sure I was capable of speech. Dr Sinclair said that they would speed up the start of chemotherapy. It had already been planned as a formality, now it was a necessity.

I tried to attach some importance to the word 'microscopic'. It suggested a minimal amount of cells that could be mopped up in no time. But any number of cells is bad news – microscopic or massive, the amount is academic. Cells multiply, a few become many, they spread, they go out of control.

If Joe was to stay positive and happy I had to keep a confident exterior, so I forced myself to look unworried when I got back. The time when he knew that doctors' conversations usually had a direct effect on him had not yet come, so he asked no questions. Alex still wasn't back and his parents were due to see Joe. Their visit was a strain, because all I could think about was sharing the news with Alex, there was no question of telling anyone else before he knew. I could call him at the office, but knowing his state of mind I was reluctant to give him news over the phone which could affect his concentration when he was driving back.

Alex's parents had left by the time he returned. I still couldn't tell him immediately. First he needed to see that Joe was all right, spend some time with him after their parting. Finally, when Joe was busy with a toy, I was able to draw Alex aside and tell him quietly what Dr Sinclair had said.

ALEX I felt terrible that Ann had had to deal with such bad news without me. It seemed ironic that while I was at the office telling everyone that Joe's kidney had been removed successfully, hopefully with no trace of cancer left, and that there seemed every chance he would live, Ann was being given information which made the long-term prospects more doubtful.

I don't think I understood fully at first what microscopic tumour cells in the bone marrow really meant. I knew that anything cancerous in the marrow was dangerous, since it was effectively an express route to the rest of the body, but like Ann I seized on the word 'microscopic' and tried to convince myself that this made the problem more treatable.

That evening, one of the house officers, Simon Horsley, very kindly asked if I would like to talk to him about the implications. Ann decided to stay with Joe while I went into the doctors' office with Simon. He was very sympathetic but also quite blunt about the situation: the fact that the 'rogue' tumour cells were in Joe's marrow meant that the cancer could literally spread anywhere. Chemotherapy might help, but I got the impression that Simon felt Joe's prospects had been vastly diminished by this news.

Again I felt as if I were living in a dream. The details of the doctors' office seemed to float in my mind as I thought about what this meant. Simon was one of our favourite doctors, a few years younger than me, with great style, a good sense of humour and a sensitive but no-nonsense manner with children. In spite of this, I know I had to fight against directing my hostility at him. 'You don't care,' I thought. 'He's not your child, he's just another patient, you don't give a damn.' I knew this wasn't true, but it was as if he was taking our hope away. Perhaps it's easier to hear bad news from doctors you don't like; perhaps then you can really hate them.

WEDNESDAY, 22 APRIL – THURSDAY, 23 APRIL 1987

ANN Before chemotherapy could start, Joe was to have a Hickman line implanted. This was a fine plastic tube which would be inserted into a vein and taken down to his heart. At the exterior end there would be a clamp and a cap which could be removed so that drugs could be injected or blood taken out. It would involve another operation and more explanations for Joe.

By then he had already had several encounters with needles; he'd needed radio-opaque fluid injected for certain scans, and he'd had blood samples taken. He didn't enjoy this at all, so the basis of our explanation of the Hickman line was that though it involved another operation, it would have the advantage of meaning no more needles.

ALEX On Wednesday morning, exactly a week after his nephrectomy, Joe was well enough to be wheeling about the ward on a small wooden tricycle borrowed from the playroom. We had been told that children had remarkable recuperative powers and, despite Tuesday's news, we clung to the fact that he seemed so lively and happy as a sign that perhaps, somehow, Joe would manage to beat cancer.

He was much too big for the tricycle but he loved scooting along on it using his feet to propel himself, and early on Thursday morning, with his Hickman line operation due at 10.30, Joe was back on the trike, full of energy, taking me on a tour of St Stephen's.

Just off the reception area was a covered walkway with several ramps, one of them quite steep. Joe free-wheeled down this repeatedly, laughing and shouting, with me running alongside until I had to admit exhaustion. He probably endangered several passers-by in the process and certainly risked tearing his nephrectomy scar open if he fell off, but for a child with a life-threatening disease who was about to have his second operation in eight days, he seemed incredibly content.

ANN We had seen a junior anaesthetist the day before, but while Joe was in the bath, being rendered clean if not exactly sterile for his operation, Dr Plumbley appeared. He told us he had decided to look after Joe himself – another example of the involvement shown in Joe's case – and that he had come to give Joe his pre-med. It was one he could take orally, so Joe swallowed it sitting in the bath surrounded by toy boats and ducks. This was his first bath since his operation, a shallow one to protect his newly uncovered scar.

This time the routine for the operation was familiar. Again I was allowed to be with Joe until he'd been anaesthetized, and this time the operation, a relatively simple one, took only an hour. Joe was very slow to arouse in Recovery and after about half an hour Alex was sent in to join us. We sat on either side of Joe's trolley, talking to the nurse who was trying to revive Joe by massaging his ears. Though there seemed nothing wrong except that he was still heavily sedated, we felt very uneasy at seeing Joe unconscious for so long. It was two hours before we could take him back to the ward. I had remembered to ask for the drip to be attached to his right arm this time, but there had been no need: the drip was connected to Joe's newly installed line – another advantage of the Hickman line.

ALEX The idea of Joe having a plastic catheter in him for what might be as long as a year seemed strange and a little disturbing at first. When Lyn Martin had drawn her explanatory diagram for me on our first night in St Stephen's, I could not imagine how having a tube come out through a hole in your skin could be anything but a persistent irritant, but she assured me that both children and adults adapted to them very readily. I was worried that Joe, who had a fondness for tugging at things, might pull it out, but this was taken into account when positioning the line. For precisely this reason, many children have their Hickman line at the top of their chest, with the exterior part taped over their shoulder, but Joe's emerged from a site just under his right arm, with the end taken round his back.

The line itself had to be flushed regularly with a sterile saline solution called Hepsal, to prevent blood from clotting it, while the entry site had to be kept clean and sterile. Although it was covered with a large waterproof dressing, this meant no deep baths and no swimming. I wondered how safely I would be able to lift or hug Joe; I also wondered if I would ever swim with him again. This was to become a recurrent thought, as I felt denied the swim we had been planning on the afternoon we first took Joe to Casualty.

ANN In spite of the fact that Kenneth Grahame was a general paediatric ward, there had been a child with a Wilms tumour there only a year before. He was now three and making an excellent recovery, needing only periodic check-ups. When the ward sister phoned his mother, she very kindly agreed to talk to us. She came to see us the evening Joe had his Hickman line implanted and was very reassuring about practical matters like taking care of the line and her son's adjustment to chemotherapy.

She had had the added complication of another child to care for, and she explained how she had stayed in hospital with her son, having her daughter visit them there for part of the day, while for the rest of the time her husband looked after the daughter at home. She told us how hard it had been for her husband to cope with their son's illness and how much he had hated coming to the hospital and the details of the treatment.

We had read about families being broken up by the stresses of a child's illness, but this was our first direct encounter with another family's reaction. This couple had survived the situation because the husband had been able to counter his denial by providing positive support at home. They had been lucky in sorting out the responsibilities each could cope with best, and I felt even more grateful for the way Alex had committed himself to caring for Joe.

It was good talking to someone who had already come through the worst part of her son's illness. But her son had not had secondaries, his treatment and recovery had been more routine, and we couldn't count on the same smooth path ourselves.

FRIDAY, 24 APRIL – SUNDAY, 26 APRIL 1987

ALEX A powerful feeling during the early days of Joe's illness was of being lost, being somehow adrift in life. The person we loved most was threatened by a disease that was still largely unexplained and our whole sense of the future was shattered.

Neither Ann nor I believes in any established religion and certainly Joe's situation did nothing to alter that fact, but I have always been drawn to the ritual of various faiths – American Indian beliefs, Buddhism, Catholicism – and when I noticed on Friday morning that there was a Catholic church, Our Lady of Dolours, practically opposite St Stephen's, I thought I would like to light a candle for Joe.

I had no idea of the Catholic significance of doing this, nor indeed of what to do, but I walked rather self-consciously into the church, found the votive candles in a box under their stand, took one, placed it in the centre in a spare holder and lit it. I said some sort of personal prayer – an attempt almost by the powers of positive thought to will the cancer out of Joe's body – and was silent for a while, surrounded by statues of saints whose names were unknown to me.

I must have wanted comfort, because I rang the doorbell of the priest's office and explained that I was not a Catholic and did not think I could become a Catholic, but that my son had cancer and I wanted to know if there was any special way I should light a candle for him in future. The priest, a gentle Irishman called Father Stephen, was enormously sympathetic and told me that I should simply do whatever felt right. He offered to come to the hospital next morning to see Joe and to anoint him.

Again, I had no idea of the significance of Joe being anointed – he had never been baptized or christened – but the warmth of Father Stephen's reaction made me feel that I would like it. This had nothing to do with any thoughts of 'insurance': that even though I did not believe in God, I would cover my – and Joe's – options. I have no interest in a god you have to fear or to bargain with. It was Father Stephen's own emotions that made me want it; I felt Joe needed all the help he could get, and the more people willing him to recover, the better.

*

On Saturday morning, Father Stephen came on to the ward and found Joe asleep. I had already asked him if Joe might be scared by the anointing, but he had told me it was simply a matter of sprinkling a little water on his forehead and saying a prayer. Ann was not entirely happy about the idea of Joe being anointed and was pleased that Joe slept right through it.

Before he left, Father Stephen gave me a book of *Devotions in Honour of St Peregrine*, the patron saint of those suffering from cancer. I read it, and though the references to God and Jesus and Mary seemed as ritualistic and mythological to me as references to Egyptian and Greek gods or the Buddha, I found the beauty of some of the language helped focus my own thoughts. Throughout Joe's illness, that one small book was of enormous help to me when I wanted to think about the sway of our lives, when I wanted to concentrate my mind on my love for Joe and his place in the universe – whether he would be here for a long time, or only briefly.

ANN As Joe was making a good recovery from the Hickman line operation and there was nothing scheduled for him until Tuesday morning, Lilias suggested that we all go home for the weekend, an invitation we accepted with mixed feelings.

We felt cut adrift. It would be lovely to be in our own home, to eat proper cooked meals, sort out what we would need for the next period in hospital, and see Joe in normal surroundings again, but it was unlikely to be truly relaxing. We were so used to the support of the hospital, to having someone to consult about our most trifling worry, that the idea of being away from the ward was quite daunting.

Joe was delighted to be reunited with his toys and spent a happy afternoon playing and catching up with a few favourite TV programmes we had videotaped for him. At bedtime, without any discussion, we tucked him into the middle of our bed and got in beside him. We wanted a big family hug, we wanted the immediate reassurance of having him beside us if we woke in the night, we couldn't bear to send him off to his own room.

The next day my mother came over, and our best friend Teri arrived with her dog, Eric. It's strange how, when your life has become so bleak that the whole world feels overcast, you suddenly notice that the sun is still shining. It was a wonderful day that Sunday, so we decided to go to the Serpentine. Walking through Joe's favourite bit of 'Daddy's Park' we could almost pretend that life was back to normal, but we were due back at St Stephen's the next day and the result of the histology was still to come.

MONDAY, 27 APRIL – TUESDAY, 28 APRIL 1987

ALEX Back in St Stephen's, Joe was started on a drug he was to take daily for virtually the entire period of chemotherapy, a small white tablet called alopuerinol. This was to counter the risk of a gout-like condition which could be caused by the accumulation of dead tumour cells in the farthest reaches of the body, in particular the feet.

Joe had never learnt to swallow pills, so we debated how best to give it to him. Someone suggested crushing it and mixing it with orange juice; the problem was that it would not dissolve and even vigorous stirring left white particles floating on the juice. Joe needed a good deal of persuading to drink it, but we told him it would help to make him better, and by keeping the amount of juice and alopuerinol small and giving him a long, unmixed drink with it, we managed to win him round.

On Monday evening Mary Judge, another of our favourite house officers, flushed Joe's Hickman line for the first time. The Hickman was a relatively new invention and there was still much discussion over how regularly it needed to be flushed to prevent blockages. The mother of the ward's other Wilms tumour patient had told us that she had been advised to flush his line twice a day. We originally were told that Joe's line should be flushed once daily, but the decision had now been taken to flush it only once a week.

We watched with both fascination and alarm as Mary prepared a sterile trolley, opened a sterile dressing pack, taking care not to touch its contents with her unsterile hands, then emptied a hypodermic syringe and needle on to the sterile field and finally put on sterile gloves. The problem with sterile procedure is that the packaging of everything you require is not sterile and if you put the gloves on at the outset, they would be contaminated by the first touch of a bottle, a cotton wool pack or anything else. Mary had a nurse assisting her, pouring Betadine, a sterile cleaning solution, and breaking open the glass phial containing the Hepsal used to flush the line; it was really a two-person task.

The prospect of learning to do all this ourselves seemed more than a little daunting – it looked so easy to touch something, perhaps even your own arm, without realizing it and risk introducing infection into the line. (In fact, we did not start flushing Joe's line ourselves for several months, as the timing always seemed to coincide with our being in St Stephen's.)

While Mary was getting ready, Ann had been unwrapping the gauze and tape protecting the line's plastic cap. Not surprisingly, Joe was by now quite nervous of the proceedings and had started to cry. We told him that it wouldn't hurt him in any way, that he wouldn't feel any different and that it was simply a question of keeping the inside of the line clean, but Joe remained unconvinced. Finally Mary, who was extremely patient and understanding of children's responses to medical procedures, told him that she would go away and come back when he wasn't so upset. She left the trolley in the room and Joe soon forgot about it. If he had not been due to go to the Westminster Hospital for a CT (computerized axial tomogram) scan early the following morning, we probably would have left the flushing until then, but instead we called Mary back when Joe fell asleep and she flushed his line without waking him.

*A*NN In order to get a complete picture of what was going on in Joe's body, he was to have a CT scan and a bone scan at the Westminster. We were very happy that one of our favourite nurses was coming with us in the ambulance to help guide us around. Toni had got Joe's number right from the start and had nicknamed him Tiger or, occasionally, the King of Fulham. Like most only children, Joe was shy in the company of strangers and other children, but quite assertive while his parents were around. If Joe wasn't being bossy, Toni was worried about him. 'That's my Tiger,' she would say approvingly when he perked up enough to issue a few orders.

For the CT scan Joe needed only a mild sedative, taken orally, to help him keep still, but for the bone scan he needed a special injection that would highlight the areas the doctors wanted to check. This was given down Joe's Hickman line and he was delighted at this fresh evidence of its usefulness, but Alex and I, still terrified of the sterile procedures surrounding its care, were horrified at the casual way the doctor handled it, failing even to put on sterile gloves.

It hadn't been planned that I should stay with Joe for the CT scan. It evolved because he wasn't sleepy enough to settle down without some encouragement. Joe had to lie on a narrow padded platform that was designed to go through a large circular tunnel containing special X-ray cameras. By taking many pictures of his body in cross-section as it slowly passed through the tunnel, a three-dimensional picture, more informative than an ordinary X-ray, could be obtained.

I was wearing a lead apron to protect me from the radiation, an enormously heavy garment which covered my front and back. The operator had estimated about twenty minutes for the scan, but it must have taken more like forty. I spent the entire time on my feet, and by the end I was ready to sink through the floor.

My job was to persuade Joe to keep still for the entire time, which I did by talking constantly, trying to remember stories where people had to keep very still or quiet, and noting the rhythms of the machine. As it clicked and whirred we began to recognize the moments when the camera was working and he had to be completely still, and the moments when the platform was moving and he could wriggle if he had to.

Toni, who was watching from the operator's booth, told me later how amused they'd been by my running commentary, heard over the intercom used to communicate with patients. Alex, left behind in the waiting room, had the most anxious time, with nothing to do and no idea what was going on.

Ironically Joe became very dopey as soon as the scan was over. I can still picture him trying to stand up on the trolley where he was resting and collapsing in a sleepy heap. Probably it was tension that had kept him awake; once he was relaxed the sedative started to work.

*

Joe rallied in time for the next scan, which was to detect tumour in the bones. It didn't involve keeping still for more than a few seconds at a time, and the bonus was that he could see his limbs on a TV screen in a kaleidoscopic arrangement of green dots which slid around and reassembled interestingly when he moved. For Joe this was great fun, and we were grateful that he got through it so happily.

Next came the wait before we knew what those shifting dots might mean – whether there was cancer in Joe's bones or not.

WEDNESDAY, 29 APRIL 1987

ANN On Wednesday we finally heard the results of the histology. Since we'd learnt that there were cells in Joe's bone marrow, the overall picture had become disturbing, but there was still the image of a Wilms as a passive type of cancer, suggesting one easily treated, to reassure us.

I suppose Dr Phillips, Joe's oncologist, and Dr Sinclair, the ward's consultant, were unavailable that day, because a junior member of Dr Phillips's staff, Dr Peck, arrived in Joe's room to talk to us. Although Joe was awake he launched into an explanation of how the histology had shown that Joe had a very rare, untreatable type of tumour cell.

The shock this announcement brought was on two levels: the mere fact of what he was saying; and that he was saying it in front of Joe with no consideration for how Joe would interpret what was being said or how his parents were reacting to it. I had to break away from the conversation to distract Joe. Maybe Dr Peck thought it was an expression of indifference, because he came over to Joe's cot to attempt to explain it all to me. I was gripped by panic at what he was telling us, and by an urgent need to stop him speaking in front of Joe. As I steered the doctor towards the door, I hissed that I didn't want to discuss it in Joe's hearing. 'It's all right, he won't understand,' was his reaction.

Even now when I think of that day, the shock of what he was telling us is confused with anger at what we felt and still feel was his appalling mismanagement of the situation. His apparent lack of forethought created a climate in which we were unable to absorb and ask questions calmly about what he was telling us – and his seeming underestimation, or sheer ignorance, of how much a child will understand or intuit from an atmosphere was staggering to us. Perhaps by now he is the master of tact, but that makes no difference to me. The most devastating moment in Joe's illness since cancer had first been mentioned was made chaotic and confused because of the insensitive manner in which we were told.

I think we were too stunned at the news and the inept way it had been communicated to want to speak at first, but when Joe fell asleep, Alex and I went and sat in the adjoining cubicle, where we could watch him through the glass partition, to talk things over. We had an unspoken agreement that we would never discuss anything we didn't want Joe to hear in front of him – even if he were asleep. One can never be sure when a child is only half asleep, or even of what can be absorbed subconsciously.

The histology seemed so final, to offer so little room for hope, that there was very little to say. Alex had gleaned a bit more information than me. The cell type was so rare that there were only two hundred recorded cases worldwide. We had no idea of the survival rate – we didn't want to know, we suspected it was zero. They were still going ahead with the chemotherapy. Though there was no evidence that it would work, it was worth a shot, and there was nothing else to try.

I had spent remarkably little time crying. Waiting till I was alone seemed too contrived and didn't work for me. The tears tended to come when I was doing something alone that I usually did with Joe, so that a simple trip to buy a carton of fruit juice or a few groceries would find me fighting for control in the street.

That afternoon was the first time I cried properly, and the first opportunity Alexander and I had to grieve together. I don't know how long we cried, wordlessly clutching each other, before the hospital's minister arrived. Despite our non-acceptance of religion, we had already met him and responded to him as a nice human being who had been interested in our dilemma as to how to handle Joe's religious education. Now, summoned by the sister on duty who'd seen our distress, he sat and talked to us while we drank the tea she brought us. By the time Joe awoke from his nap, we were able to rejoin him in a calmer frame of mind.

ALEX The conversation with Dr Peck was one of the lowest points of the entire period of Joe's illness. At that time we had been in St Stephen's for only two and a half weeks – though it felt like several lifetimes – and already we seemed to have had peaks and troughs of hope and despair.

A week before, when we had learnt of the microscopic tumour cells in Joe's bone marrow, the future had seemed bleak, but during the intervening days we had somehow managed to find something positive to cling on to – buoyed up by Joe's incredible cheerfulness and by the hope that our love for him would strengthen his resistance, perhaps give his immune system the added force it would need to destroy the cancer.

Now that hope had been taken away again, and in a way we found particularly distressing, we wished we could have seen Dr Phillips, whose friendly Welsh manner and vast experience of cancer – and, perhaps as significantly, of dealing with people suffering from it – always left us feeling reassured that, even if the news were bad, there might still be some hope.

When Ann and I talked there seemed little to say, but I think we forced ourselves to concentrate on a thought we used throughout Joe's illness to keep us going: that every person is unique, with a unique body type and individual reactions. Statistics may suggest all sorts of things, about cancer or anything else, but they cannot offer proof in your particular case. There are always exceptions, and we prayed that Joe would be one now.

I am not sure if it started that day, but a powerful memory of those first weeks in St Stephen's was my reaction to a funeral parlour directly opposite the hospital. This company had in their window a tiny coffin decorated with flowers. It was far too small to be a child's coffin – more rabbit-size – but in my mind I saw it as one and it angered me.

It seemed that I could not cross Fulham Road without seeing

this particular window, and every time I passed it I glared at it, hating it, trying to will the glass to shatter, the whole building to fall in on itself. I would look straight in at the small coffin – proving to myself that I was not afraid, I could confront Death, I could beat this – and in my mind I would scream, 'You're not going to get him! You're not going to get him!'

5 Chemotherapy

Staff Nurse Toni by Joe Buffalo, aged three years nine months,
May 1987

ANN We had plenty of preparation for chemotherapy – explanations from Dr Phillips and Mary Judge, who as part of her training had had extensive experience with paediatric cancer patients in Edinburgh. But reactions varied so dramatically that, until Joe actually started treatment, we had no idea whether he would have a bad time with it or be relatively lucky and not suffer too much.

If Joe's body had been clear, he would have had one three-month course of chemo as a precautionary treatment. Now there was evidence of remaining cells, a more sustained attack was to be made, even though there was no guarantee that the drugs would be effective, and a year's treatment was scheduled.

For the first three months Joe was to have a weekly injection of vincristine (a drug derived from the Madagascan periwinkle, a fact which somehow made it seem less devastating, almost natural). Every third week, the vincristine would be combined with two other drugs, adriamycin (also known as doxorubicin) and actinomycin, to make a stronger dose. Later in the treatment he would be able to drop the weekly doses and have only the triple dose every third week.

We knew there would be side effects – nausea was almost inevitable, though its intensity varied enormously from patient to patient and it was unlikely on the weeks when he just had vincristine. The other predictable side effect was hair loss, which could be caused by two of the drugs prescribed for Joe, vincristine and adriamycin.

We had to give some thought to how to prepare Joe for all of this. If we told him the drugs would make him sick, it was almost a guarantee that he would be. If we didn't warn him, it would be a shock and more distressing than necessary. We also had to prepare him for his hair loss.

ALEX Despite the quite appalling nature of these side effects the decision to subject Joe to chemotherapy hardly seemed like a decision at all. In terms of conventional medicine, it appeared to be the only hope for him; our other option was to sit back and let him die, perhaps within a fairly short time.

We knew nothing about chemotherapy until it was explained to us. Similarly, I remember that until my sister developed multiple sclerosis, I would have been hard pressed to distinguish it from muscular dystrophy; there are whole areas of life all but the bravest of us shy away from, unless forced to confront them personally.

'Chemotherapy' simply means treatment by chemicals. The drugs involved are powerful toxins, which destroy cancer cells but also provoke violent reactions, such as nausea, and kill healthy red and white blood cells in the bone marrow, thus weakening the body's immune system. Some adult patients and no doubt some parents of children with cancer (though we have not met any) choose not to have chemotherapy, but to live with cancer and to try to find some other means, whether from within themselves or through alternative medicine, of clearing their bodies of the disease.

If I had been the one with cancer, I would have felt more at liberty to make that choice, though I suspect I would still have opted to go ahead with chemotherapy. Because it was Joe, both Ann and I felt that we should at least try it: if the treatment caused him unbearable suffering, we could always stop it. Also we were aware that, should Joe die, we would experience more guilt if we hadn't tried it than if we had.

ANN The day after our conversation with Dr Peck, Joe had his first treatment. We no longer knew what to hope for. A cure was unlikely now, but maybe the chemotherapy could at least control the cancer. For the first time we began to think in terms of buying time. There was so much research being done, and so many breakthroughs being made, that maybe somewhere the drug that could save Joe was being perfected. Our most important object was keeping him alive in the hope that a cure would become available.

We had been assured that the single application of vincristine would be trouble-free, but as a precaution Joe was given an anti-emetic (to stop nausea and, at least in the case of children, help the patient sleep through much of the worst period) and put on a drip to prevent dehydration should he be sick. Before the drugs were given it was customary to take a blood test to make sure his general condition was good. This could now be done with the Hickman line, and the giving of the vincristine, also through the line, was quick and undramatic.

Though the anti-emetic made him sleepy, Joe had no reaction to the chemo, and woke much too early the next morning in a very lively mood.

ALEX Joe was awake just before 6.00 a.m., the morning after his first vincristine treatment, full of beans and keen to play. My friend and employer, Mozafar Aminian, had visited us the previous evening with some very generous gifts for

Joe – an electric train set and two Lego kits. At the time Joe had been asleep, as a result of the sedative he'd been given, and on a drip, and the presents had remained unopened.

Now he spotted the Hamleys bag instantly and wanted to investigate 'Sofar's presents' (Mozafar was always thrilled that Joe attempted his Iranian name, whereas even most of his adult English friends called him Michael for ease). Shortly after six o'clock, I moved a chair next to Joe's bed, opened the first of the Lego boxes and stared in bleary-eyed horror at the entirely visual 'diructions' (a favourite word of Joe's, combining 'directions' and 'instructions') for the construction of a cement-mixing truck.

This was the first mature Lego Joe had been given – previously, he had had the simpler Duplo and Fabuland varieties with their larger plastic bricks and less ambitious designs. Now, before I was even properly awake, I had to sort out what seemed like hundreds of tiny bricks and parts and ascertain solely from colour variations in the diagrams which piece went where. Joe later mastered Lego assembly really well, but I always felt it was some sort of intelligence test I was failing.

I was nonetheless delighted that he was so bright less than twenty-four hours after treatment. It seemed to bode well for the future: at this point I grasped at any sign that Joe was strong and happy as evidence that his response to cancer might be exceptional – he might survive.

If the day started well, however, its mood – or mine, at least – deteriorated in the afternoon. I wanted to buy Joe a present as a treat for having his first chemotherapy (the dawning of a whole system of chemotherapy treats, which Ann and I got a great deal of pleasure out of buying and Joe certainly seemed to enjoy receiving). Joe loved *Thomas the Tank Engine*, so I thought I would find him a Thomas engine for his new train set. Where better to look than 'The Train Shop' – Joe's nickname for Harrods?

I left St Stephen's and, first, walked across to Our Lady of Dolours to light a candle for Joe and to pray, in my own way, that chemotherapy would be successful. I then went to our car, which I had not moved since we had brought Joe back to St

Stephen's on Monday. It was now Friday; the car's interior light had been left on and the battery was completely dead.

This incident would hardly be worthy of mention were it not for the utter despair it elicited from me. When your child has cancer, you somehow feel the rest of the world should work for you without any effort – you feel you ought to be protected. I stared at the battery with a totally illogical feeling of hopelessness, then finally, with much anger, managed to rouse myself to unbolt it from its mounting. I hailed a taxi, told the driver our address and slumped in the back with the battery.

When the driver tried to start a conversation, I think my heart sank – taxi dialogue can push you close to insanity even when life is fine. But this man had a sympathetic tone and I found myself telling him about Joe and the battery, and was struck by how powerfully he was saddened by our situation. Not for the last time among taxi drivers, he refused to accept payment. It makes me tearful even now to write this, and it always made me tearful at the time – that a child with cancer somehow cut across all the commerce and bullshit that surrounds everyday life.

I liked to think then that hearing about Joe did not simply sadden people but also helped to put their own problems in perspective. Certainly it was comforting – though also painful – to be at the receiving end of such kindness and concern, but it did not and could not provide what we wanted: for reality to be different.

It is hard to convey how long a day could seem at this point, how a sense of hope one minute or simply an hour spent playing happily with Joe could turn rapidly into fear and doubt.

On Saturday, Joe seemed to have recovered fully from his first treatment and was on the hospital room floor learning to control his electric train set. I had bought him Percy, the little green locomotive from *Thomas the Tank Engine*. Joe was running him round and round the circular 'Double-O' gauge track we had laid out, then chugging him on to a siding. By the middle of the day, however, Joe had mentioned that his legs were tired and soon after started to complain of a pain in his left thigh. Our hearts sank; it seemed unlikely, but could this be another tumour starting already – this time in his leg?

We called Lucy Moore, who examined him and told us that the aches were probably a side effect of the vincristine, which could impair muscle action to some degree. We wanted to believe her, but I know that some doubt remained in our minds.

Sunday was worse. It was 3 May 1987, tomorrow was May Day bank holiday, and we were told that we could take Joe home for a couple of days. We were already worried about his legs, but shortly before we were to go, I noticed a swelling on Joe's face, just below his jawline on the left-hand side.

It was very slight – more a lack of symmetry than anything. I wanted not to believe it; even before I had properly taken it in, my mind was saying 'tumour' to me. I hoped I was just being paranoid, but when I pointed it out to Ann – calmly, so as not to distress Joe – she could see it also.

Again we called Lucy. Again she examined Joe; she could feel a small mass on his left parotid (salivary) gland, but was reluctant to offer an opinion. I told her my fear – that it was a new tumour – and sensed that she might share it, though she suggested it might simply be an inflamed gland. In any case, she told us that we may as well go home for the rest of the bank holiday weekend, as Joe had had his first chemotherapy treatment and there was really nothing to be done until Dr Sinclair came back on Tuesday.

At home we were immensely depressed. Mozafar came over with some American chocolate cake – which Joe always referred to as 'Sofar's cake', whoever got it for him. Gran and Fred arrived, too, having driven round London in search of a new battery for our car. Joe enjoyed their company, but I could not keep my eyes off the lump under his left jaw, gloomily convinced of what it was and wishing it would somehow disappear.

On Bank Holiday Monday Ann's mother, Alice, visited, but Joe was very listless, lying around on the sofa or the floor with no clothes on. When I drove Alice to Goodge Street tube station for her train home, she was clearly upset about him and worried about his condition. She echoed mine and all our family's and friends' thoughts when she said, 'It doesn't seem right that Joe should be so ill. Older people, they've had their lives, but not a lovely little boy like Joe.'

That night, as the night before, back in our own bed with Joe snuggled between us, I held his hand while he slept and read the book of *Devotions* Father Stephen had given me. The words seemed strange and prompted all sorts of connections. One line, 'As I gaze on you in the sanctuary, to see your strength and your glory', always created a double image of the peaceful Spanish missions Ann and I had visited in California almost ten years ago, and of Joe in Spain, playing on a hotel patio, surrounded by lush flowers in the heat.

I wished in a way that I could believe in a bearded, paternal, Sunday School God – a wise old father figure I could turn to and ask for help – but I simply read the words and put my own, far looser interpretation on them, praying that whatever forces move the universe, they would be merciful to Joe Buffalo:

> *On my bed I remember you*
> *On you I muse through the night*
> *for you have been my help;*
> *in the shadow of your wings I rejoice.*
> *My soul clings to you; your right hand holds me fast.*

Entrance Psalm, Ps. 62. 'A Soul Thirsting for God'

On Tuesday we returned to St Stephen's, relieved to be back in the hospital environment and that the holiday weekend was over. Dr Sinclair examined Joe's face and was very concerned by the lump, which had grown visibly over the past forty-eight hours. He wanted Joe to have an ultrasound first thing in the morning, and to move the first triple-drug chemotherapy treatment forward by a day to tomorrow.

In many ways, Dr Sinclair was one of the 'old school' of hospital consultants, a kindly but often extremely adamant man in his fifties, with an ever-present pipe and a manner designed to keep his staff on their toes. (Their revenge, at least on one occasion, was to hide his pipe!) For children, he performed magic tricks with coins – which impressed me rather more than they did Joe; for parents, he offered diagnoses and advice in rather absolute terms. Now, we were glad that he was so decisive and that there would be prompt action, though at the same time his reaction rather reinforced our own fears.

*

On Wednesday morning Joe was examined by Peter Cox, Professe
Wastell's registrar and an extremely likeable man with two your
daughters of his own. Although a surgeon most used to operatir
on adults, he had a joky, relaxed manner which had immediate
put Joe at ease the first time they'd met, and now Joe was qui
happy for Peter to shine a torch in his mouth and prod about.

Like Dr Sinclair, he was convinced that the mass was
tumour on the left parotid gland. He had been called in to advis
on the feasibility of surgery; he was clearly willing though ne
keen to operate on Joe's mouth and joined us in hoping tha
chemotherapy might destroy the tumour.

In the afternoon, we went down to Ultrasound, where Joe wa
becoming more popular with each visit, partly because he seeme
to enjoy ultrasound and also because he always took his 'friends
such as Cookie Monster, with him. The examination now wa
not so much to confirm the presence of a tumour – the mass wa
quite visible – but to log its extent as a marker against whic
any reduction in size brought about by chemotherapy could b
measured.

This time, the doctor actually examined Joe on the woode
tricycle he'd ridden down on. As he spread jelly (used to ensu
contact with the skin) on Joe's face, then rubbed the ultrasour
sensor – which was not unlike an electric razor – over it, Cook
Monster observed in his gruff voice, 'I see, Joe – now you ai
shaving!' To which Joe replied, sounding very authoritativ
'No, no, Cookie. This is not shaving, this is an ultrasound test t
see if my mouth is all right!'

Back in our room, the trolley bearing the three chemotherap
drugs was wheeled in at about 4.00 p.m. Cookie Monster wa
certainly needed now, not merely as a comforting friend for Jc
but also, to some extent, as a distraction for me. Ann and I wer
anxious about the treatment on a whole variety of levels – ho
Joe would respond to the drugs; how sick he would be; wheth
chemo would combat the cancer at all – and the simple fact c
putting the furry blue Cookie Monster glove puppet, with i
ping-pong ball eyes, on my hand and adopting his deep growl
voice (constant repetition of which could lead to a sore throat
somehow made the situation seem less dire.

Cookie was a link with happier times. We had bought him in a department store in New Hampshire when we had spent the two months there with Joe at the end of 1984. He was the only one of his kind left and though we saw other Cookie Monster puppets in other shops, we never saw one quite the same as ours (the fur was always a different shade of blue, or the eyes were not the same). Instead of operating his arms, your hand worked his huge black mouth, so that Cookie could talk very effectively and even bite your finger – or demolish real cookies – when called upon to do so. I remembered amusing Joe with him over fried breakfasts at a café called the Post Office in Provincetown, an extraordinarily lovely, two-street, fishing village and tourist trap up on the tip of Cape Cod. Joe had been about fourteen months old then and laughed to see Cookie snapping at french fries. Now, in St Stephen's, under rather different circumstances, Cookie would sing Joe's name over and over again, mixing up the letters, or tell him, 'Joe Buffalo, I love you.' And Joe would answer, even if he were a little tearful and afraid, 'I love you, Cookie.' Or, if the world was really worrying him: 'Be quiet, Cookie Monster!'

ANN Joe sat on my lap while the drugs were given through his line, preceded by an anti-emetic, and he was actually asleep before everything had been injected. When he woke up about two hours later, he was in very good form, happy and hungry. After a quick discussion with the nurses we decided to let him have something off the supper trolley. Unfortunately, this small amount of food seemed to be a trigger for his nausea and Joe suddenly and dramatically started to vomit.

Alex and I had to form a production line of papier mâché sick-bowls, and for about the first twenty minutes it was a non-stop process. A nurse rushed in with inco pads to cover the bedding and it was not until the intervals between the vomiting had lengthened a bit that there was a chance to change his bedlinen and clean him up. Though it calmed down, Joe continued to be sick all evening, falling asleep for a while when he had his top-up dose of anti-emetic and waking again a couple of hours later.

Around midnight he fell asleep properly and slept all night

through without incident, then started to vomit again when he woke the next morning.

We felt very guilty about having given him the food that started the vomiting, but in time we learnt that if Joe were going to be sick, eating or not didn't make much difference, and we decided to let him follow his instincts. Eventually we discovered that, like travel sickness, the nausea associated with chemotherapy is brain-centred and food intake has little influence. In fact, the vomiting was more tolerable while there was something in his stomach. If it was empty, he produced bile or what the staff called 'coffee grains' – granules of blood from his stomach lining.

This first triple treatment provoked the most intense reaction. There were a variety of anti-emetics and sedatives to try in various combinations and eventually, by trial and error, a regime that suited Joe was found, which greatly reduced his discomfort.

The most disturbing development came later, perhaps three or four months into chemotherapy, when Joe started being sick in his sleep. At first he had always been awake, or else had stirred enough to try to sit up, but suddenly he was vomiting while lying down asleep at night, without being conscious enough to move or call us. Alex and I were terrified he would choke, and immediately organized a shift system so that one of us stayed awake beside him all night to sit him up when this happened.

The house officer we discussed this change with was quite blasé about it. She said he had a good 'coughing mechanism' and was perfectly safe. This wasn't something we were prepared to leave to chance, and besides, coughing mechanism or not, it would be hateful for him to be sick in such circumstances.

We had told Joe, that first time, that chemotherapy might make him feel a bit ill, but that it wouldn't last too long. Though his reaction was far more extreme than we had hoped, we were assured that it could have been worse and that occasionally patients didn't recover completely between one dose and the next.

Naturally, Joe did not enjoy any of this and eventually would become quite distressed as soon as the doctor prepared to inject

at Joe started to call the 'sick medicine'. This was quite a
ngthy process, as the drugs couldn't be introduced too vio-
ntly into the system, and fortunately Joe tended to fall asleep
they were being given. One, adriamycin, a bright red liquid
at looked like some wicked witch's potion from a Disney
rtoon, had to be injected over a period of three minutes, with
e doctor timing the release of tiny drops with the aid of the
cond hand of a watch.

The most impressive part of all this was that even when he
ew what was in store for him with chemotherapy, Joe still
proached it quite calmly, planning which toys he wanted to
ck, if we were coming from home, and showing no resistance
getting in the car or going into hospital. Considering the fight
put up over the taking of some quite innocuous medicines,
s amazing that we didn't have to drag him kicking and scream-
g into St Stephen's. In the way that children have of sensing
at the priorities are – and when they can push their luck –
e knew it was too important to make a fuss about.

ALEX The tumour on Joe's face had originally grown from
almost nothing to the size of a mumps-like swelling in the
ace of about forty-eight hours. In the forty-eight hours follow-
g the first triple-dose chemotherapy, the reverse happened –
e lump went back down.

This seemed an almost miraculous sign that chemotherapy
ight work. Given the fact that there had been no real expecta-
on among the medical staff that Joe's rare tumour type was
eatable, even they permitted themselves some cautious excite-
ent. Nine days later, a further ultrasound investigation
vealed that the mass on Joe's parotid gland had diminished by
ore than half.

We had been told that there would be no way of knowing what,
any, success chemotherapy was having until a series of tests,
cluding another CT scan, at the end of the first three months;
w Dr Phillips allowed that Joe might have some small chance.
e was careful not to raise our hopes too high, but his affection
d concern for Joe shone through any pronouncement, and his
es suggested a confidence which had not been there before.

*A*NN I was told that Joe's hair loss could begin very soo after chemo started, so I needed to prepare for this ver quickly. I decided to have Joe's hair, which we always kep fairly short, cut into a crew cut right away, in order to create sense of transition between thick hair and no hair. Joe ha actually had his first triple dose of chemotherapy before I coul get his hair organized. Luckily we had a couple of friends wh were trained hairdressers and we asked Spike, who by then wa more involved in running night-clubs than salons, if he coul help. He had cut Joe's hair once or twice before, with Joe – wh enjoyed the attention – sitting on his lap. This time, I think Jo shared our feeling that it was a more significant occasion tha usual, because he insisted on sitting on my lap while Spike kne beside us to work on his hair.

It was a very sharp cut and Joe was quite impressed by it. had meant to take a photograph of his new look, but the ha: loss started so quickly that I didn't get round to it in time. A da or two later I noticed a tuft of hair on his pillow and in hardl more than a week his hair was more or less gone. I wished ther had been an opportunity to get his hair cut earlier, but we ha spent so much time in hospital that it had been impossible. I wa worried that Joe was more likely to connect his hair loss wit the cutting than the drugs.

Fortunately, very young children have no vanity and aren given to looking in mirrors. In all the time, nearly a year, tha Joe was bald or had only very sparse hair growing back, n child ever remarked on Joe's appearance. He was extremel lucky to have friends still at the age when they accepted peopl as they were – for older children the loss of hair can present a sorts of psychological and social problems. But with Joe th main need was a reassuring explanation of what was happening

I told him that the medicine he was taking was very stron; which had already been demonstrated by the way it made hir sick, and that it could make his hair fall out, but that the ha: would grow back again when he could stop taking the medicin Joe received this information very quietly. He didn't seem di tressed, but I knew he hadn't adjusted to it and needed time t think it over. I had rounded up all his hats, and suggested that :

might be fun to buy some new ones, maybe a baseball cap as it was the summer, but he wasn't interested in the idea and never showed any need to cover his head.

During the weeks of his illness Alex and I had tried the well-publicized child psychiatrists' ploy of using puppets to communicate with Joe. Professionals had found that children who wouldn't talk to an adult could suspend disbelief and talk quite openly to a puppet, even though it was obviously being manipulated. Once or twice when Joe had seemed rather reflective we'd used his Cookie Monster puppet to sound out his feelings, and had been impressed at how well Joe had understood what was happening to him. While we were trying to think of the most tactful way Cookie might approach Joe's hair loss, Joe actually announced: 'It's all right, Cookie. My hair's going to grow back when I stop the sick medicine.'

We felt reassured by this, and it was a remark he repeated often, to adults and children who hadn't even introduced the subject. Maybe it was more of a protective mechanism than we thought, because there was an incident later which suggested that Joe wasn't as relaxed about it as he appeared.

We were at home. I had turned on the television to watch the news and then wandered into the kitchen for something. Suddenly Joe called out, 'Mummy, come quickly, there's a boy like me on TV.' I raced back into the room to see part of a report about a new children's cancer ward being opened. There was a little boy on screen, obviously a chemo patient, who had no hair. Joe seemed immensely satisfied by this proof that he wasn't alone. The one thing I hadn't thought of telling him, because he had no contact with other cancer patients at this time, was that exactly the same thing happened to other children.

6 *Living with Uncertainty*

'3-Girl-SuperTed and her bottom', by Joe Buffalo, aged four
years eleven months, 10 July 1988

*A*LEX More than anyone or anything, Joe himself helped us
live from day to day. It seemed as if whatever was thrown
at him – 'sick medicine', tests, more tests, periods of virtual
isolation – he would bounce right back, adjusting to the strange
new pattern of his life by joking with Cookie Monster, learning
to enjoy the considerable influence he seemed to wield over
nurses and doctors, and only occasionally admitting his frustration with a sigh or a weary 'Oh, boy!'

We lived with a sort of exaggerated sense of the denial of death everyone exercises, no matter how subconsiously. Every adult knows that one day he or she will die, but our minds block that fact from us very effectively – perhaps sometimes too effectively – for most of our lives. We were absolutely aware that Joe might die, but our minds clearly had their own defence mechanisms and we seemed able to assimilate even the most negative information, part-accepting and part-denying it, in order to get on with our lives together.

Joe, on the other hand, did not know what death was; he had never asked about it and it was only when, in mid-May 1987, he found a dead wasp at my sister's house that the question came up.

'What is it?' he asked. We were upstairs with my brother-in-law, Peter, in his rather cluttered workroom. The sun streamed in through the windows, straight on to the dead insect on the floor.

'It's a wasp, Joe. It's dead.'

Joe didn't like wasps. 'Can it still sting me?'

'Only if you tread on it or touch it. It can't move any more because it's dead.'

I wish I could remember exactly what Joe's next question was, but I would be lying if I presented it as his precise words. It might have been, 'What is "dead"?' Or he might more simply have asked, 'What does that mean?'

'It means it isn't a wasp any more. It got tired of being a wasp and now it's something else.'

He stared, fascinated, as it lay perfectly still in the summer dust on the floor. We may have pushed it along a little, to show him that it was no longer moving.

'All creatures die, Joe,' Peter said, picking it up to dispose of it out of the window. 'Some live a long time and some live a short time.'

'People die, too,' I told him. 'It's like starting again as whatever you want to be. A wasp can come back as another wasp, or it can choose to be a lovely dog like Tish [Lynne and Peter's pet], or it might want to come back as a person.'

Joe seemed to absorb this information with the mixture of excitement and doubt that children bring to major concepts. When we went back down to Ann and Lynne, he announced: 'We found a dead creature upstairs!'

Later, Ann and I discussed whether to explain death to Joe in terms of his illness and decided against it. His interest in the wasp, though it coincided with his cancer, seemed very much the normal questioning of a three-year-old. We did not in any way want to add confusion or doubt to his world and he seemed so happy, for the most part, that we did not believe he was troubled by fears he could or would not voice. Throughout the course of Joe's illness, only one doctor we encountered seemed to believe that our way of talking about death with Joe was unhealthy and urged us to tell him directly that he would die, but from the vantage point of having lived through his death, I think neither Ann nor I would do anything differently if we had to decide again.

Summer 1987 was a summer of chemotherapy. The treatments, and their effects, punctuated the months. We soon discovered that the vomiting and hair loss were by no means the only side effects of the drugs. About a week after Joe's third chemotherapy treatment, when we had been back at home for a few days, Joe started to run a fever and became increasingly listless.

We took him back to St Stephen's (one of the great advantages of their relaxed approach to administration was that Joe was not officially discharged each time we went home, and we could simply take him straight up to Kenneth Grahame Ward), where Joe was given a blood test – the blood drawn through his Hickman line, which was to become a familiar procedure. When the results of the blood count came through about an hour later Joe was pronounced neutropaenic, one of those magically intimidating medical terms, which simply means that his immune system was drastically lowered. The neutrophil count was only one of the various regular counts taken of Joe's blood, but it was apparently the clearest guide to his level of immunity. It should have been about 3,000; on this occasion it was 70, which meant that he had very little resistance to disease.

We were to become very familiar with neutrophils, the white blood cells whose function it is to destroy foreign matter in blood and tissues and thereby combat infection. I had never heard of them before, and to this day have not seen even a picture of one (they might have an extraordinary, microscopic beauty or they might be the dullest of blood cells), but they took on an almost mystical function in our lives. As a result of chemotherapy and, later, radiotherapy, Joe's neutrophil count went up and down like a roller-coaster, but simply knowing what it was alerted us to periods of danger from infection and periods when we could relax. When so much else was uncertain, here at least we had some small illusion of control.

Not that control was easy. The next step, having discovered that Joe's blood count was low, was to place him – and us – in reverse barrier nursing. This essentially meant putting us in a hospital room which had been specially cleaned (in fact, a perfunctory floor-wash and quick wipe-down of table-tops and other surfaces was all that ever took place).

The idea then was to maintain the room as a 'sterile' environment and keep foreign dirt and the risk of diseases out, by having everyone who entered wash their hands and put on a sterile gown, face-mask, cap, overshoes and gloves, and by wiping or spraying all objects taken into the room with an alcoholic sterilizing solution. The rigour with which this procedure was followed varied enormously, and it has to be said that consultants were the worst offenders, presumably believing themselves to be beyond transmitting mere mortal diseases.

Joe did not seem unduly concerned by this new form of confinement, perhaps because we threw ourselves into it with almost a pioneering spirit, determined that it wouldn't get the better of us. One of the worst aspects was that we had to choose between a tiny room which had its own toilet or our regular, double room, which didn't. We tended to go for the latter, as the additional space was very welcome, but the price was that every time Ann or I wanted to use the loo, we had to discard our gown, mask and overshoes, leave the room, and then scrub up and put on fresh sterile clothing on our return.

Reverse barrier nursing would be a disastrous experience for anyone even remotely claustrophobic; as it was, it seemed that the hottest days of summer 1987 always coincided with our having to wear masks and gowns. And for once – perhaps only to us – it seemed like a hot summer.

ANN The first time Joe was neutropaenic there was a case of chickenpox on the ward and the doctor on duty decided to give Joe an immunoglobulin shot to protect him. This had to be given intramuscularly, so Joe's Hickman line couldn't be used. Joe was very upset about this, and we felt miserable and scared. Joe had been won over to the line because it meant no more needles, and now, only two or three weeks later, he had to have a hefty injection. We felt as if we had misled him, but this was something we hadn't anticipated.

Greater than this sense of betrayal was the fear. We had not been warned about the possibility of neutropaenia in advance, and Alex and I were still digesting the implications. The fact of Joe's cancer had been terrifying in itself, and now we had been told that the most routine ailment – even an infection carried by a pet – could become life-threatening while his body had no defences. We considered the irony of him surviving the cancer only to die of chickenpox. Suddenly we had a completely new set of anxieties, the world was full of danger.

Chemotherapy introduced a string of fresh concerns into our days. There was the constant fear that Joe would become neutropaenic, the fact that the muscle-weakening doses of vincristine were making his legs so wobbly that he staggered around like a little old man and had caused a squint so dramatic that a tumour affecting his eye was briefly suspected, and the worry of the weight he lost during the three-weekly bouts of nausea.

With his weight already low, and his poor appetite, it was a struggle to build Joe up between each session of chemotherapy. We were terrified at the prospect of seeing him get thinner and thinner. It would have been ideal if we could have put him on a wholefood diet, and before his illness I had managed to restrict him mostly to additive-free food, but it soon became obvious that if we wanted Joe to eat, it would be on his terms. Fortunately his taste, though eccentric, was mostly good. For the first few months of his illness we had to adjust to an obsessive pattern of eating which sometimes had us dashing out to a late-night shop for some item he suddenly fancied. Luckily there were two shops close to St Stephen's that stayed open till 11.00 p.m., and at home we had a store that closed at midnight. If he took a fancy to something we would stock up, because often he would eat nothing but that for days.

At one time he would only eat cheeseburgers tucked into pitta pockets. A major passion was for avocado, which he had either mashed or cut into cubes with pitta bread or tortilla chips. This craving lasted so long that the canteen at St Stephen's actually ordered a crate especially for Joe and sent one up on the food trolley every mealtime – he is possibly the only patient ever to get avocados on the NHS! Then, for over a month, he ate only tuna and mayonnaise sandwiches which had to be cut into triangles, not squares. On the whole he craved quite healthy food, though the nutritional balance may not have been perfect, but he did ask for things like sausages and salami sticks too.

Sometimes we would spend hours playing elaborate games to seduce him into eating. I would pretend I was going to eat the mouthful of food I had ready on a fork, and Joe would enjoy stealing the food while I glanced away. Alexander would play a more elaborate version of this involving a Care Bear lion which jumped as high as Joe's favourite Pepperami stick, saying: 'It's my house, and I can jump as high as my house.' As he said this, the lion would look away. When he looked back his house would be a bite shorter, and the game would go on until the sausage was gone.

Alex also invented 'bricks and shoes', Cookie Monster's name for sausages and baked beans. This time Cookie was the hopeful thief of Joe's meal, frustrated when Joe beat him to every mouthful he loudly planned to steal. These games often took hours and were quite exhausting and repetitive, but if they resulted in Joe eating, they were worth the effort.

ALEX Time passed at a strange, unreal pace during the first three months of Joe's chemotherapy. I tried to develop a Zen-like approach to hospital life and embrace whatever was going on at the moment. I was grateful to be with Joe, both in the sense of being allowed to stay with him all the time and in the fact that he was still alive, given my initial fears, and I tried to make even the smallest task seem meaningful. If we decided to wash the hospital room floor, I would try to wash it as perfectly as it could be washed. If I was cooking for Joe in the decidedly unsterile ward kitchen, I would pour boiling water over virtually every available object and develop an elaborate system of remembering what I had touched and what was in theory safe for Joe. If he and I played together, I would try to enter totally into the game, even when on occasions the game would become so repetitive or go on for so long that I felt myself to be on the verge of madness.

With no hesitation, I would characterize my behaviour during this period and during the whole of Joe's illness as obsessive; that was my way of coping with the uncertainty. But at the same time, I felt relatively relaxed about living on the ward – more so than Ann – and enjoyed the security of having medical advice constantly at hand. I also enjoyed the contact with the nurses, particularly the students, and perhaps flirted with them a little. Their obvious love for the children and the dedication with which they seemed to throw themselves into their work impressed me and made me question what sort of contribution I had made to other people in my life.

As a result I became very angry, when we stayed at St Stephen's during the June 1987 General Election campaign, to hear Conservative ministers and MPs lying through their teeth about their commitment to the National Health Service and how safe it was in their hands. Their claims that it was being fully-funded were a nonsense when all around us there were shortages of the most basic items, from clean linen to toilet rolls. The levels of pay for virtually everyone in the service – nurses, domestics, doctors, porters – were absurdly low, and whenever 'radical' solutions were put forward by Government (such as a 15 per cent across-the-board increase for nursing staff), the benefits in real terms were either eroded by the conditions attached or by the fact that the basic wage was so low to start with that the percentage increase was still miniscule.

We sensed at times that the hospitals were straining at the seams to maintain their patient care, and that their ability to cope was very much due to the determination of the staff to compensate for shortcomings elsewhere. Joe was never denied any treatment due to cut-backs, but we were acutely aware of the nightly telephone checks on bed availability at other hospitals and the fact that on some nights in London there were virtually no spare paediatric beds available in the event of an emergency.

We felt immensely grateful to the NHS for providing total care for Joe, as our right, at a time when the last thing we needed was the anxiety of wondering how we would pay for expensive, long-term medical treatments. Simply deciding whether to subject him to the rigours of those treatments was painful enough without taking cost into account, and the experience reinforced in me – not simply because of Joe, but through watching other, less advantaged families on various wards – an absolute belief that public medicine is the only fair and humane way of providing health care in a society. Private medicine in Britain has always sponged off the back of the National Health Service, in terms of training and transfers to NHS hospitals when private hospitals find themselves unable to cope with acute cases; more worryingly, private health plans rarely offer genuinely comprehensive, unlimited care for patients such as Joe with cancer or my sister with multiple sclerosis.

ANN Naturally my reservations about being in hospital at all contributed to my hostility to the whole process of reverse barrier nursing: the little loopholes and oversights, the way the regime varied depending on who was on the ward at the time, Dr Sinclair coming in in his street clothes with no protective gown, the dirty curtains, the fact that the first couple of times Joe was neutropaenic no one remembered that we should all wear overshoes, so everyone was walking germs into his room.

Some of the staff obviously considered that Joe would have been safer at home, since people have a greater immunity to family germs, and that the hospital was altogether a dangerous place for him. I think the opposing logic was that in hospital he could be observed and treated with antibiotics immediately, should any infection occur. But he was so much safer from infection at home that it seems madness that we were pressured to keep him in hospital.

At the time we accepted it because we weren't confident

enough of the alternatives, yet he was frequently being barrier nursed while there were suspected meningitis cases on the ward – sometimes in the adjacent cubicle. This was a tremendous source of anxiety for us and we found ourselves treating other parents with suspicion in case they might pass on their children's germs to us and we might transmit them to Joe.

In the Westminster Hospital, I discovered, where there were children with no neutrophils at all, there were sterile areas in which, once properly prepared, families and staff could move freely, and the children ate only irradiated food. At St Stephen's, the handling of food was rather haphazard. At first we were advised only to give Joe food in sterile containers, such as tins or sealed vacuum packaging. This was limiting in terms of what Joe liked – no fresh fruit was allowed, for example – and often meant the food had an unfamiliar and disagreeable texture.

Later the rules were relaxed to allow a wider variety of foods – as long as they came from outside the hospital, in case the food on the hospital trolley had picked up germs in transit – which were prepared by us in as sterile a way as possible. This involved pouring boiling water over plates and utensils in the little ward kitchen, usually burning ourselves in the process, and washing all packaging before opening it. We scrubbed the counter and covered it with layers of paper towels, but however careful we were, it wasn't exactly scientific.

I think Alex liked the idea of participating in something as concrete as barrier nursing because it made him feel he was helping to keep Joe safe in a very active way, but I went through the motions with little confidence. It was Alex who devised all our routines, the way we changed from outdoor clothing to protective covering, the elaborate preparation of clean food. His attitude made the confinement to one room tolerable to him, but I found it claustrophobic and every time the rules changed I felt more frustrated and cynical.

ALEX Early on, I tried to go back to work. Partly I thought that focusing on something other than Joe's cancer for a while might be good for me, but the main reason was that with a mortgage repayment due at the beginning of June and no funds to meet it, I was worried.

I went back into the office to see how plans for The One World Festival were progressing. Mozafar, whose idea it was, had initially performed a miracle in persuading the Wembley Stadium group to finance the development of the project, in addition to providing Wembley Stadium itself for the British end of the international concerts. We had support from BrightStar, the satellite company which had serviced Live Aid. Our beneficiaries were two well-established charities, the Save The Children Fund and Y-Care International, part of the YMCA movement – though perhaps we should have taken as an omen the fact that about a week after Terry Waite, the chairman of Y-Care, had agreed to serve as honorary patron of the festival, he had been kidnapped in Beirut. We had the possible involvement of foreign governments and other stadia around the world. The one thing we didn't have was top-name rock bands – and since this was to be a day of satellite-linked, international rock concerts, that posed a major problem.

The fact that it was now May and the festival was set for 11 July created an air of some tension. On the day I returned to the office, a crisis meeting was set for 2.30 p.m. at Wembley. I had been involved with Mozafar from the start in trying to get the festival going, but now I felt somewhat redundant. I knew that my heart wasn't in it any more, but I was prepared to try. However, shortly after arriving at the office, Mozafar told me that I needn't go to the Wembley meeting.

Perhaps I was feeling paranoid – I was certainly on edge – but I erupted. I stormed into his office, shut the door and told him I thought it was a lousy thing to do to me, to exclude me from a crucial meeting when I had been involved for so long. 'I can't believe you're behaving like this,' I said. 'I think you treat your friends shittily. You know Joe might be dying and you know how hard I've worked for this, and now you tell me I'm not wanted. I don't need any of this kind of uncertainty at the moment!'

I think I grabbed him by the collar of his jacket and shoved him up against a window, I was so angry. I knew I had a rage inside me as a result of Joe's illness, and this was its first manifestation. I felt unbelievably hurt and betrayed, but I also realized that my anger was not entirely directed at Mozafar, who had been a good friend in the past, and immediately I pushed him, I burst into tears.

The confrontation cleared the air a little (what I didn't know at the time was that everyone who worked in the office was outside the closed door listening to it avidly) and I went to the meeting at Wembley. Although it was essentially a 'crunch' meeting, the fact that it forced us all to face a few home truths seemed very positive. The scale of the festival was almost maniacally over-ambitious and by the end of the afternoon had been cut back to a much smaller event at Wembley Arena, with more modest foreign links, which seemed at least in the realms of possibility.

I returned to the office the next day with a renewed enthusiasm, feeling that, with Joe so ill, I might now bring a real passion to the involvement with Save The Children. I seriously underestimated my emotional state, however, and in the middle of a follow-up meeting that morning with a TV producer, I burst into tears again. I had been arguing some particular point with him and he may simply have wanted me out of the discussion, but he provided me with the perfect escape when he said: 'You shouldn't be here, you should be at home saving your own child.'

I told Mozafar that I wouldn't be coming in any more and left the office that lunchtime with an overwhelming sense of finality and relief, aware that somehow – by borrowing money against the hopeful sale of our flat – Ann and I would avoid bankruptcy and that, far more importantly, I was now completely free to spend all my time with Joe.

I realized then that I had probably returned to work only to prove to myself that it wasn't what I wanted. My biggest fear with Joe's cancer was of it developing anew while I was away from him; I think this served to aggravate a more fundamental problem in my personality, which is a difficulty in accepting that the world turns without me! I knew there was no miracle I could perform to save Joe even if I was with him constantly, but being there made me feel less impotent. The rightness of my decision to leave the office seemed to be confirmed that afternoon when I arrived home to find Ann considering taking Joe back to

St Stephen's because he seemed less well. I was glad that I could get him in the car straight away and that from now on there was not even a glimmer of external commitments to complicate my involvement with his care. Perhaps I was also exorcizing some of the guilt I know I felt over having seen so little of Joe during the period when his cancer first developed.

*A*NN Joe's illness had meant a complete disruption of the pattern of our lives and we swiftly adjusted to the idea that nothing was predictable any more. Joe might or might not be well at a certain time, might or might not need tests or hospitalization, might or might not be able to see friends or go places. Everything had to happen on a day to day basis, if it were feasible when the time came.

Though we had kept the possibility of Joe returning to nursery school in mind, it became less and less likely. He had bounced back from his operation, but it seemed that there would always be something to make attendance unreliable. When Joe became neutropaenic for the first time, we realized it was hopeless. With a poor immune system there was no way he could mix with other children on a regular basis. Sadly I called the nursery school, which had kept his place open, to explain that it was impractical for Joe to return. I was sorry that this little bit of normality had gone from our lives, but for the moment Joe was better off in the security of home.

But with Joe at home all the time again, and so possessive that he wouldn't go to sleep until we did, it seemed that Alex and I were never alone together. We didn't feel confident enough to leave him with anyone he didn't know well, and anyway we hated leaving him at all at that time. We took it in turns to go out, and occasionally Alexander's parents came over from Bexhill to sit with Joe, but it was a long way to come for babysitting, so it wasn't a regular arrangement.

It began to seem that, although we were physically together almost all the time, we only existed in relation to Joe, and that our anxiety was causing a distance between us much greater than the one usually created when you have children.

Fortunately, as far as Joe's care was concerned, we seemed to have the same instincts. Though our attitudes to some of the staff and regimes like barrier nursing were different, we never disagreed about important issues, such as which treatments Joe might have or how we were going to explain them to him. If some course of action were suggested at St Stephen's, we often had to give permission with only the minimum of discussion, but it seemed that we were never in conflict over Joe.

The problem was that there weren't enough opportunities for more general discussion of how we were feeling, of how frightened we were, or the possibility of having a normal relaxed conversation about general things. We were together and yet isolated; I felt as if our relationship were seeping away. Some days I wondered if we would have anything left if Joe died. Thinking about the possibility of Joe dying started to mean more than the loss of my child. I began to think it might mark the end of my relationship with Alex too. I was looking forward into a void.

ALEX The extended stays in hospital, together with the fear and doubt surrounding Joe's cancer, certainly put huge and unnatural strains on my relationship with Ann. It had felt quite loving and secure prior to his illness, though not without the problems anyone might encounter after many years together – problems of balancing a remarkable degree of companionship and the joys of parenthood with the need to maintain some passion, some excitement, the need to continue to grow both individually and as a couple.

I know that from the moment of the initial diagnosis, I was afraid of what the outcome for us might be if Joe Buffalo died. That possibility seemed to throw everything up into the air; I dreaded the thought of no longer being a daddy and I worried greatly about how Ann might react to the loss of Joe, bearing in mind that her husband and father had died of cancer. I had first known her around the time of her husband's death and the pain she experienced then was considerable. How much more would she grieve for Joe, whom she loved even more?

I think too, if I am honest, that I must have doubted my own commitment to her. We had been through many ups and downs in our relationship and had come close to parting when Joe was one year old and I, high on the excitement of making two feature films in a year, felt seduced by the idea of starting a new life and a new family with someone I had met in California. I experienced then an almost megalomaniac belief in my ability to have a life in two countries. Echoing a thought I had had the night Joe was born, when I had said that I felt as if they could fire bullets at the three of us and they would simply bounce off, so strong was our love, I rationalized my supposed parental commitment to my Californian friend with the words: 'I can be a father there and here. It's only a few hours on the plane to London; I can still see a lot of him. Joe is very strong, and he'll know I care about him even from here.'

Now, with me proven so utterly wrong, I had no hesitation in dedicating myself to Joe's care. Perhaps the earlier threat I had posed strengthened us now. I learnt later that many fathers opt out of caring for their families when faced with a situation as drastic as ours – there are too many mothers left to cope alone with the vast mental and physical demands surrounding child-hood cancer. I had no intention of creating another abnormally stressed, single-parent family, but I feel no self-righteousness in saying that, because I did have very real and deep fears about the future and what path we might ultimately take.

*A*NN Our very different approach to barrier nursing was an extreme example, but there were other ways in which Alex and I were in conflict during Joe's illness.

I became very disconcerted early on to find Alex taking Joe's temperature a couple of times a day and in the night (this was easily done even if Joe was asleep, as we used the underarm method). I always relied on the traditional maternal hand on the forehead. If Joe felt hot, I followed up with the thermometer, otherwise I assumed he was OK. When I remarked that the hospital hadn't asked us to keep a check on Joe's temperature, Alex replied that they hadn't had to ask, that he'd decided to do it anyway.

I couldn't decide if this meant that I was thoughtless and

neglectful, or that Alex was becoming obsessive. I began to feel as if he were turning Joe's illness into a competition to see which of us was the most wonderful, dedicated parent. It seemed to represent a desperate need to participate in Joe's care; perhaps it is a need that for me was taken care of by the simple fact of being a mother, because I was more content to coast along relying on my instincts.

There was one morning when a thermometer wasn't necessary. Alex woke me at about 7.00 a.m. to tell me he was worried about Joe, who was burning hot. Alex took his temperature and immediately phoned the hospital. The night staff were still on duty but the night sister told us to bring Joe in right away. Alex and I pulled on our clothes, woke Joe, gave him some Calpol and carried him out to the car wrapped in a quilt. Joe, who usually woke after us, later recalled this as happening 'in the night'.

At St Stephen's we learnt that Joe had an infection and was neutropaenic (the only time he was really unwell while he was neutropaenic), and we started preparing Joe's room for reverse barrier nursing. Joe was so hot that he threw off all his clothes. Even starting a course of antibiotic and regular doses of Calpol couldn't cool him down completely, so a nurse brought in an electric fan to help make him comfortable.

Alex's parents visited us at that time, bringing presents of two Lego kits. Because of the infection, they were not allowed into the room but given chairs in the corridor where they could watch Joe through the glass partition. By this time, Alex and I were feeling less tense about Joe's general condition, but for them it was a distressing sight – a naked little boy, thin and wilting, sitting attached to his drip. But Joe still had the energy to be interested in his presents, and be cross that the medicated cloth we had to wipe them with had smudged the pictures on the Lego boxes.

The following recollection of this incident was recorded at home in Brighton one evening while Joe was in traction, early December 1988, about a month before his death:

JOE: Do you remember when I was so hot in the night, I had to go to hospital in the night and had to have a fan and I was absolutely freezing? But while we were doing Lego, we used a bed sheet and putted it on the floor so we could do Lego?

ALEX: Yes, I do.

JOE: Do you remember when I was so hot I had to go to St Stephen's, I didn't have to have a test or anything, just have a fan?

ALEX: I do remember that, was that when we were in the big room?

ANN: I think it was.

JOE: Yes, and when we used to live in London, I was getting so hot, I had to go to hospital and have a fan. Let me show you what kind of fan. Not the paper kind of fan which you wave at your face, this kind of fan [draws picture].

ALEX: An electric fan.

JOE: The one which goes around and around very fast.

ALEX: Maybe we should get one of those for here one day.

JOE: Yeah, but let me show you one thing which was good about it.

ALEX: What was that, Joe?

JOE: If we put paper capes on Melissa and Cookie Monster and Leglin and put them next to the fan, we could see their capes blowing. [Joe used to make his puppet friends into superheroes when he wore a towel as a cape, pinned with two 'I am 3' badges, and became his own creation, 3-Girl-SuperTed.]

ALEX: [Laughs] I remember – we used to do that, didn't we?

JOE: Yeah, we did. And that was very fun. That was very fun, Dad!

ALEX: Well, maybe we can get a fan one day.

JOE: Yes, because I think that will be better than Calpol, because it is an awful waste of Calpol. [Calpol is junior paracetamol, which we used to reduce Joe's temperature when he was feverish.]

ALEX: Well, does Mummy think we should get a fan?

JOE: Yes, because the fan will be better than Calpol. We could just turn it on when I get much too hot.

ALEX: Right. You are so gorgeous.
JOE: Yes, I are . . .

ALEX During this period, I decided I must return to work on my novel. It was not so much the fact that it was due at Hamish Hamilton at the end of August 1987 and that date was fast approaching – I knew that the nature of our circumstances would excuse any tardiness in delivery. It was more that I felt, despite everything, a massive commitment to it and an excitement about the pages I had written. Also, having severed my links with Mozafar's office, I felt I still needed something outside the hospital and Joe's illness on which to focus my attention and anger.

I realized there was a danger that the book would simply become a form of therapy for me, but I thought that my awareness of that should help prevent it becoming a problem. The novel was then called *Mackerel Sky*, though I retitled it *The War Zone* once it was finished, and its central theme of a teenage daughter's incestuous relationship with her father was a strange subject to be writing about as the father myself of a sick child on a general paediatric ward.

It is always difficult to know what first sparks an idea, but I think *The War Zone* had grown from two sources. One was definitely Joe Buffalo's birth and the massive impact that had on rooting me to the world: for the first time I felt fully committed to being here, to involving myself in society, to being a small, integral part of a whole. I felt passionately about everything that might affect my child, both emotionally and politically, and certainly the book is in large part a response to the destructive forces of Thatcherism and Reaganism over the past decade, to the deconstruction of a caring society and the elevation of greed and ambition as the motivating factors in life. Above all, I hated the hijacking of 'morality' by Thatcher and her ilk – their belief that as long as something looks clean, then it is wholesome; the way that the old lies were being resurrected as the new truths; the ability of people whose personal and business ethics might be totally grounded in convenience, deceit and a discriminatory view of the world to present themselves as the guardians of our souls.

The other inspiration for the novel was more direct, and again linked to Joe's birth. The thought of becoming a father made me watch other fathers and I became acutely aware of the quite electric relationship between many fathers and their teenage daughters. I watched the gentle flirting that goes on and talked to various women friends about their feelings about their fathers. These were always intense, and I found myself fascinated by the whole area of family as the environment in which you shape your attitudes towards relationships, whether through close ties with sisters and brothers or one parent or the other, or through an atmosphere of hostility and mistrust.

As I had worked on the book and found the voice for it – through its young narrator, Tom, who feels betrayed and excluded by what's going on between his father and sister – I had come to feel quite passionately that what I was doing was worthwhile, if very disturbing. Now, with Joe sick and possibly dying, I felt a whole new commitment to it: if I was to spend time away from him at all, it had to be on something I really cared about. While we were staying at St Stephen's, I would go home for at the most two or three hours and just try to write like a fury. I would tell myself: 'If Joe dies, I want to be able to look back and say, "Yes, the time spent on the novel, which I could have spent with him, was not wasted." '

The other factor very much in my mind was a sense of responsibility to the truth – not to propriety, but to a more fundamental, emotional truth, the sort of thing you admit to yourself only when pushed to the limit, as I felt by the prospect of Joe Buffalo's death. And a responsibility to the victims of incest, not simply to use their pain for some sanitized tale at the end of which all the ends are neatly tied up.

On Kenneth Grahame Ward, despite the trust we enjoyed with the staff, Ann and I were never told if sexual abuse cases were being treated – which would have been a break with hospital confidentiality – but we certainly were aware of children who had been physically abused (one of the hospital code phrases for this is 'non-accidental injury'), including a three-month-old baby whose legs had both been broken. When I returned to the ward after a couple of hours spent writing, I wanted to be able to feel that my novel presented at least one aspect of the ways in which we ensnare and abuse each other – and, perversely, love each other, too – as accurately and as truthfully as my abilities permitted.

*A*NN In early August 1987, Joe saw *Snow White* for the first time. He loved the film but we noticed that if his attention flagged at all, it was while the dwarves were on screen. I found them quite tiresome, but I was surprised that a three-year-old didn't think they were funny. His favourite character was the Queen, in her guise of Wicked Witch. When we got home he and Alex spent hours playing an elaborate version of the poisoning scene, with Joe substituting his own creation, 3-Girl-SuperTed (SuperTed's girlfriend), for Snow White and Alex playing the Wicked Witch. As we didn't have any apples, Alex had to improvise and with a croaky voice pressed 3-Girl-Super-Ted to try one of his 'ripe, juicy nectarines' instead. 3-Girl-SuperTed would eat the fruit and expire, only to be saved by Boy SuperTed, as Joe called him, at the last minute. On the first evening Joe devoured five nectarines this way, and the game was to remain an excellent way of persuading him to eat some fruit.

Later, Joe introduced another form of the game in which he would announce that he was 3-Girl-SuperTed and that he was dead. Alex and I had to exclaim in wonder at the beauty and goodness of 3-Girl-SuperTed until Boy SuperTed and his sidekick Spottyman arrived and brought her back to life. Though he had obviously combined the end of *Snow White* with the *SuperTed* mythology, Joe's interest in playing dead and the adoration that went with it was disturbing under the circumstances. Maybe healthy children play that sort of game too, because Joe never showed a conscious awareness that he was terminally ill.

Snow White was so popular with Joe that we took him to see it twice more in the next few months. The third occasion was definitely overkill. By then Joe was completely bored unless the Witch was on screen, and the moment she fell off the edge of the precipice at the end he stood up and said, 'Let's go.' He had no interest in the happy ending.

*A*LEX *Snow White* and *SuperTed* both played a large part in Joe's imagination throughout his illness. Later in the year, in November 1987, Joe started telling us his dreams and we decided to record them in a 'dream book'. The first two were totally concerned with characters from these two sources, and would seem to show Joe exploring the darker side of his subconscious – or at least identifying with the villains:

SUPERTED DREAM WITH TEXAS PETE/
THE BAD DREAM

Joe and Texas Pete kidnap a boy – the boy in the funfair story [a *SuperTed* episode shown on TV]. They take him to the ghost-train in the *SuperTed* story. They do horrid things to the boy, everybody does. Joe enjoys doing these horrid things – attacking and hurting him. SuperTed doesn't come into the dream. Joe gets on well with Texas Pete in the dream; he's a member of Texas Pete's gang. [Joe says that this dream doesn't frighten him, but that it's a bad dream.]

November 1987, first told to Daddy on the pier in Brighton

THE WICKED WITCH DREAM

I go in the Wicked Witch's car and look around. It's a black Toyota – like our car, a different colour, orange. A stripy one. The Wicked Witch is in the car and says, 'Hey, Joe, what are you doing?' She's the same as in the film but she doesn't have her Wicked Witch clothes on. She is wearing soft-bit clothes [a bra] – the Wicked Witch has soft bits [breasts]! She is wearing a bra and a *Tin Tin* jumper, but not orange like mine – white. She has long nails and the same face as in the film. I don't touch her soft bits. Now she doesn't know my name. She says, 'Hey, what are you doing?' and I say, 'Just looking around,' and get out of the car. [Joe says this dream is a good dream – it doesn't frighten him.]

9 December 1987, some months after seeing Disney's *Snow White*

7 *Summer 1987*

'A bird kissing another bird (or about to)', drawn by Joe Buffalo,
aged three years eight months, at St Stephen's, 22 April 1987

ALEX: An almost random sampling of notes from my diary
recreates more accurately than anything the shape of our
days during summer 1987, the highs and lows, the strange jumble
of fear with the more mundane details of trying to sort out the
many practical problems facing us. There seemed at times to be
an overall sense of progress, of hope – but it was a hope too
desperate to trust entirely.

These extracts by no means include all the chemotherapy
treatments or incidences of reverse barrier nursing; we were all
staying at St Stephen's unless otherwise stated.

Monday, 25 May 1987 (Bank Holiday) I go home for a while. *Mackerel Sky* plan. Bath.

Joe hugged me when I got back – in good form, tired but dancing (on drip) to TV.

Mary – Joe's blood count improving, but neutrophils down. Have to wait.

Wednesday, 27 May 1987 YMCA – swim.

I go home – estate agents, etc. [We were trying to sell our flat to clear the mortgage and other debts.]

Drink with Lyn, Anna, Carol, Simon, Graham, Mike. [Various members of staff from the ward had invited us to the pub opposite the hospital gates.]

Thursday, 28 May 1987 Joe – hospital garden – briefly. (Dr Sinclair thought it a bad idea.)

Joe's blood count safe for chemotherapy – neutrophils 1,800.

Saturday, 30 May 1987 Painting the basement steps – then RAIN! [I was trying to brighten up the flat for sale; as soon as I got back to St Stephen's, it poured with rain and I had to repaint the steps the following day.]

Tuesday, 2 June 1987 Echotest on Joe's heart – Brompton Hospital. [This was to monitor Joe's heart muscles, which could be adversely affected by one of the chemotherapy drugs.]

4.30 Dr Harris, St Stephen's. [Ann and I had asked for family counselling; this was to become a fairly regular weekly appointment.]

7.30 Carol's leaving party – Hollywood Pub. [We felt privileged as parents to be invited to a staff nurse's leaving party, which was a fairly wild affair, including a stripping nurse and the near-rape of a Tarzanogram!]

Wednesday, 17 June 1987 Sold the flat.

Friday, 19 June 1987 11.30 Joe – triple chemotherapy.

Dr Phillips pleased with Joe's progress – CAT scan + bone marrow biopsies in a couple of weeks.

Monday, 22 June 1987 Joe's blood count low – will be given a small transfusion.

Wimbledon – 1st day completely rained off.

Tuesday, 23 June 1987 Joe – haemoglobin transfusion.

Into reverse barrier nursing.

Sunday, 28 June 1987 Joe – Hyde Park – popcorn & ice cream. [We took Joe out for the afternoon from the ward.]

Wednesday, 1 July 1987 Joe – ophthalmologist. [Joe developed quite a serious squint in his right eye; the general feeling was that this was another side effect of vincristine's muscle-relaxing properties, but this was not certain and surgery was considered as a possibility for the future.]

Thursday, 9 July 1987 Reverse barrier nursing.

Ann at home with cold.

Bricks & shoes – sausages & beans for Joe all the time. [I cooked these in the ward's kitchen while a nurse kept Joe company – he was not happy to be left alone.]

Friday, 10 July 1987 Reverse barrier nursing.

Ann at home with cold.

Dry run with valegan – Joe sleeps for 4 hours.

W. Brompton Cemetery – walk. [Joe was sedated with valegan to test his response in preparation for a brain scan on Monday; I left him on the ward and walked in the sun in the cemetery, again forcing myself to confront the possibility of Joe's death and trying to prove to myself that I was not afraid of it.]

Saturday, 11 July 1987 Reverse barrier nursing.

Joe smashes his toe with drip stand. IVAC. Sleeps till 11.00 p.m. Then bricks & shoes at 1.00 a.m. – after fire alarm. [The fire alarm would often ring in the hospital; on this occasion we could actually smell smoke on the ward and I worried about moving Joe if there was a fire, as he was still on a drip and his immune system was low.]

Monday, 13 July 1987 Ann back with us.

MNR scan at Marylebone clinic (magnetic resonance scanning).

Valegan doesn't work – Joe stays awake. [This was the only scan that Joe never had; Dr Sinclair was concerned that Joe's squint might be an indication of tumour activity in the brain, but despite the test run on Friday, Joe would not succumb to sedation and the scan was abandoned.]

Tuesday, 14 July 1987 9.00 Westminster – CAT scan/bone marrow biopsies. [The CAT scan went ahead despite the fact that Joe was still officially in reverse barrier nursing with a suppressed immune system.]

Battery flat – last straw. [I had left my car lights on again; I was often in a very tense state when we arrived at hospital.]

Wednesday, 15 July 1987 Still reverse barrier nursing.

V. tense – waiting for scan results.

12.00 Sleep. [I am not sure whether this means that Joe slept or I did; Ann and I were often physically exhausted throughout Joe's illness.]

Mum & Dad come up – masks & gowns.

Thursday, 16 July 1987 Dr Sinclair – CT scan/biopsy results. Cancer out of bone marrow, secondary tumours gone, but mysterious 'holes' on scan. One on lung, one on liver, one on lumbar vertebra, one on hip, two on femur.

Bone scan & gallium scan next week, ultrasound on liver tomorrow.

6.00 Neurologist to look at Joe's squint; no reflexes in knees (vincristine).

Friday, 17 July 1987 10.30 Orthoptist – Joe. No deterioration in eye.

2.30 Ultrasound on Joe's liver – doctor thinks it's clear, only an extended blood vessel.

Graham's leaving drink. Chelsea Harbour, Lots Rd. Ferret & Firkin. [One of the ward's playworkers was leaving and invited us to his farewell party; during this period it was as if the staff at St Stephen's provided us with a social life that we did not wish to pursue elsewhere.]

Sunday, 19 July 1987 Plaza – 5.00. *An American Tail* – Joe. [Or as Joe called it, 'A Meciran Tail' – this was the start of a period when there were quite a few animated feature films around and we took Joe to the cinema more often; he was also starting to follow narratives for the first time.]

Tuesday, 21 July 1987 9.30 Joe – Charing Cross Hospital – bone scan.

Thursday, 23 July 1987 Joe – gallium scan – Charing Cross Hospital.

Monday, 10 August 1987 6.30 Century Theatre – *Snow White*.

Friday, 14 August 1987 Chemotherapy – first for 5 or 6 weeks.

Saturday, 15 August 1987 JOE BUFFALO'S BIRTHDAY.

Recovering from chemo – OK in afternoon. *Batman* suit. *Robin Hood* and *Raccoons* videos.

Joe's Fourth Birthday

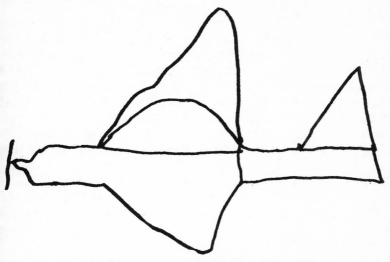

Aeroplane by Joe Buffalo, aged four years, 1987

ANN Just before Joe's fourth birthday, he received a greatly valued present. Our friend Annette, expecting Joe to be in hospital, had left it for him on Kenneth Grahame Ward and when Joe arrived for a brief visit to have his line flushed he was thrilled to find a package waiting for him. Its contents were not a very great mystery because a fluffy face was peering out of the gift box, and when unwrapped properly Joe found a gorgeous raccoon puppet complete with striped tail. The choice of a raccoon was a particularly happy coincidence. Annette had no idea that one of Joe's favourite television programmes was a cartoon series called *The Raccoons*. Joe immediately decided to call his puppet Melissa, after the heroine of the programme, and the name suited her very well.

I wondered if there was room in Joe's affections for another puppet and even felt a bit sad that Cookie, who was rather threadbare, might be rejected. I offered Joe my theory that Melissa had come to help Cookie out because keeping Joe company all the time was such hard work for one puppet. Joe seemed to think this made sense and it was interesting that the two toys always enjoyed equal status with him.

Alex and I both did their voices, and we managed to create a fairly consistent relationship for them. Cookie was always very practical and reassuring, Melissa was usually very confident but occasionally needed support from Joe. Sometimes they explained things to him, and occasionally Joe had to console or explain things to them. They really were invaluable in helping Joe through all the hospital routines and dull days, comforting and encouraging him, and giving us another angle on how Joe was feeling.

However much of a hurry we were in, Alex and I both became conditioned to grab Cookie and Melissa. If Joe were suddenly summoned for an X-ray while we were in hospital, they would go with him; if we just went up to the entrance hall to collect our mail at home, they still came too. They were his constant companions.

A child's birthday is quite an anniversary for the parents too, with its memories of the actual birth. We felt especially reflective on Joe's fourth birthday, and I thought briefly of the irrational regrets I had had when he was born that if Joe took as long as I did to settle down, I'd never live to see my grandchildren. Those thoughts came back to me vividly now. When Dr Phillips, who was in charge of Joe's chemotherapy programme, first explained the treatment and its likely side effects to us, he mentioned that it would almost certainly leave Joe sterile. Again I felt enormous sadness at this loss of potential grandchildren, but this time there was a ghastly inevitability to it. If the treatment worked and Joe lived, I probably wouldn't be a grandmother. If the treatment did not work, I definitely wouldn't.

The idea that I might have another child who would provide grandchildren rarely occurred to me. Though Joe had been conceived and borne with no problems, I had had a miscarriage when he was two, and at forty-two another baby seemed less likely. Though I had not given up the hope of having another child, the fact that Joe was an only child was an advantage to all of us during his illness. Alex and I were spared the conflict of balancing Joe's needs with those of brothers and sisters, and Joe had our undivided attention.

ALEX It was hard to feel entirely positive about Joe's birthday. There had been a time when I thought he might not live to four, but now that the day had come, it seemed only to emphasize the passing of time, the enormity of the problems facing Joe.

Like Ann, perhaps even more so, I was very struck by the fact that chemotherapy would make Joe sterile. I remember talking about this with Dr Harris, our counsellor, who felt that I was focusing on a rather abstract problem, given the nature of Joe's illness and the distinct possibility that he would not reach adulthood in any case. But I felt, if he was going to live at all, the quality of his life was vital, and sterility might affect his whole sense of himself, both sexually and in terms of being a cul-de-sac, if you like – the last of a line. Joe had always given me a sense of continuity, of being a small hiccup in a larger cycle, and while I had not always wanted a child, the fact that I might one day have one had been important to me.

The birthday certainly made me think about his future – which was perhaps a rather pointless exercise, since there was nothing to be gained from guessing what it might be. I know I could not escape projecting myself a year ahead and wondering where we might be and whether he would have a fifth birthday; but more immediately I tried to concentrate on making this one as happy for him as possible. I had always enjoyed Joe's birthdays, particularly the parties Ann and I had organized for him, and I hoped that he would be well enough to have one now.

ANN I felt that the birthday was a hopeful milestone for us. There had been a time when we didn't know if Joe would reach four, but August arrived, he was making good progress and, apart from his lack of hair, we thought he was looking quite well.

The problem was that his birthday, on Saturday the 15th, coincided with chemotherapy. We could think of nothing more miserable than having chemo on your birthday, but we were in a dilemma. Though we were sure the staff would agree to postpone the chemo until the following Monday, we were moving to Brighton in a few days and there was so much to organize that we couldn't spare any weekdays. We really needed to get chemo out of the way over the weekend.

Alexander and I decided to arrange a small birthday party for Joe the following Friday, alerting friends but explaining that if Joe were neutropaenic it might have to be cancelled at the last minute. Although Joe was interested in the idea of a birthday and presents, his sense of time was still not very exact, so that I was able to tell him his birthday was soon without him wanting to count the days. I decided not to identify Saturday as his birthday in case he felt really ill: it would be better to exercise a mild deception and celebrate an 'official' birthday the next day.

That weekend he was given his chemo drugs on Friday, and though he was still feeling sick on Saturday morning, by the afternoon he was feeling fine, his fastest recovery from chemo. We had his presents wrapped and hidden away, and while he dozed I arranged them on a table at the bottom of his bed. When he woke up a group of nurses from the ward came in and, to Joe's great embarrassment and groans of 'Oh boy,' and 'Be quiet,' they sang 'Happy Birthday' and presented him with a jigsaw puzzle, a red car and a wonderful SuperTed card specially made by Staff Nurse Karen Addison. Joe had a habit of throwing off all his clothes when he felt sick, so he sat in bed wearing nothing but a Thomas the Tank Engine hat that had been among his presents, looking pale and skinny but immensely happy. His favourite present was a Batman outfit from Gran and Fred which he insisted on wearing right away.

It was all so normal, a little boy excited about his presents, but the little boy was attached to a drip, and he was spending his birthday in hospital.

ALEX The evening before Joe's birthday party, we had been invited to a barbecue a friend, Rosemary Reid, was having her parents' house in Chobham. Joe had recovered from his 1emo and had not yet had a blood test to see if he was neu-opaenic, so we decided to chance socializing and took Joe in 1e car to Chobham.

Rosemary and her boyfriend Philip cooked a wonderful meal 1d seemed pleased at how lively Joe was. It had been one of the ottest days of the year and we could almost fool ourselves that e were a normal family, enjoying a pleasant evening with good iends, sitting out under the night sky; but the fact that Rose-ary's parents had a swimming pool made me acutely aware of 1e impossibility of swimming with Joe while he had his Hickman ne, and although I enjoyed myself in the water, I prayed to 1e stars that Joe might be able to swim with me again – at osemary's or anywhere – on a night such as this.

ANN On the day of his party, Alex took Joe into St Stephen's in the morning for his blood test, while I got the food rganized. As usual the birthday cake was a joint effort. I made 1e cake and put on an icing base, leaving Alex to do the reative bit, the decoration, when he came back from hospital. ɔe was very keen on cars at the time, so I had purchased some ny wooden racing cars, and Alex was going to transform the 1ke, shaped like a four, into a race track. I wasn't sure how he as going to accomplish this, and I don't think he was either, hich was making me rather nervous as, when he and Joe eturned with the news that Joe's blood count was healthy bout an hour before the guests were due, the cake was still ndecorated. But there's nothing like a deadline to get things appening, and by the time the first guest arrived, Alex had nished.

It was a lovely party, just three special friends, who had all rought a baby brother: Alice with Sam, Statten with Max, and aty with Tom.

aty was a whole year older than Joe, but Alice and Statten had oth had their fourth birthdays that spring. I remembered the

time just before any of them were born, and thought about th
hope and expectations of three pregnant women. Seeing othe
children, so robust and full of life, made me aware of a sense o
being robbed. Our life together wasn't working out the way i
was supposed to. Even if Joe survived, part of his childhood wa
being taken away from us all by his illness.

Alice especially seemed to represent happier times. Joe and
had often visited her and her mother, Mary, and these outing
were always special because they lived 'in the country'. Th
treat started the moment we left home. First, the tube to Water
loo or, better still, a taxi if we were running late; and then a rid
in a train – more like a tube train than a proper train, admittedly
but one that went from an interesting mainline station througl
real countryside.

Actually, Alice lived in rural Surrey, relatively close t
London, but her home was the nearest to a storybook cottage
have ever seen. Approached down a bumpy track, it suddenl
appeared, square and pretty, backed by a huge garden and i
field where elderly horses grazed. In my memory it was alway
sunny when we were there. I see Joe and Alice in a sand-pit; Jo
and Alice sitting on the patient (and stationary) horses' backs
Joe and Alice admiring white ducks in a village pond; all four o
us walking through a nearby bluebell wood, the light diffused b
overhead trees, a mysterious soft blue. Then, back on the trai
again, and Alex there waiting for us when we got home.

The last visit we planned had had to be cancelled – on the da
we should have been taking the tube to Waterloo, Joe had th
operation to remove his kidney. The party marked the first tim
the children had seen each other since Joe became ill, and it wa
comforting that it was a noisy, lively, almost normal occasion.

After everyone had gone, Alex collapsed on the sofa and fel
asleep. Joe lay alongside him on the floor in imitation and doze
for a few minutes too. I thought about how all Joe's friend
seemed to have brothers or sisters now, while we only had Joe
We had so much to lose. But on that day we had some encourag
ing test results behind us, and an exciting new life in Brighto
to look forward to. It was a time to be positive.

9 *The Move*

A house by Joe Buffalo, aged four years four months, late 1987

ALEX Because of our financial problems, moving house while
we were all effectively hospitalized was a necessity rather
than a question of choice. My bank manager, Alex Wishart, had
proved enormously sympathetic and helpful in arranging an
overdraft, and National Mutual had suspended our mortgage
repayments for three months, but time was running out and we
simply had to move.

Despite the apparent impossibility of selling our Knightsbridge
flat a year earlier, when we had hoped to move to Spain, this
time the second couple who viewed it said they would buy it and
we began to feel that, with so much else to deal with, at least the
move might work out smoothly. We knew it was going to be
difficult finding somewhere we liked for the sort of sum that

would be left after we had paid off our mortgage and debts, but we scoured estate agents' lists in any case, hopeful that we would be lucky. I hated spending time away from Joe and Ann on something as soulless as looking at property, but I tried to spare them any unnecessary outings.

Initially, I tried to find a flat close to St Stephen's, as we liked the area and realized that even if Joe's cancer were completely eradicated, we would be spending a lot of time there in the future, but the prices defeated me. Then I chanced upon a council house for sale in Putney, and while I had reservations both about the possible culture shock involved in moving from Knightsbridge (which we didn't particularly like) to a council estate, and the fact that I felt that selling council properties at all was a bad social policy, the house itself was bright and spacious and had a garden which I thought Joe would enjoy. It was also right on the edge of Putney Heath – good for bike rides and games of football – and only fifteen to twenty minutes' drive away from St Stephen's, in good traffic. Ann and Joe came and saw the house twice and liked it, so we went ahead with arranging a survey and the purchase.

My doubts began to grow as we got closer to exchanging contracts. The day the surveyor's report arrived, I went to see a movie, Woody Allen's *Radio Days*, and was very struck by the shots in the film of the ocean breaking right at the end of a street. I am still not sure how much of a part that film played in altering the course of our move, but next morning, feeling compelled to scan the property pages of the previous Sunday's newspapers, I came across a Regency house for sale in Brighton that was within our price range. It had to be a misprint, I felt, as a similar house in London would have cost several hundred thousand pounds, but when I phoned to check, I was assured that the price was correct. I went through to where Ann was playing with Joe and asked, only half-seriously, I think, 'How would you like to live in Brighton?'

As we drove out of London about an hour later, I tried to imagine what it would be like to live somewhere else, which was hard when I had always tended to measure my sanity in terms of my proximity to the London chaos I loved – particularly Soho. By the end of that evening, a Tuesday, I had largely fallen in love with Brighton, or at least with the idea of living by the sea and the wonderful Pavilion. It seemed as if it might be a great deal healthier than London, Joe certainly enjoyed its more obvious attractions – especially a seafront rocket ride, which rose up on hydraulic arms and circled round endlessly (the operator appeared very moved by Joe's lack of hair and rather obvious 'chemotherapy look' and gave him extended, free rides) – and I think both Ann and I were attracted by the idea of a totally fresh start. I had come, somewhat illogically, to associate Knightsbridge with the cause of Joe's cancer, and I wanted desperately to be out of our flat – even if Joe had to die, I wanted it to be elsewhere. Brighton represented hope.

*A*NN It took me longer to adjust to the idea of moving to Brighton than it had to Alex's idea a year earlier, that we move to Spain. Then I had agreed to it in half a minute. This time it took me about half a day. When Alex originally suggested it on a Tuesday morning I thought first about the distance from St Stephen's, then from our friends and family. But I had had similar reservations about the possibility of moving to Putney Hill; Brighton was only a bit further down the road, relatively speaking. We had lived so long in central London that even moving to Knightsbridge from Soho had seemed like a retreat into suburbia. If we had to buy down, doing it in Brighton should be a lot more fun.

Alex said he thought we should go down to Brighton that same afternoon to look at a property he'd seen advertised in the Sunday paper. I refused on the grounds that a friend was coming to see us that evening and I had already had to put her off once. When she rang half an hour later to say that she couldn't make it, it seemed like a sign. 'OK, let's go to Brighton,' I said.

We had an informal arrangement to talk to the family psychiatrist at St Stephen's if we were in the hospital on a Tuesday. I decided to call her, just in case she was expecting to see us. I started to tell her we really needed to spend the afternoon house-hunting, feeling too like a truant to add that we'd be doing it in Brighton. 'I'm glad you called,' she told me, 'I have some good news. Dr Sinclair asked me to pass it on because he thought I'd be seeing you today.' The results of the tests on Joe's bones had come through. The holes were still a slight mystery, but there was no cancer there: possibly they were the sites of tumours that the chemo had already dealt with. We hadn't expected the results so quickly, so it was a marvellous bonus to get such wonderful news. Before we left for Brighton, Staff Nurse Lyn Martin called from Kenneth Grahame Ward to give us the same message. We set out feeling it was a special day.

Joe, who had not enjoyed house-hunting or the idea of leaving the only home he remembered, began to show his first interest in moving when we told him we were going to look at houses in Brighton. His recent trips there had been a great success and I realized right away that if we lived there we would be spending far too much time and money on the rides and video games. On that first day we only looked at one house, lovely but too small, and situated almost opposite the Palace Pier with all its temptations. So Joe had more rides, we picked up some information from estate agents, and went home feeling quite committed to this new scheme.

Three days later we made an offer on the house we liked. We hadn't done any research into the nicest or best-served areas of Brighton, just viewed a few houses that turned up on agents' lists, and found one ten times nicer than anything we could have afforded in London – well placed for the sea, the station, the shops, and the children's hospital, which we hadn't even known existed until after it was all decided. The house seemed so inviting and the move went so quickly and so smoothly, that we felt it was meant to happen.

Three weeks and one day after Alexander had first thought about Brighton, we moved in. In fact, although our solicitors probably broke some records getting it all organized, we hadn't actually completed the purchase, but the owners, Kim and Phil Ryan, who have remained our friends, let us take possession anyway.

Joe was greatly excited by it all. When we were house-hunting in London, Alex had done a lot of groundwork to spare him, but in Brighton Joe discovered a new enthusiasm. He had had opinions about all five of the houses we saw, and liked the one we were moving into best of all. I thought the fact that Kim and

Phil had a little boy, James, a year younger than Joe, had a lot to do with it: it was a house that was obviously hospitable to children. Joe told everyone that he was going to live in James's house, and developed such an anticipatory look when he said it that I began to suspect he'd misunderstood the whole arrangement. One day I said to him: 'Joe, you know James won't be leaving his toys in the house when he goes, don't you?' Joe looked uncertain. 'Well, we're going to pack all your things and take them with us, aren't we? We aren't leaving them behind for anyone else,' I went on. Joe had to agree to the logic of this, and seemed to look forward to living in the house just as much, but I'm convinced that the reason he'd first liked it was that it contained a good cache of toys.

His enthusiasm was very evident the afternoon we moved in. Alex had already gone off to try to get the phone re-connected, while Joe and I waited in a friendly neighbour's house for Kim to arrive with the keys. When Kim opened the door, I barely had time to exchange a word with her. Joe grabbed my hand and pulled me all over the house. Downstairs first, into the basement and out on to the patio, then back upstairs, in all the rooms, ending up in the attic room that was to be Alex's workroom. There was no furniture and no toys, but Joe seemed extremely happy; thrilled to be in Brighton and excited to be living in a proper house.

The removal vans arrived and there was chaos for hours as the men hurried to unload; they had to get home to London that night. It was ten o'clock before they were gone. We had a traditional moving-day supper of fish and chips and then the three of us all collapsed into our bed, unceremoniously left in the middle of our new bedroom. When we woke the sun was shining through the light curtains and there were seagulls calling out. Our first day in Brighton.

10 *Brighton*

Postcard drawn by our friend and agent Charles Walker, thanking us for dinner and an afternoon spent kite-flying and sword-fighting with Joe; October 1987

ANN The pattern of Joe's treatment continued much as before, even though we had moved. Before we made a final decision about Brighton, we had asked if Joe could remain a patient at St Stephen's. The answer was yes. We had been reluctant to change hospitals when he was in the middle of being treated by people completely familiar with his condition and in whom we had developed a great deal of trust, and for similar reasons Dr Sinclair and Dr Phillips were equally reluctant to hand him over to new doctors. Dr Sinclair immediately offered to make contact with the children's hospital in Brighton, the Royal Alexandra, so that Joe's weekly blood tests could be carried out there; and, since the hospital had a cancer ward, Joe would have contact with experienced staff.

We felt a little embarrassed at the role the Royal Alexandra was forced to play in our lives: the Cinderella hospital that did the boring blood tests while St Stephen's kept control of the interesting facets of Joe's treatment. But as far as continuity and Joe's sense of security with his existing doctors were concerned, it made sense. Given the way that all medical staff – doctors, nurses, technicians, physiotherapists – tend to circulate in search of promotion or experience, there is no realistic basis for assuming that London hospitals are better than provincial ones, yet to two London chauvinists, our first visit to the Royal Alexandra was an unfortunate confirmation of all our fears.

From the moment Joe arrived on the ward for his first blood test, he was bombarded with a flood of baby talk he had never experienced before. His Hickman line, which he always called his line, was constantly referred to as a wiggly worm, or his wiggly, a bit of tweeness he found quite incomprehensible. Apparently wiggly worms weren't flushed in the way Joe was used to; they had 'big drinks'.

We had always believed that children are quite capable of using a proper vocabulary and that, in the case of the Hickman line, giving its correct name and explaining its function was a good deal more helpful in demystifying it than any amount of cute language. At the time the line had been installed Joe was not particularly articulate, and yet he had understood perfectly what it was for, and had been justly proud of his mastery of the medical jargon.

Now, in a children's hospital, on a cancer ward, where if anything we should be dealing with more enlightened people, we found ourselves having to translate bewildering euphemisms back into normal English. Once Joe had cracked their code he dealt with the matter himself. 'You mean my line,' he would say if anyone mentioned a wiggly worm. On one occasion, when he was a bit older, he stunned a nurse who'd been foolish enough to talk about 'a big drink of salty water' by saying reprovingly that he hoped she meant saline, because he didn't want sea water in his line.

All of this may reflect personalities more than medical expertise, but Alex and I were a little disconcerted by the attitudes we encountered even over the simple matter of a blood test. At that time Joe's Hickman line had developed a leak and had been repaired, and no longer gave blood so reliably. On the occasions when blood wouldn't come at the first attempt, the staff at the Royal Alexandra wanted to resort to a needle immediately, causing Joe great distress, which seemed out of keeping with people used to caring for very sick children. With patience the line would always yield blood, and yet that patience, not an expendable luxury even in an overworked department, but an absolute essential in treating an apprehensive child, was frequently lacking. Our early impression of the cancer ward at the Royal Alexandra was of a staff perhaps understandably de-sensitized by constant contact with terminally ill children.

This first impression was, of course, far too simplistic, and in due course we became aware of the department's many virtues, as well as its failings. In particular, they demystified our approach to Joe's bouts of neutropaenia, giving us the confidence to keep him at home instead of admitting him to St Stephen's for reverse barrier nursing. They also taught us to maintain his Hickman line ourselves, a simple task made complicated by the need for minute attention to sterile procedures, but which was liberating in reducing our dependence on hospitals.

In other words, it was probably no better or worse than any other ward in any other hospital, but our first crucial impressions were unfavourable, and we were constantly thankful that St Stephen's, where everyone had always made us feel that Joe was as special to them as he was to us, still wanted to care for him.

ALEX Joe's initial response to living in Brighton had less to do with the sea than with the video games on the Palace Pier. We had no hesitation about indulging him in this new-found enthusiasm, though I certainly enjoyed taking Joe there far more than Ann, who found the atmosphere of the video arcades noisy and smoky. It is hard to deny a child with cancer anything, but we did try to resist simply giving in every time Joe wanted to go to the pier, partly because we were extremely broke and it was quite possible to spend £5 within a matter of minutes.

Joe's favourite arcade – which he nicknamed 'The Circus' – was a large, domed affair at the far end of the pier, and the healthy part of these outings was while he walked or rode his bicycle with trainer wheels over the wooden boards, listening to the seagulls overhead. I loved being close to the water and hoped that the sea would somehow have a recharging effect on Joe's body, but I also felt that the motivation and aggression required to play the video games might help him too.

I had heard of a young child with a brain tumour being encouraged to visualize the cancer cells in terms of Space Invaders which his body's defences could zap, and I tried to make similar connections for Joe, who particularly loved a game which involved blasting a monstrous, fire-breathing video dragon as it twisted in mid-air: 'The bug in your tummy that started making you ill is a lot like that video dragon,' I would tell him. 'Try to think about it wherever it is inside you, and every time you zap it, you'll get stronger.'

Not that we spent all our time inside the arcades. Joe was very fond of dressing up as 3-Girl-SuperTed and racing me along the seafront on his bike or running up and down the length of the pier with the wood and glass windbreak between us. I usually had to play Texas Pete in these games – the villain of the original *SuperTed* cartoons, but a combination of aggressor and saviour in Joe's adventures.

On one occasion I offered to race Joe round the exterior of the largest of the video arcades, with each of us taking a different side. Halfway round, I realized that I had underestimated the length of time I would be separated from Joe, and began to worry that he might panic – he was only just four. I doubled back, hoping to catch him up round the other side, but lost him completely. Now I started to panic, suffering what is probably every parent's nightmare, running up and down the pier, unsure of which direction he might have taken, with visions of him somehow falling into the sea or reaching the road. I thundered through the arcade we had been circling, shouting, 'Has anybody seen a little boy with a towel pinned to him?'

Finally, as I was heading back for the seaward end of the pier, two children of about twelve told me they had seen Joe at the side of the road by the traffic lights. I raced back to the street, dreading the irony of an accident making Joe's cancer irrelevant, and spotted Joe crossing the road towards a traffic island in the middle. There were two or three cars approaching, which I think had already slowed down for him, but I screamed at him anyway to stay where he was until I got there.

He was crying when I reached him, and I was close to tears myself, angry at my own stupidity and uncertain, when Joe told me that he had waited for the green light to cross, whether he meant the green pedestrian signal or the green light for the traffic. In fact, he had acted very sensibly and had been making his way back to the car, thinking that's where he would find me, but I know this incident made a mark on him, because he would mention it occasionally a year or more later, and we would try to make a joke of which of us had been the more frightened. I include it here not merely because it demonstrates how the normal trials of parenthood don't vanish just because you have something as significant as cancer to deal with, but also as a reminder of how active and independent Joe was at this time, compared with how physically dependent he was to become.

ANN The incident on the pier had a subduing effect on both Alex and Joe. As Alex told me what happened that evening I could imagine exactly what he'd been through. Once, when I lost Joe for about a minute in a department store, I had experienced that same panicked, frantic search. On that occasion Joe had miraculously turned up standing right behind me, completely unconcerned. It was the sort of incident that seems to happen at least once in every parent's life, and I considered it was just good luck that it had never happened to me in such a devastating way.

Knowing how vigilant Alex was in looking after Joe, I felt only sympathy for how he must have felt, anger was irrelevant, but Joe was quite offended by my calm reaction. 'Be cross with Daddy,' he told me recriminatingly. I said I didn't need to be cross, because I could see that Alex had already suffered enough by being so frightened when he couldn't find him, but this didn't convince Joe. 'You're very, very naughty,' I shouted at Alex,

'don't ever let anything like that happen again!' A rather in-
adequate reprimand, but, for Joe, honour was satisfied.

ALEX When Joe did finally notice the sea, it was not in any
way that we might have expected. He started talking to it!
Joe and I were on the pier one day, and I may have remarked on
being able to see it again through the cracks in the wooden
boards, when Joe suddenly announced: 'Hello, Sea – we're back!'
On the spur of the moment I replied, 'Hello, Joe,' in the sort of
voice I imagined the Sea might have – a low, sloshy, lugubrious
rumble (heavily influenced by my readings to Joe of Eeyore in
Winnie-the-Pooh, I suspect) – and a conversation began.

I wish I could remember precisely what we talked about that
first time, but in any case the Sea became a major imaginary
character in Joe's life. Just as Cookie Monster and Melissa
filled a certain need for Joe, the Sea took on its own role: rather
grand, always pleased to see him, reassuring about whatever he
was going through and gently teasing about his enthusiasm for
the video games. On that first occasion, I'm sure the Sea would
have asked Joe how he was, and Joe would have explained, as he
did, 'I've been ill. I had a bug in my tummy. It means I have to go
to St Stephen's for chemotherapy.' (Over a period of time the
'sick medicine' became 'chemothepary' and then 'chemotherapy'
– a transition Joe was proud of, but of a word I wish he'd never
had to know.)

Joe always greeted the Sea immediately we went down to the
pier or the beach, and I think talking to it was a way for him to
come to terms with its immensity – for me, too, the sea was
awesome, a vast, god-like force, stronger than any of us, yet
somehow calming and comforting. He certainly became a lot
more interested in simply exploring along the beach. I remember
one occasion in particular, in November 1987, when the evening
sky was especially dark and we had a torch with us; up ahead,
there was a huge black shape, just visible against the sky. We
approached, wondering if it was a beached whale – like Boris,
the whale tiny Amos the mouse finally rescues in another of
Joe's favourite books, *Amos and Boris*. When we got closer and
examined the shape with the torch, we realized that it was just a

large stone breakwater, but I think both Joe and I liked to think we had found a whale on the beach.

The friendship with the Sea took on a whole new perspective next time we drove up to London for chemotherapy. As we were leaving our house (a major operation which involved loading the car with our TV and video, a suitcase of clothes for the three of us, a selection of Joe's toys and books, the typewriter and various notes and books so that I could get on with my novel), I suggested driving down to the Sea to say goodbye. 'No,' Joe said. 'The Sea's coming with us.' So we drove down to the front and from his car seat Joe called, 'Come along, Sea – we're going to St Stephen's!' I made a whooshing sound as the Sea disappeared into the car, and Joe, showing a marvellous regard for logic, said goodbye to the Sea's 'friends' – the rest of the water left behind.

Thus began a ritual of going to collect the Sea whenever we left for St Stephen's. On Kenneth Grahame Ward, Joe would explain to the staff how the Sea had come with him and was keeping him company in the hospital's pipes and sinks. This seemed like such an unusual and entertaining idea that some months later, in early 1988, Joe and I started writing a story together which became our children's book, *Henry and the Sea*.

*A*NN Moving to Brighton didn't spoil Joe's social life. He already knew James Ryan and through him we were introduced to Benjamin and his sister Naomi, and Daniel, all near neighbours. Coincidentally some other friends, parents of Vanessa, one day older than Joe, had moved to Brighton a year before us. When the old restrictions of trips to hospital and neutropaenia didn't intervene, Joe had an almost ready-made circle of friends.

September was a month when Nigel Andrews, the film critic of the *Financial Times*, often asked me to deputize for him. Though I had warned him earlier in the year that Joe's illness might prevent me working, he didn't take the obvious course of finding another journalist but still very kindly gave me the chance to do his column for three weeks while he went to the Venice Film Festival and then took a holiday. If there had been any instability in Joe's condition I would not have been able to accept work that involved tight deadlines, especially as it now meant commuting to London for screenings, but Joe was in good form and Alex was available to look after him, so I was able to see it as a welcome break, a way of keeping a separate identity.

Joe viewed my work in a rather odd way because, on his rare visits to the cinema, he always saw cartoon features like *Snow White* or *The Aristocats*. I don't think he really accepted the concept of live action films. Once, soon after I started writing for the *Financial Times*, I had to review one of the *Care Bear* movies. I took advantage of the occasion to take Joe with me, and he enjoyed the film a good deal more than I did. But though it was fun for him at the time, it created an unfortunate misunderstanding about the nature of my work, and Joe obviously suspected that I spent my days watching children's cartoons that he ought to see too. It took me a long time to convince him that the films I saw were, by his standards, grown up and boring.

But that September he developed a new attitude to my absences. With all of Brighton to explore, and with Alex completely at his disposal, Joe was determined to have a good time. One afternoon, when there were no films screening, I rushed back, eager to see them, and found the house deserted. Later they arrived home tired and excited after a trip to Devil's Dyke to fly kites with new friends, James Kerry and his mother, whom they'd met almost by chance because James attended the infant school in our street.

In the first few weeks, Joe's happiness had already proved the move a success.

ALEX There were times during autumn 1987 when it seemed as if we never stopped moving. We drove to St Stephen's at least once every three weeks for chemotherapy, which always involved us staying there for three or four days, often for longer. We never had more than a week or so in Brighton at a time, but it began to feel like home, even if our explorations of the town were severely limited – Ann and I rarely went out together with Joe, but rather maximized our use of time by taking Joe individually and giving each other a break. Even mundane chores

like going by bus to pick up the car from being serviced could be
fun when Joe came along; one of the things I miss most now
about being a parent is that chance of seeing the world, however
briefly, through your child's eyes, that and the pride I always
took in having Joe with me.

Despite growing financial pressures and the fact that my
novel would solve none of them in the short term, I threw myself
into finishing *The War Zone*, greatly encouraged by my friend
and agent, Charles Walker, who visited us in Brighton and in St
Stephen's on several occasions, and by a letter from my publisher, Christopher Sinclair-Stevenson, telling me not to worry
about the missed deadline. I worked in the attic room of the
house (the first time I had had a workroom that didn't double as
a bedroom or something else), from which I had a splendid view
of the autumnal mood-swings of the sea beyond the rooftops of
Brighton. Often while I was working there, Joe would climb the
stairs to see me, bringing me sandwiches and a beer for lunch, or
coming to gaze at the illustrated map of Bequia (the Caribbean
island we had visited when Joe was eight months old) I had on my
wall, which he always referred to as 'The Treasure-Map Island'.

When we were at St Stephen's I was able to continue writing,
thanks to the hospitality of two of our ex-neighbours from
Knightsbridge. Bob and Anna Scott spent most of their time in
Switzerland and had kindly left the keys to their London flat
with me so that I could work there. It felt strange, to be returning
to our old buildings in Beaufort Gardens when we no longer
lived there, but I would drive over for an hour or two while Joe
was sleeping or playing with Ann and discipline myself to start
writing almost immediately.

The wrench of being away from Joe at all, especially when he
was in hospital, seemed a powerful force and I found that I could
switch into the right frame of mind in moments. I tried to use the
emotions I was experiencing daily about Joe's illness – most
notably my anger and hostility – and translate them into the
context of the novel. Towards the end of the book, for instance,
when Tom, the young narrator, confronts the fact that his father
has been having sex with his sister, I drew on the waves of
unreality and inescapable horror that I had felt upon first hearing
the diagnosis of Joe's cancer:

This is where my life turns, even more so than with Jessie, this is where the madness has to be confronted, its ugly adult form is showing its head. It's actually happening, it's been happening and we're not in some TV show, on some council estate with the kids screaming and the cats shitting and the smell of cooking and half a discount store of stereo and video and computer junk in a corner – see, I'm an elitist at heart, I revert to type. But this is my life we're talking about and it's tiny, flat and insignificantly fucked up.

From *The War Zone*

There were other, perhaps stranger, parallels between life and the novel. I had opened the book on a birth in a car which collides with a huge, fallen oak on a Devon road. I had actually never seen a tree wrenched out of the ground and had done my best to imagine it; then, on the night of Thursday, 15 October 1987, southern England experienced its worst hurricane for 250 years, and Brighton was suddenly a weird landscape of felled trees.

The storm had woken me in the night with the banging of a neighbour's window as it swung violently open and shut, but I had persuaded myself, as a newcomer to the coast, that this was simply the sort of weather you got by the sea. Next morning, when I went out, the roads around our house were literally impassable due to fallen trees, and the beautiful old churchyard of St Nicolas at the end of our street was like a scene from a horror movie, its eighteenth- and nineteenth-century gravestones cracked and torn out of the earth by ancient tree roots. As Ann, Joe and I went to investigate (along with all our neighbours; there was the kind of party mood extraordinary events seem to create), I was treated to an over-abundant confirmation of the exposed roots and gaping earth I had fantasized for *The War Zone*.

Joe was certainly struck by the drama of it all, though, of course, at four years of age, he may have thought that such devastation happened quite regularly. We made a home movie of him in the churchyard and on the beach a few days later, on 22 October 1987, in which he used his raccoon glove puppet Melissa to report on the hurricane:

JOE: [a high-pitched voice, as Melissa] This is Brighton.

ALEX: It's Brighton, is it?

JOE: [as Melissa] This really is Brighton!

ANN: Is this the churchyard after the hurricane, Melissa?

JOE: [as Melissa] This is churchyard.

ALEX: What's Melissa saying?

JOE: [as Melissa] The trees have fallen down!

ALEX: The trees have fallen down? That's terrible.

JOE: [as Melissa] The trees have really fallen down. Of course they have really fallen down.

ANN: How did it happen, Melissa?

JOE: [as Melissa] It happened with all the wind.

ANN: All the wind came, Melissa?

JOE: [as Melissa] Yes.

ANN: It must have been a very strong wind.

JOE: [as Melissa] I'm finished, Daddy.

On the beach:

JOE: [again doing a strange, high-pitched, excited voice, much like his Melissa voice] Hello! All the trees have fallen down, and the sea is there, and Joe is there, and Ralph Stuart [Joe's toy hedgehog] is there, and Melissa and Cookie Monster are there. That's the end!

11 *Christmas 1987*

'Joe loves Daddy and Melissa loves Daddy', written by Joe Buffalo, aged four years four months; *Peanuts* Christmas card, 1987

ALEX We approached Christmas 1987 in a mood of considerable hope. Apart from the side effects of the chemotherapy itself, Joe had been remarkably well and active for some months, and while everyone at St Stephen's was cautious in their optimism, there was definitely a sense that Joe was making progress. Back in October, I had written the following note in my diary:

Friday, 2 October 1987 Wonderful news – Dr Phillips says Joe should have 2 or 3 more chemotherapy treatments, then if the tests are clear he can stop around Christmas! Happy Christmas!

ANN In Early December, Joe was due for his quarterly tests – a CT scan, bone scan and bone marrow biopsy. These took place at three different hospitals. Now that we lived too far from London to take Joe directly from home, this involved being based at St Stephen's for a few days with trips to the Westminster and the Royal Marsden to use equipment there.

Joe's bone marrow biopsy could be done on Kenneth Grahame Ward, so it should have been the most straightforward. As the test involved taking a sample from the hip bone, Joe needed to be sedated in advance and then given a local anaesthetic when the test was actually done. Because Joe had a long history of being resistant to sedatives, Alex and I were concerned that he be given an adequate amount to get him through. Only the week before, Joe had had to be sedated at the Royal Alexandra. An ingrowing toenail had become painfully infected and it had been decided that it should be cut away. To our surprise the consultant, Dr Cree, had performed this very minor operation herself, and we had been impressed by her commitment to the all round care of her patients.

What had also impressed us was that she had sedated Joe very effectively for just the right amount of time, and we had asked for details of the dosage so we could pass them on to St Stephen's. Unfortunately the only reaction we got there to what we saw as a sensible exchange of information was that they didn't like ketomine, the sedative Dr Cree had favoured, and didn't want to use it.

The drug of their choosing was given to Joe that afternoon in his room after Alex had left to get some writing done. Joe and I waited for a doctor from the haematology department who was going to take the bone marrow sample, with a house officer from Kenneth Grahame Ward present. When the haematologist arrived, Joe was still completely alert and decidedly unhappy about events when we took him into the treatment room.

Joe had to lie on his front so that the needle could be inserted in his hip. A local anaesthetic was going to take care of the pain of the needle, but this did nothing for Joe's state of mind, which the sedative should have calmed but clearly had not, and he was crying and distressed. I held his hands and stroked and soothed him as best I could, and though he was obviously frightened he lay very still. I felt so proud of his brave reaction – I wouldn't have blamed him if he'd tried to get up and run away – and angry that such an unpleasant and totally avoidable incident had occurred. Later, I was told that the local anaesthetic has no effect on the bone, which must be penetrated to reach the marrow, so that the experience had been even more painful and disturbing than I had realized. I regretted then not making a fuss and refusing to let them go on, but practical considerations, such as the delay – maybe several days – before the haematologist would be available again, had intervened.

The following week I discovered that I might as well have made them stop, because the result of the biopsy had been so unreliable that the test had to be repeated. Joe's progress so far had allowed us to be optimistic, but there was always the knowledge that the cancer could return. Though Dr Phillips explained that the result of the biopsy was ambiguous, it was obvious that he was very concerned about what it might signify. Apparently there are two kinds of bone marrow biopsy: the aspirate, which analyses fluid from the bone, and the trefine, which is more thorough and involves taking a solid sample of bone. Dr Phillips told us he was arranging for Joe to come in the following week so that he could have the trefine.

When I asked why Joe had not had the fuller test in the first place, I was told that he had been too distressed for the doctor to carry it out. Since Joe's resistance to sedation was common knowledge on the ward, and Alex and I had tried to prevent exactly the shambles that had occurred, I was furious. I had no idea at whom to direct my rage – would a house officer make a decision about a sedative, or would that be the registrar's responsibility? I was angry with someone, but I didn't know who.

Now Joe would have to go through the whole thing again, and was to have a full anaesthetic. With a healthy child I would have been concerned that he had as little exposure as possible to sedatives and anaesthetics, but in Joe's condition the standards were different – he simply could not get through some of the tests he needed without help, and the side effects of the drugs involved were almost trivial compared to those he had in chemotherapy.

The second test went smoothly, but there was no chance of getting a result until after Boxing Day, and the possibility that there might be tumour cells in Joe's bone marrow turned the hopeful Christmas we had anticipated into a time of tension and fear.

ALEX The day after the unsuccessful bone marrow biopsy at St Stephen's, Joe had his CT scan at the Royal Marsden, which proved an equally distressing experience. Although we were angry about the way the biopsy had been handled, our faith in St Stephen's was still immense and their unusually flexible and sympathetic approach to Joe's care made dealing with the more rigorous disciplines of other hospitals a strain for us. The Royal Marsden is perhaps the pre-eminent cancer hospital in Britain, yet we found their staff ill-prepared to deal with children. When Lilias, the registrar on Kenneth Grahame Ward, called them to arrange the scan, she found it impossible to convince them that Joe would require a sedative, despite the fact that he had been sedated for his two previous CT scans at the Westminster.

In the light of the previous day's experience with the biopsy, Lilias was as sceptical as we were that Joe would co-operate sufficiently for the scan to go ahead, but we decided to try in any case, since it was impossible to arrange a scan elsewhere before Christmas.

We were due at the Marsden at 10.00 a.m. on Thursday, 10 December. I drove Ann, Joe and Sharon Doughty, a favourite nurse who was accompanying us from St Stephen's, the short distance up the Fulham Road in the car, as ambulance transport was in short supply and in any case was always too early or late.

We had only a brief wait at the Marsden, where we tried unsuccessfully – and with Sharon's support – to convince the staff that Joe would require sedation. We explained that it had been considered necessary at the Westminster (our approach in these situations was always to use favourable experiences at other hospitals – usually St Stephen's – as a precedent and try to insist on the same treatment now), but were told that the Mars den did not agree. We pointed out that although Joe was a well-behaved four-year-old, the scanning equipment was quite imposing and that it was unrealistic to expect a child of his age to lie perfectly still for the minimum of twenty minutes the scan would take. This was countered by a claim that a six-year-old girl had lain still for her scan – to which we responded that there was a huge difference in this context between four and six.

At least we were both allowed to accompany Joe into the scanning room, but despite our best efforts – including supportive jokes and remarks from Cookie Monster and Melissa – Joe was distressed by the sight of the scanner, which is not unlike something an astronaut might be put through at NASA, and refused even to lie down.

When he started to cry, it was decided that perhaps sedation might be the best solution, but no member of staff who was authorized to administer it was available at the Marsden. I then telephoned St Stephen's to find out whether one of the Kenneth Grahame house officers could come up to the Marsden with some sedative. I spoke to Lindsey Corrie, who had just finished ward rounds and whose friendly and totally sympathetic manner was refreshing after an hour or more of the Marsden, and drove there to collect her and bring her back.

When we arrived, Joe seemed pleased to see a familiar face and was relaxed about Lindsey administering the sedative through his line. Lindsey stayed while the scan went ahead (as much for moral support as anything, I suspect), and once Joe had recovered a little from the sedation, we all drove back to St Stephen's.

The problem in a situation like this was that, except at St Stephen's, where for the most part we felt actively involved in decisions concerning Joe's treatment, our instincts and experience as parents often seemed to count for little. There is a risk, obviously, of interfering too much, and we tried not to be too demanding or demonstrative in our dealings with unfamiliar doctors and nurses; but at the same time a parent's knowledge of how his or her child might react is likely to be accurate and in many instances can save not only time and effort, but more importantly avoid distress to the child.

*A*NN Though he did not enjoy the week of tests, Joe was consoled by the knowledge that it was nearly Christmas. Because he was now attached to two hospitals, he was invited to parties at St Stephen's and the Royal Alexandra. I was sorry to see at both parties that he was shy of joining in games like pass the parcel, but he enjoyed himself and was thrilled at the Royal Alexandra to receive a marvellous SuperTed doll which could shed its fur to emerge in trunks and cape. We were very amused at that party to see Joe relax as the afternoon progressed. After being quite reserved during the games and tea, he became very excited at the sight of the microphone the visiting Father Christmas used, and as everyone was going home, he seized it and started reciting 'Baa baa black sheep' over and over again.

This was the first Christmas that Joe was fully aware of the Santa Claus myth. The year before he had been thrilled by the idea, but had been so determined to stake out Beaufort Gardens and watch Santa Claus arrive, that he had refused to get out of our car after a Christmas Eve outing. 'We're going to sit here and wait for Santa Claus,' he'd announced, and it had taken Alex twenty minutes to persuade him that there wouldn't be any presents delivered until Joe was indoors and asleep. This year Joe understood that Father Christmas expected privacy.

We had taken him to see Father Christmas at Hanningtons, our local department store, which had an excellent grotto based on Raymond Briggs's *The Snowman*. Joe had seemed to understand that the Father Christmas he saw there was a kind of deputy, not the real thing, and didn't seem at all put out when, because he'd enjoyed it so much, we paid a second visit and met a completely different Father Christmas.

On Christmas Eve we had all been invited to visit James Kerry and his mother, Adele. That evening there was to be a children's service at St Nicolas Church, which was close to our house. Though I don't believe in any organized religion, I had admired the beautiful, ancient church ever since we had moved, and thought this would be the perfect opportunity to enjoy its atmosphere properly. Adele agreed that this would be a nice start to the evening, and we all arrived at the church to find the congregation being handed lighted candles. The children's candle-lit faces certainly looked charming in the dark church, but I spent most of the service cringing away from Joe whose candle seemed to be dropping hot wax all over me.

We sang a few carols and the vicar read the story of the Nativity. Joe was more interested in his surroundings than the ceremony, but not at all intimidated. I had made a few unsuccessful attempts to explain to him what festivals like Christmas and Easter signified to some people, but my own disbelief had made it difficult for me to communicate the stories. But I did want him to know something about other people's faith eventually, so that he could decide for himself, and because I felt that religion had had such a powerful influence on music, literature and art that half our culture would be lost to him without some kind of religious education.

Though the service was delightful, I felt that maybe the time was not yet right for any of this. After half an hour, Joe whispered: 'When can we go?' I imagined the service would be short, perhaps an hour, so I told him we would leave soon, deciding to take him out if he got restless. Only a minute later the vicar announced that the service was over and we left, praising his good sense in making it so brief – just the right length for excited children with short attention spans.

At James's house he and Joe had an interesting conversation about stockings versus pillowcases for Father Christmas. James had a very splendid large stocking that Adele had made for him; Joe had decided to choose one of our pillowcases, and that evening, back home, we had an urgent discussion about exactly where we should place it. Joe had slept with us all the time he was ill, and I think we needed the security of having him close at night just as much as he needed us. But now Joe was worried that if Father Christmas looked into his room and saw the bed was empty, he might think he wasn't in the house. We decided to compromise by leaving Father Christmas's snack – biscuits and Coca Cola, chosen by Joe, with carrots for the reindeer – in Joe's room, and pinning the pillowcase to our bedroom door as a hint that Joe was with us. On Christmas Day Joe woke to find his pillowcase filled, with two huge packages beside it:

JOE: [very sleepy] Can you get me my sack?

ANN: Joe, I can't believe you don't want to go and get it yourself!

ALEX: I think you should go and get it, Joe, because Santa likes boys to go and see what he's done with their sack. Do you want to come with me?

JOE: Sea!

ALEX: [as the voice of the Sea] Oh yes, Joe.

JOE: Did you wake up and open your eyes?

ALEX: [as the Sea] I'm afraid, Joe, I missed Santa Claus, I was sleeping.

JOE: No, no, you're not supposed to wake up. Mean, if you wake up, Santa Claus would take all your presents away!

ALEX: [as the Sea] Oh, maybe it's just as well.

JOE: [excited at seeing his sack] Look at this!

ALEX: [as the Sea] I did hear the reindeer, Joe, I heard all the jingling.

ANN: [reacting to the presents] Gosh, that's a big one, it wouldn't go in your pillowcase.

ALEX: Look at that, Joe, I think Santa must have had to take your pillowcase off the door because he couldn't get all the presents in.

JOE: [very excited] And look at this nother one here!

ALEX: That's from Mummy and Daddy.

ANN: Yes, we put that there last night, but we didn't see the other stuff. Do you want to open that one last?

ALEX: Shall we get it all on to the bed?

JOE: Can you get that for me, and I get the big present? [Laughter]

JOE: SuperTed!

ALEX: [as SuperTed] Yes, Joe.

JOE: It's Christmas Day now, it's not Christmas Eve any more.

ALEX: [as SuperTed] Happy Christmas, Joe.

ANN: [also as SuperTed] Bubbling blancmange!

ALEX: [as SuperTed] What? What was that?

JOE: That was my mummy saying, 'Bubbling blancmange!'

[Extracted from a tape made on 25 December 1987. We had taped Joe opening his presents the previous Christmas; it was these tapes that encouraged us to tape various conversations with him at other times. Joe was usually unaware that the tape-recorder was on.]

ALEX Christmas Day was definitely a success as far as Joe was concerned, and was perhaps not as tense as we had feared, though it was impossible to escape wondering whether Joe would still be alive next Christmas.

He was overwhelmed (momentarily) by all his presents, and particularly liked the junior snooker table which Father Christmas had brought for him. I, in turn, loved the Peanuts Christmas card Joe had given me, which was in fact a little book containing the traditional poem, ''Twas the night before Christmas', illustrated with pictures of Snoopy, Charlie Brown and friends, and inscribed by Joe: 'Joe loves Daddy and Melissa loves Daddy X X.' I read the poem aloud to him while we were still in bed, and indulged for a moment in a sort of glorious Victorian fantasy of Christmas.

Joe was not an early riser even on Christmas Day, and by the time he had opened all his gifts we were late setting out for Christmas lunch with my family, which came as no surprise to them. Just as it was our first Christmas in Brighton, it was my parents' first Christmas at Bexhill-on-Sea, and we drove along the coast, thrilled to see what we could of the ocean through a fairly heavy mist.

Gran and Fred were delighted as always to see Joe Buffalo, but I found being with them and with Lynne and Peter made me somehow more aware of the fragility of my family now. By the time I drove us home, the mist had really rolled in and I simply followed the headlights into a shifting blur, happy that Ann and Joe were dozing peacefully in the car, but in a way as uncertain about the future as the darkness ahead.

ANN If we'd kept strictly to Joe's chemotherapy timetable he would have spent Christmas in hospital. Fortunately everyone involved thought this was a terrible idea, and it was agreed that we would bring him in the day after Boxing Day, which, because Christmas was on a Friday that year, was not until Tuesday the 29th.

We arrived at St Stephen's to learn that the second bone marrow biopsy had been completed and was clear. We had already heard that all Joe's other tests were clear, so this was an encouraging piece of news, and a great relief after the tension of Christmas. Joe still had a small tumour on his lung, but it had been dormant for months and seemed to be regarded as the least threatening of his problems.

On 31 December 1987, Joe was still recovering from his chemotherapy. Alex and I wondered how we should celebrate the New Year. It was an occasion we always found faintly depressing, but it seemed important that we acknowledge it in some way, so Alex bought a bottle of champagne, and when midnight came we took paper cups of champagne out to the night staff, then sat in our room and drank a rather sober toast to 1988 and Joe's good health.

So far, the news about Joe was still good, but we were both wondering how he would be by the next New Year. Joe could be virtually recovered by then, or – maybe – dead. There was no way of knowing. At five past midnight, Joe, who had been quite listless all day, suddenly announced that he was hungry and wanted beans on toast. It seemed significant that he had rallied just when the year started, and as we watched him cheerfully eating his snack, his nausea completely gone, we hoped that it was a promising sign.

12 *False Hope*

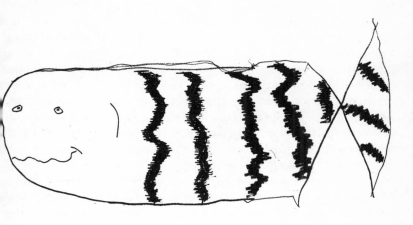

Fish by Joe Buffalo, aged four years two months, 1987

ALEX The new year began well, with Joe back home in fairly good form. I was writing hard, trying to finish *The War Zone* by my birthday at the end of January, but always enjoying the time I spent with Joe above anything.

One particularly special afternoon occurred early in the month, when we visited the Brighton Dolphinarium. Ann and I had very mixed feelings about this place, as the dolphins seemed never to see natural light and there were documented reports of a high proportion of dolphin deaths over the years. We had taken Joe once before and he was keen to go back, being extremely fond of dolphins; so, on Monday 11 January 1988, Joe and I spent half an hour wandering round the aquarium, looking at the small shark and the catfish, which were his favourites, and then went in to see the dolphin show.

While it was sad to see highly intelligent creatures being forced to perform circus tricks, it was also possible to admire

their extraordinary beauty and strength, and Joe got enormou
pleasure simply from the spray that showered us when they leap
out of the water and dived back in. Then came the point in th
show when a child from the audience was invited to ride alon
in a small dinghy, pulled by a dolphin with its nose through
ring at the end of a rope.

Joe desperately wanted to be chosen, and stood up, but I fel
slightly doubtful, since it involved the child being taken back
stage by the trainer, fitted with a life-jacket and led out alon
a platform to get into the boat. Joe still had his Hickman lin
in, and I had dreadful fantasies of the sort of infection he migh
get if, for any reason, he slipped and fell in the water. As i
was, simply being in the Dolphinarium exposed him to a smal
risk of infection from the stuffy air, the presence of other chil
dren, and the dolphins' far from sterile pool and bucket of dea
fish.

The problem was solved, to Joe's dismay, when a young girl i
the audience beat him to it. She disappeared backstage, ther
was a pause, then a few moments later she reappeared, crying
having obviously suffered second thoughts. The trainer aske
for another child and this time there was no stopping Joe – h
climbed down across the seats and I handed him over to th
trainer, briefly muttering that he had a catheter fitted to hin
that must be kept sterile and hoping that no accidents woul
befall him.

Thankfully, all went well. Joe was led out in his life-jacket, wa
asked his name and clearly announced into the microphone, 'Jo
Buffalo!' The trainer held Joe's hand as he climbed down into th
dinghy, then the dolphin appeared, poked its nose through th
ring, and Joe was on his own, being drawn through the water a
remarkable speed. He looked marvellously proud and quite inten
on what was happening, both aware that he was suddenly th
star of the show but also serious about this encounter with
dolphin. I felt as elated as he did, sorry only that Ann wasn't witl
us to see it and that I didn't have her camera with me.

When it was over, Joe seemed to have attained a new sense o
independence and confidence, and I told him that he had don
something I had never done – been pulled in a boat by a dolphin
We bought an inflatable toy dolphin on the way out, which Jo

immediately named Clarabel, and went home so that he could tell Mummy about his adventure.

ANN When Joe got home he was radiant. He loved to ring on the doorbell and have me answer, which could be annoying if I had to break off what I was doing in the basement and go upstairs, even though Alex had his keys and could easily let him in. But when I opened the door that evening, Joe was holding his new dolphin and looked so excited that I could tell instantly that something important had happened, and my vague feelings of irritation vanished.

Joe came in, talking a mile a minute about his ride with the dolphin, and how he'd had a second chance, and how his new dolphin was called Clarabel. He seemed so animated and grown up – a boy who rode with dolphins – that I immediately caught his mood. I knew how much competition there was to be the chosen passenger, and realized that Joe must have completely forgotten the shyness he often felt among strange children to have asserted himself so successfully.

Our mood of elation lasted the whole evening, and Joe couldn't wait to call Gran and Fred to tell them about his ride. Not having seen the show, they must have initially pictured him tossing about on a dolphin's back, and Joe greatly enjoyed retelling the story of how it all happened, and how it felt to sit in the little boat, the centre of attention.

The dolphins made an enormous impression on Joe, and a few weeks later he had one of those uneventful but delightful dreams that can give such pleasure:

DOLPHINS DREAM

A happy dream. Joe was at the pier, but it was bigger than it is 'numally' [one of Joe's favourite words, a combination of 'normally' and 'usually']. The dolphins were jumping above the water – the sea.

9 March 1988

*A*LEX On Thursday 21 January I typed the last pages of *The War Zone*, just as Ann was packing our things to go up to St Stephen's for Joe's chemotherapy. We drove to London and Joe was given his drugs that evening. The next day I had lunch with Charles, my agent, and handed the book over, feeling relieved to be finished, hopeful that it was as powerful as I had striven to make it, but also more than a little scared that it might be too disturbing for many people – and might stun the friends we had made among the staff at St Stephen's when it was published.

Ann and I had hoped that Joe would have recovered sufficiently from chemo to go home by Saturday afternoon, when my parents had planned a pre-birthday dinner for me, inviting Lynne and Peter, too. It seemed almost as if any family gathering was fated not to succeed, because as Saturday progressed, Joe's condition changed in a way it never had before. By Saturday evening I was incredibly scared – perhaps irrationally, though I think the presence on the ward of a child with meningitis contributed greatly to my fear that he might actually die that weekend.

*A*NN That Saturday in St Stephen's was like a rehearsal for what lay ahead of us. At first everything seemed normal. Joe had had his chemo on Thursday evening; he was sick during Friday and hadn't completely recovered when he woke on Saturday morning. We didn't worry too much because he often snapped out of the nausea quite suddenly, and we'd just have to cancel the dinner if he didn't.

Then, in the early afternoon, Joe's condition changed completely. He stopped feeling sick, but became very listless and rapidly deteriorated into a state of semi-consciousness, looking so white and lifeless that we were terrified. The doctor on duty examined him carefully and could find no explanation. He took a blood sample and sent it off, marked urgent. Alex and I sat by Joe, tense and afraid.

The one question I had not yet asked about Joe's illness was, if he died, how would it happen? Probably that was an unanswerable question, as it would depend on which aspect of the cancer

aused his death. Now I was wondering if this was it. I was
eartened by the doctor's assurance that he could find nothing
angible wrong with Joe who, in spite of his disturbing appear-
nce, was very strong. But his condition was so unfamiliar, and
e looked so weak and ill, that the thought that he might die
vouldn't go away.

Alex was so anxious that he almost passed out, collapsing
eside Joe's bed. A nurse helped to revive him, and he went to
hone his parents looking pale and scared. Joe had no symptoms
he doctor could treat, so we just waited helplessly, our minds
welling nervously on the meningitis patient in the room next to
urs.

That evening, Joe seemed a little better. He was still droopy,
ut his semi-conscious state seemed to have turned to a more
natural sleepiness. The next morning when he woke he seemed
erfectly normal and happy. No one could ever explain what had
appened to Joe: it was just one of those things, and it was over.
Ie felt fine that Sunday morning, but Alex and I were exhausted
y anxiety and a restless night. We went back to Brighton
lmost too drained to feel relieved.

ALEX Having finished *The War Zone*, I put my mind to the
fact that we were frighteningly broke and in debt, with no
bvious, immediate source of any income. I wanted to write
nother book, but that would not solve our cash problems
uickly enough and in any case I felt I needed to spend more
ime with Joe than I had for the past couple of months.

For the first time in our lives, I applied for state benefits. Not
nly did we have no savings, but we owed considerable sums to
he bank and credit card companies, and although I had tried
ard to find some scriptwriting commissions for sponsored films
- work which should have been fairly flexible in terms of my
ommitment to Joe and our unpredictable but frequent periods
f hospitalization – none was forthcoming, and my heart wasn't
n it.

On a Wednesday morning early in February, I went to our
ocal Social Security office to sign on. Despite the friendliness of
he staff I encountered, the whole process itself is calculated to

remove any sense of self-worth or identity almost immediately and to place you on the defensive in terms of your entitlement to any benefit – 'welfare chiselling' is considered a far more heinous crime than the massive tax avoidance and evasion practised by virtually any company or individual who can afford an accountant.

I felt a little gloomy about the occasion, but also strangely privileged, not only in the sense that my career had always been unpredictable and there was no reason to think that it would not recover, but more so in that, measured against the scale of Joe's illness and the possibility of losing him, there was the extraordinary strength of fearing little else: we were facing the worst, what else could happen that really mattered?

I walked back up the hill through the churchyard to our street, and arrived home to find a letter from Christopher Sinclair-Stevenson, my publisher at Hamish Hamilton, about *The War Zone*, which completely lifted my spirits. I had had no idea how he might respond to the novel and had tried not to dwell on it too much, but the first paragraph alone made me feel that the time I had spent on the book had been worth it:

> Dear Alexander,
> First of all, very many congratulations on *Mackerel Sky*. [It was a later part of this letter and further discussion with Christopher that persuaded me to change the title to *The War Zone*.] I read it over the weekend with mounting excitement. I think that you have far exceeded my expectations – which may sound a very backhanded compliment – but it has the most extraordinary raw tough immediacy about it. It is a novel absolutely of our time, inevitably shocking, disturbing but extremely impressive. I am astonished that you have managed to finish it in the middle of so many personal problems . . .
>
>   Extracted from a letter of 8 February 1988

I remember that I hugged Ann and Joe, who were both in the room with me, re-read the letter, and felt that somehow, if my feelings about the novel were justified, perhaps my feelings about Joe living would be proved right also. I realize as I write

this how foolish it may sound, but essentially Ann and I knew
that we were clutching at straws when it came to Joe's survival,
and any straw was a good straw.

During this period, Joe's character and sense of the world seemed
to blossom. He had been somewhat of a late talker, but was now
extremely articulate, with an impressive vocabulary, although
he still spoke with a slight lisp.

Perhaps he was at an age – four and a half – when he would have
made great progress in any case, but we felt that our concern for
him, the activity around him and his constant contact with
interested, sympathetic adults, contributed to a more sophisticated response to life than that of other children his age. Also, and
this is an observation many people who have worked with terminally ill children have made, it is as if the children themselves
know what they are facing and attain a calm and a wisdom more
commonly associated with the very old. We still did not accept
that Joe would die and had not told him that he might, but we had
talked about death extensively and perhaps he had some subconscious or intuitive appreciation of his situation. Whatever the cause,
he was someone it was a joy to be around: loving, amusing, full of
life, sharp-witted and very much in control of his environment.

A^{NN} Joe knew that Alex and I got paid for writing, and
began to associate our typewriters with literally making
money. He used to enjoy bashing at random at the keys of my
typewriter, rather generous with the paper, his favourite layout
being a few lines to each sheet with plenty of space between
them. One day, when I'd told him something he wanted was too
expensive to have right away, he announced that he was going
to 'do some writing' and thumped out three pages on my machine.
He told me he was earning some money for toys and, when I
asked how much he thought he'd make, he pointed to each page
in turn: 'Three pounds, three pounds, four pounds,' he explained.
'I'd better do another page!'

I loved the idea of each page having a definite earning power,
and imagined a situation in which, every time I finished a page,
a ten-pound note popped out of my typewriter like a cash register.

I don't know how Joe arrived at the sums he mentioned, as he never had much grasp of the value of money, so that whether a toy cost fifty pence or fifty pounds, it probably had the same worth for him. I finally managed to give him some concept of comparative sums by relating them to the cost of Lego kits. He knew their different sizes meant different prices, so I would tell him that something was about as much as a little Lego, or a medium one, or a very big one. This misfired when he started to view these comparisons as a trade, and thought that if he gave up asking for the battery-operated motorbike that cost as much as two really huge Legos, he could have the Legos in its place.

ALEX In early February, Joe wrote his first, very short story. Although by now he loved books, knew the alphabet and could type, one letter at a time, if we told him the letters, he showed little aptitude for reading or writing. We wondered if this might be a negative response to our own absorption in books; in any event, we did not press him hard, convinced that children learn at their own pace and aware too that if he were to die, what was the point?

JOE'S WORM STORY

Once upon a time there was a little worm. He had a very grand house which had lots of mud. There was a boy named Joe who liked to be very dirty. He used to take the worm down to the sea in his little Lego house, to protect the worm from the birds. Then he would go home with the worm, and that is the end of the story.

Written by Joe Buffalo Stuart
('Once upon a time' typed by him) 10 February 1988

When he had dictated his story to me, we were very struck by the phrase 'very grand house', and wondered where it had come from, until we recalled something similar in *Winnie-the-Pooh*, which I was reading regularly to him at this time.

A few days later Joe added to his story, showing the same regard for creating a very definite ending:

There was a storm when the worm and Joe were going home. Joe and the worm were so happy to be home.

The day after the storm a flier worm was flying a plane and Joe's worm was sitting in the back of the plane. Then they landed and Joe's worm got out of the plane. He saw a chicken, then he went and said hello to it and that's the end of the story.

On 16 March 1988, Joe dictated to me his own 'Pooh's Hum', clearly inspired by the hums in *Winnie-the-Pooh*, yet also a distinctly original work listing some of the things Joe liked most about life and closing with an image which stunned me with its beauty as he said the words:

POOH'S HUM (BY JOE)

Tiddley pom
I like TV
Tiddley pom
I like Calpol
Tiddley pom
I like light
Tiddley pom
I like having a bath
Tiddley pom
I like having a soggy
Tiddley pom
I like staying awake at night
to sing to the stars
Tiddley pom
I like staying awake at night
to tell stories to the stars

['Calpol' is junior paracetamol; 'soggy' was Joe's word for shit.]

One of the most enjoyable evenings during early 1988 was spent making a tape to send to our friend Cherie Hoyt in America (in fact, the tape was never sent: Joe sounded so happy that we could not bring ourselves to part with it). It was a Saturday night and we had all gone to bed early. For once, Joe knew that we were using the tape-recorder and responded much as he had to the microphone at the Christmas party – by hogging it.

He 'read' his worm story for Cherie, actually remembering it almost word for word as he had dictated it, then proceeded to drive us half crazy by endlessly singing a song, 'C is for Cookie', performed by Cookie Monster on a *Sesame Street* alphabet video tape Joe was very fond of:

JOE: [singing the words for the hundredth time] 'C is for cookie, which is good enough for me; C is for cookie, which is good enough for me; C is for cookie, which is good enough for me; oh, cookie, cookie, cookie starts with C!'

ALEX: Can you hear that sound, can you hear that scream? That scream was Cherie jumping out of the window. Aaaagh! Cherie's gone flying out of the window, driven to insanity by 'C is for Cookie'.

JOE: [laughing] Why did she jump out of the window? [Starts singing again] 'C is for cookie . . .'

ALEX: This tape's been taken over by terrorists.

JOE: 'C is for cookie, which is good enough for me; C is for cookie, which is good enough for me . . .'

ANN: [joining in] '. . . Oh, cookie, cookie, cookie starts with C.'

ALEX: I can't stand it!

JOE: [imitating Cookie Monster on the *Sesame Street* tape] You know, a crescent moon looks like a C, but you can't eat that. So, 'C is for cookie, which is good enough for me . . .'

ALEX: [as Cookie Monster] Joe, I'm going crazy. I'll never eat another cookie again.

JOE: 'Oh, cookie, cookie, cookie starts with C.' I've got a idea. Please, I've got a good joke! Who's fighting when a man is not fighting?

ALEX: I don't know.

JOE: I tell you who's fighting when a man is not fighting. A . . . a . . . a Pacman! [laughing]

ALEX: [laughing] I don't think I understand that one, Joe. I think you have a sort of William Burroughs sense of humour: it's bizarre. What about that one we were talking about – what doesn't have a shadow?

JOE: A shadow doesn't have a shadow!

ALEX: That's right.

JOE: [laughing] A raccoon doesn't have a raccoon!

ALEX: Joe doesn't have any sense!

extracted from a tape recorded in March 1988

If Joe was unhappy at this time, or worried about his illness, he didn't show it. In fact, he seemed remarkably cheerful most of the time, as were we. His dreams of this period, which we continued to collect in his dream book, suggested common childhood anxieties such as separation, but nothing which seemed to trouble him unduly, though in retrospect the crab in the second dream might seem to represent death, or somehow to presage the paralysis which was to strike Joe in mid-April:

THE HAM SHOP DREAM

[Joe was very fond of sliced ham and, before we moved, used to go with Ann to buy it from a particular butcher in Knightsbridge, which he called 'The Ham Shop'.]

We are in a restaurant: Mummy, Daddy and Joe. 'My Mummy's mummy was in the dream – Nana.' We are eating in the car, after the restaurant. Joe says he didn't come in the car: 'I just found the car on my own.' Mummy and Daddy go to the car with Mummy's mummy, and Joe goes back to the restaurant to get a plastic cup to use in the car, but the restaurant is closed. Joe starts crying and running everywhere looking for The Ham Shop. He finds The Ham Shop, but the door is too small: 'It's like Jerry the Mouse's door in *Tom and Jerry*. I thought The Ham Shop place could help me, but it had a too-small door.' [Joe says that this was a sad dream. 'When I woke up my eyes were water and I had a big hug with Mummy.']

January 1988

JOE'S FRIGHTENING DREAM

Joe is playing tennis with a lady he doesn't know, on a patio (not ours) or in the park. Mummy and Daddy may have been there – 'Exactly, they were.' Then Joe and the lady are playing football, and the ball rolls under some trees. Joe goes to get it, but there's a crab there, a frightening crab, about two feet long, and it grabs Joe's legs with its pincers and holds him for ever and ever. [Joe often made changes to his dreams later, when we talked about them. In this case, on 4 April 1988, Joe explained that the crab grabbed his leg 'because probably it was a helpful crab and it wanted to get the ball for me.']

Told to us 16 January 1988, but Joe says it's a dream
he used to have in London, too

*A*NN Though Joe wouldn't be five until August, it was time to think about getting him a place at a local school. We very much hoped that he'd be fit enough to go by the new school year in September and, anyway, there was a certain amount of competition for places. We asked around and made up a short list of three that appealed to us and were close by. It seems sensible under any circumstances not to involve a young child in a long daily journey to school, and in Joe's case we felt it would increase his sense of security, and ours, if he were close to home. I don't know if that was why he was so keen to inspect St Paul's, the school in our street. He often watched the pupils in the playground and, besides, his friend James Kerry went there – though pretty well any school we chose would contain at least one of his friends.

Alexander and I were happy to take him to see St Paul's, but thought it would be too good to be true if such a convenient school were also the most suitable. When we visited it, we found the staff so sympathetic, and their willingness to let Joe attend part-time if that suited him best so sensible and flexible, that we immediately accepted the place they offered him. St Paul's was a church school with a very moderate attitude, so Joe would eventually learn the Bible stories that troubled me so much.

It was still early in the year and we were planning for September. It was always a little frightening to plan too far ahead, as if we were tempting fate, but if life did proceed smoothly Joe would have to go to school, and we were glad to have something organized.

ALEX Although there had been talk of stopping Joe's chemotherapy at Christmas, the decision had been made to continue until the originally proposed one-year course was complete, in April 1988. This may have been partly the result of the concern over Joe's bone marrow, or simply a precautionary measure.

The tumour on Joe's lung had not grown but had not diminished in size, and whereas I know Ann and I hoped that by Easter the chemotherapy might have eradicated it, it emerged that Dr Sinclair was considering other options.

In not the most satisfactory way to learn of a major decision affecting your child, I encountered Dr Sinclair in the St Stephen's car park, one Friday evening in early March 1988, as he was leaving and we were arriving for chemotherapy. I liked Dr Sinclair enormously – I liked his obvious love of children and even his rather traditional consultant's bluster – but on this occasion he annoyed me greatly when he announced, as I was unpacking the boot of our car, that since the only tumour remaining in Joe was on the lung, he thought it wisest to remove it surgically.

Lung surgery on a child is a rather daunting prospect to most parents, I would have thought, and because of the nature of our meeting, I had no chance to discuss the implications with him. Ann was already up on the ward with Joe, so that by the time I told her, Dr Sinclair was no longer even in the hospital and we could only discuss the situation privately and worry over the manner in which surgery appeared to have been decided upon without our being consulted.

I was not clear whether Dr Sinclair had liaised on this with Dr Phillips, who co-ordinated Joe's chemotherapy programme, and both Ann and I felt extremely upset about the fact that, since it was the start of a weekend, we would not be able to contact either of them to find out exactly what was being proposed. In fact, it was Dr Cree who put our minds at least partly to rest when, having returned to Brighton after chemo, I mentioned our concern to her. She told me that since the chemotherapy was not dealing effectively with the lung tumour, surgery was probably the best option, as radiotherapy on the lungs is detrimental to breathing. This simple explanation was enough to quell our doubts: no matter how great your faith in any particular doctor, you just need to know what is going on.

The next, or rather continuing, area of conflict with Dr Sinclair occurred over a CT scan. A couple of days after we returned home, we received a telephone call from one of the house officers at St Stephen's telling us that Dr Sinclair had asked him to arrange a partial CT scan of Joe's lungs before his next chemotherapy treatment.

Again, we had a sense of decisions being made without our involvement, and of the course of treatment to which we – and Joe – had become accustomed being varied without sufficient explanation. We immediately wrote a letter to Dr Sinclair, stating that, as we understood it, Joe was to have had a full range of tests, including a CT scan, in April anyway, and that we would prefer not to subject Joe to yet another scan, as he always found them distressing and required sedation:

> Obviously we are prepared to be guided in all these matters, but we would greatly appreciate a chance to discuss this additional scan with you. Our main concern is that Joe should not have to undergo yet another test when he could wait until this full course of chemotherapy is over. We did ask to speak to you today, but understood that you had already left the ward. We would be very grateful if you could call us at some point.
>
> With best wishes,
>
> Alexander Stuart   Ann Totterdell
>
> Extracted from a letter to Dr Sinclair, 10 March 1988

Joe Buffalo at about three months, above; and rowing on the Great East Lake in New Hampshire when he was fourteen months old, right.

Ann, Alexander and Joe at a family party for his third birthday, above. Playing in Harrod's ball pool, aged three and a half, right, shortly before his cancer was diagnosed.

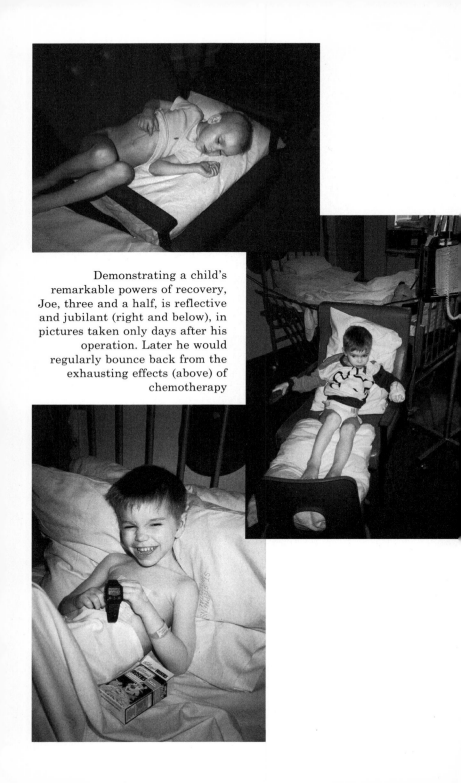

Demonstrating a child's remarkable powers of recovery, Joe, three and a half, is reflective and jubilant (right and below), in pictures taken only days after his operation. Later he would regularly bounce back from the exhausting effects (above) of chemotherapy

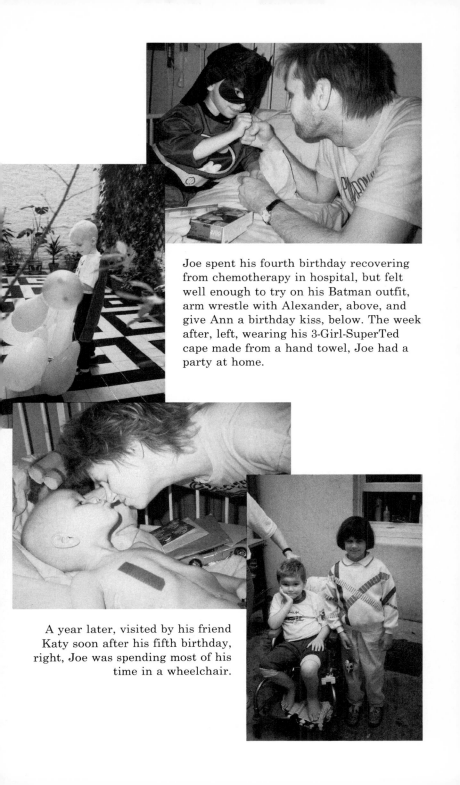

Joe spent his fourth birthday recovering from chemotherapy in hospital, but felt well enough to try on his Batman outfit, arm wrestle with Alexander, above, and give Ann a birthday kiss, below. The week after, left, wearing his 3-Girl-SuperTed cape made from a hand towel, Joe had a party at home.

A year later, visited by his friend Katy soon after his fifth birthday, right, Joe was spending most of his time in a wheelchair.

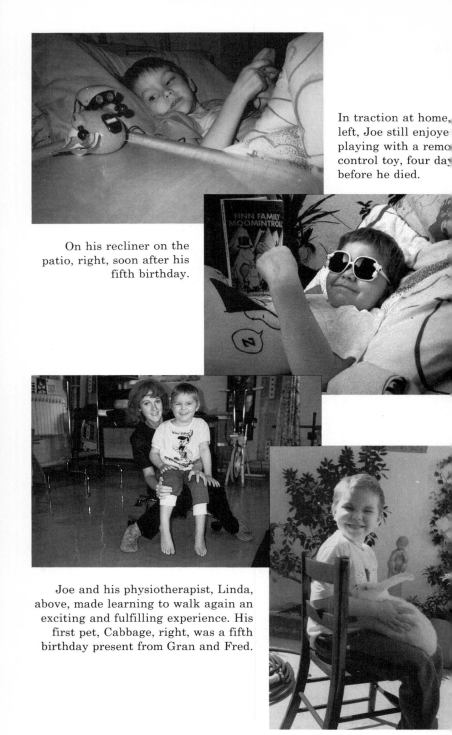

In traction at home, left, Joe still enjoyed playing with a remote control toy, four days before he died.

On his recliner on the patio, right, soon after his fifth birthday.

Joe and his physiotherapist, Linda, above, made learning to walk again an exciting and fulfilling experience. His first pet, Cabbage, right, was a fifth birthday present from Gran and Fred.

Dr Sinclair wrote back, telling us that he had discussed Joe's condition with Dr Phillips and that they both agreed there should be a limited scan of Joe's right lung, in order to see exactly what was going on before proceeding with further treatment.

Clearly, this was a reasonable argument, except that the lesion on the lung had been known about all the time and so still did not explain why a scan was suddenly required now, rather than in a month's time. In part, I think Ann and I felt rather as if we were being treated like children in the matter of our own child's most vital medical care. We also considered the possibility that Dr Sinclair had simply made a decision and was determined to stick to it; but worse was the fear that perhaps he knew of some new tumour activity within Joe and was not telling us. When you live in fear, any mystification or lack of openness on the part of the doctor simply adds to your dread.

Originally delayed by some confusion over which hospital to book it at, the scan never took place. Joe's condition changed dramatically towards the end of March and we found ourselves faced with more immediate, and far more frightening, concerns.

13 *The Nightmare Returns*

Daddy, drawn by Joe Buffalo, aged four and a half, early 1988

ALEX In the last two weeks of March 1988, Joe started mentioning a pain in his right shoulder. Since the original diagnosis of cancer and the removal of his left kidney, which had caused him the initial discomfort, Joe had been remarkably free of pain and had suffered more as a result of chemotherapy than as a direct result of the cancer. He had occasionally mentioned aches in his legs and a specific ache in his left arm between the shoulder and elbow, but none of these had persisted, and had generally been attributed to the effect of vincristine (one of the chemo drugs) on his muscles.

Now we began to worry, only slightly at first, that he was experiencing a consistent pain which, though it seemed to shift in location to some small degree, centred on a fairly clearly defined area of his back. The pain came and went, but when he had it, it made him cry, and the only way of easing it was with a hot water bottle or a hug from Mummy. Joe had never been a child who cried easily – even as a baby, he would cry for a feed, then settle as soon as he had Ann's breast in his mouth – so we found this development deeply troubling. Ann and I would look at each other and wonder what it was, and when either of us said, 'I hope it's nothing serious,' we both knew what we meant: please, let it not be the cancer returning.

On the Thursday before Easter, the last day of March, I took Joe down to the seafront for the afternoon. We drove to the Brighton Marina to look at the yachts for a while, then went back along the road towards the pier, past various amusements and fairground rides.

Joe was keen to try some new rides and seemed happy enough, though he had mentioned the pain in his shoulder the previous day. In the past, he had amazed me by enjoying some of the fastest rides more than me. We had once gone on a sort of high-speed, mini roller-coaster called 'The Dragon', which had had me clinging on to Joe and the rail, my shins rammed up against the bar, while Joe laughed with glee.

Now he wanted to try a similar ride, and while I had some misgivings, I liked him to feel as active as any other child, and so asked the attendant operating it how fast it was. I told him I had a child who had cancer, and he assured me it was not particularly fast. I bought two tickets and sat with Joe, the safety bar in front of us.

The ride started and as it got faster and faster – much faster than I had been led to expect – I could feel Joe's back being forced against my arm by our acceleration and I could see that he was in pain. I shouted at the operator to stop the ride, but he couldn't hear me, and we carried on round, a fear entering my mind that if there was cancer somewhere in Joe's back, the pressure on it might be causing him horrific pain and might cause permanent damage.

The ride stopped, and I think by then Joe was crying, whether from pain or from the anxiety he sensed in me, I'm not sure. I was furious at the attendant for misleading me and swore at him, but in reality I was much angrier with myself for taking the chance at all. I have a large capacity for stupidity, but I hope it was not simply that: I wanted to treat Joe as much like a healthy child as possible, but sometimes I took things too far.

Two days later, on Easter Saturday, 1 April 1988, Charles Walker came to Brighton to visit us, and we drove a few miles along the coast to Angmering for the afternoon. Joe paddled on the sand flats in his wellington boots, then we drove to see the castle at Arundel and a particularly lovely thirteenth-century church at Clymping, then started back to Brighton.

By the time we got home, Joe was complaining of feeling very tired and lay on the sofa, resting. We were all downstairs in our kitchen–basement area, and while Ann cooked dinner, Joe mentioned that his back was hurting him again. We gave him a hot water bottle and he snuggled on the sofa, but the pain seemed to get worse and he started to cry.

Charles and I tried to amuse Joe while dinner was prepared, but by the time we were ready to eat he was in considerable pain and there was an enormous air of tension in the room. Ann and I had not been looking forward to the Easter weekend in any case, as the previous Easter had been our first weekend in St Stephen's after the diagnosis. Now, in front of Joe, we could say little to Charles of our fears, but I think they were pretty evident, and certainly the sight of Joe in so much pain was especially disturbing when he was normally so cheerful.

At some point in the evening Charles went upstairs to the bathroom and, as he was about to come back down, collapsed momentarily at the top of the stairs. The fact that he had fainted scared the hell out of us at first, but in a sense I think it relieved the tension we were all feeling. It was obvious that something had changed for Joe, and while none of us knew what it was, it was too easy to imagine the worst.

ANN The following Monday we called St Stephen's to report our worries about Joe's pain, and Lilias suggested that we bring him in on Tuesday, which was clinic day, to be examined. We drove up to St Stephen's, and after Joe had an X-ray that had been arranged for him, he played on the rocking-horse in the corridor until Lilias was free.

That day, the pain wasn't troubling him at all and he was riding on the horse very happily when she arrived. Lilias said she could look at him where he was, and she prodded him and made him move his arm about while he sat on the horse. She could find nothing wrong with Joe and wondered if he could possibly have strained his shoulder in some way. He seemed so much better that day, quite free of pain, that we accepted this decision quite hopefully and took him home again, agreeing that we should just keep Lilias informed of his condition.

During the week, Joe's pain crept back. He was reaching the end of his third three-month course of chemotherapy and we wondered if he was simply exhausted by it. I decided to encourage him to rest for a few days, and I had no trouble persuading him to let me tuck him up on the sofa with his Lego for much of the day.

On Friday afternoon we were visited by Karen Bravery, a staff nurse from the Royal Alexandra. She had extensive experience with childhood cancer and, though her call was mostly social, we were very glad that she had an opportunity to observe Joe. I had noticed the day before that he was getting a bit unsteady on his legs, reminiscent of the wobbliness the early heavy doses of vincristine had caused.

While Karen was with us, Joe got off the sofa to go upstairs to the bathroom and we immediately saw that he was walking on his toes. He had occasionally done this during the vincristine period, and Karen told us about another patient who had walked on her toes for the entire duration of her chemotherapy. But we all found the incident disturbing, and Karen left advising us to persist with St Stephen's over the pain.

That weekend, Joe's wobbliness increased and he mentioned the pain in his shoulder again. On Monday morning I called Karen before I called St Stephen's, to ask if the pain could be investigated at the Royal Alexandra. She said that medical etiquette would make it impossible for them to take any action without St Stephen's permission, so it would be best to take him there. She added that if they had trouble arranging a swift CT scan, which might be necessary, the Royal Alexandra had a good relationship with the Royal Sussex County Hospital and could arrange one at very short notice in Brighton.

I called Lilias and she suggested that we bring Joe up again and plan to stay a few days for observation. We started the lengthy process of packing the car – there was no going home for anything we might forget – and got up to St Stephen's in the late afternoon.

The ward seemed very busy and there was only the house officer left on duty for the night. The three house officers we had known had just moved on, after their four months on Kenneth Grahame. The three new house officers were unknown to us, but when Louise came to our room, very late in the evening because she had been so involved with other patients, she examined Joe very thoroughly. Her only omission was that, though we had told her how wobbly his legs were, and that he had actually fallen over just before we left home, she didn't see him walking. It was late and Joe was tired, he didn't want to get up, and she said that there would be plenty of opportunity to observe him the next day.

A little while after she had left us, Joe decided he wanted a toy. Although the ward was dark, he insisted on going to the playroom. As he staggered down the corridor, I ran round to the ward desk to see if Louise was there. I wanted her to see how unsteady Joe was, but there was no sign of her, and I couldn't go and look for her and leave Joe on his own. In fact, that was the last time I saw Joe walk for many months, and no doctor on Kenneth Grahame ever saw him walk again.

The next day, Tuesday, Joe had more X-rays, a message was sent asking Dr Phillips to come, and Dr Sinclair arrived to examine him. No one seemed to have drawn any conclusions from Joe's symptoms, but Dr Sinclair was trying to arrange a CT scan. It looked as if it wouldn't be possible before Friday or even

Monday, an eternity under the circumstances, so we passed on the offer made by the Royal Alexandra and suggested we took Joe back to Brighton if a scan could be arranged there.

Though the suggestion was politely received, we could tell it was going to be ignored. There was some logic in this as the observations made while a scan is in progress are the most valuable, especially if they are made by a doctor who has observed CT scans on the patient before. But this seemed to pertain far more to subtle changes than the possibility that there could be something dramatically and unmistakably wrong. We were frustrated, but there was nothing more we could say.

After Dr Sinclair had left the ward, Lilias came back. She examined Joe some more and we asked if she would look at him on his feet as we were so concerned about his weak legs. We helped him up, but his legs buckled under him, he couldn't stand or straighten them. 'It's his hamstrings,' Lilias told us. 'They're weak because he's spent so much time in bed.'

Her explanation did not seem very plausible, but there was little we could do. We were waiting for the CT scan and Joe had just been examined by Dr Sinclair. We hoped that Dr Phillips would come soon, but he had to divide his time between patients at four different hospitals, so he was hard to contact.

By this time, Joe had stopped wanting to walk, he was tired, he had difficulty keeping his legs straight in bed, his shoulder still gave him pain – and we were frantic. Now we had to wait for the CT scan to find out what was happening. For the moment, the observation consisted only of a nurse taking his temperature and blood pressure regularly.

That evening, Joe wanted to move across his bed to a new position. He did it with such difficulty, rolling his body and hauling himself with his arms, that Alex went racing on to the ward to find a doctor to witness it. The only person he could find was a student nurse. He brought her in and she watched with concern, promising to tell the sister on duty as soon as she could.

Wednesday passed and no doctor came near Joe. I bitterly regretted the recent change of house officers. There had been three changes in the year we had been attached to Kenneth Grahame, and each time we had made friends with the new young doctors. Because experience on a children's ward was a requirement of their general training, they did not necessarily have any commitment to paediatrics. At first I had found it disconcerting to be on a ward devoted to children and realize that only the registrar and the nurses had paediatric training, and that the other three doctors were there simply to earn their medical Brownie points. But though there had been a couple who didn't have a natural rapport with small children, most of them had got on very well.

We had enjoyed knowing all the house officers we had encountered, and it had been interesting and often helpful to hear them apply their experience to Joe's case. I thought wistfully of them: Mary, Lucy, Simon, Kathy, Anna, Leon, Mike, Henry and Lindsey. All moved on now. Any one of them would have come into our room just to say hello. Any one of them would have been concerned about what was happening to Joe. But now the doctors were conspicuous by their absence. Not only did we not know the new house officers, but they were hardly ever in evidence. Suddenly, when we most needed support, there was no one to talk to. The ward was very busy, but that was nothing new. I had never known a situation before where we literally did not set eyes on a doctor all day.

The next morning, Thursday, we were asked to the doctors' office to speak to Dr Sinclair. He told us a CT scan had been arranged for Monday and asked if Dr Phillips had seen Joe. Lilias had sent him a message on Tuesday, but he had not responded. Now Dr Sinclair asked her to try to contact Dr Phillips again.

We felt a little better, knowing that something was happening, but we were still unhappy about Joe's general condition and the lack of interest taken in him. I complained to Lilias that it was late Thursday morning and that Joe hadn't been seen by any doctor since Tuesday afternoon. Joe had come in for observation specifically because he had a pain in his shoulder, which still troubled him, and the temperature and blood pressure taking seemed irrelevant to that.

Lilias seemed embarrassed by my complaint, but her reaction

was lame. 'Sorry about that,' she said. 'We've been very busy, there's a meningitis case on the ward.' I might have retorted that there was always a meningitis case; it certainly seemed that way. I felt it had far more to do with the fact that none of the new house officers knew Joe or had any involvement in his care. Unless specifically asked by Lilias to see Joe, there was no reason for them to make time for him. However, there seemed no point in saying any of that, and I left her, assuming that Joe might get some attention now.

In fact, Joe still did not see a doctor until the next day. I was outside our room early Friday afternoon, talking to Anna, the playworker, who was explaining that Ronald McDonald, the McDonald's clown, was visiting the ward. She told me she would make sure Joe got a special visit, as he wasn't up to joining the other children in the playroom. As I listened, I saw Dr Phillips walking down the corridor. I felt my spirits lift when I saw him. At last Joe would get some proper attention.

'I've only just got the message about Joe,' he told me. 'I'll look at his X-rays and be right in.'

ALEX Dr Phillips's examination of Joe on that Friday afternoon – 15 April 1988, the anniversary of Joe's nephrectomy, the operation to remove his cancerous kidney – had much the same impact on us as hearing for the first time, a year and three days before, that Joe had cancer. We had been dreading this period, with its calendar reminders of so much anguish and doubt, and now it seemed as if our fears were more than justified.

When Dr Phillips came into our room, Joe was lying on his bed as he had been for the past few days, but now completely unable to sit up. Lilias and several nurses accompanied Dr Phillips, so that when he drew us aside after the examination, we could talk quietly while everyone else kept Joe occupied. The warmth and concern with which Dr Phillips regarded Joe were evident as always, but there seemed now a darkening of his spirits which we had witnessed only once before, when he was so concerned about Joe's bone marrow at Christmas.

He told us that he thought Joe had a tumour on his spine and that he wanted us to transfer immediately to Charing Cross Hospital, so that Joe could have a myelogram in order to get a clear picture of what was happening.

The likelihood that Joe had a new tumour – in the bone and, most significantly, sufficiently advanced to be causing such pain and such difficulty with movement – scared us utterly. Without even having to think it through, the implications in terms of Joe's chances of living were obvious. We were still in the room with him and had to hide the horror we were feeling, but, as we had noticed before, sometimes when the news is truly bad you do not allow yourself to fall apart, because adrenalin or some determination to fight for your child, whatever the situation you are confronted with, overpowers any temptation to let go.

The letting go comes later, when you have assured yourself that your child is not frightened, when you have fully absorbed what you have been told. Then, you allow yourself the fear and the release of crying, but at the same time your anger rises. Your mind starts to function almost as a hunter, desperately searching for a solution that no one else has thought of, for a reason to believe that things are not as bad as they look, for some glimmer of hope.

For the moment, we felt numbed. Joe needed our attention, and we needed the reassurance of just holding him and hugging him. An ambulance had been called to take us to Charing Cross and, thankfully, while we packed a few of Joe's toys, not knowing how long we would be there – an hour, two, three? – Ronald McDonald came in to entertain Joe.

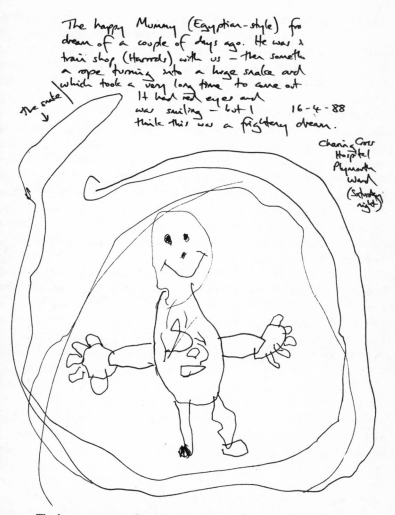

The happy mummy, from Joe's dream about an Egyptian mummy
and a snake; drawn by Joe Buffalo, aged four years eight months,
on Plymouth Ward, Charing Cross Hospital, on 16 April 1988

ANN In the ambulance I get control of my fear. Alex and I sit with Joe, explaining that we will be going back to St Stephen's in a day or two. He looks unhappy. He doesn't like the prospect of a strange hospital, and knows as well that there are more mysterious tests ahead.

Quietly Alex asks if I have a present for Joe. I usually carry a few little surprises to cheer him up if things are getting tough for him. I remember the *Meg and Mog* book I have bought as his next chemo present, and slip it to Alex. He presents it to Joe, who unwraps it looking more relaxed, and immediately asks me to read him the story.

At Charing Cross we don't move forward so much as react and follow. We are led everywhere. Joe cannot sit up and so is wheeled on a stretcher. We walk beside him, armed with Melissa and Cookie Monster, barely taking in the vastness of Charing Cross – an impersonal, multi-storey hospital we have visited before with Joe, for bone scans, but have never got to grips with.

We are taken straight to the X-ray department. Joe is to have a myelogram, which involves the injection of a contrast material around his spinal cord, and, though he isn't happy, it goes quite smoothly. We have to wait for the fluid to spread along Joe's spine. The doctor warns us that Joe will be best off lying flat on his back for the next twenty-four hours, as this will help prevent the bad headache the myelogram can cause. After the X-ray is done we are taken up to Plymouth Ward, the children's ward where we are to stay.

Mr Richards, the consultant neurosurgeon, arrives. He tells us that there is a tumour in Joe's vertebrae pressing on his spinal cord which could completely paralyse him in less than twenty-four hours. He is angry. He tells us that he always stresses to doctors that if a cancer patient complains of back pain they must investigate the spine. He tells us that he can operate on Joe to remove the tumour but that, because of its position, it is a major operation – a 'megabugger' is his phrase. It will mean going through his rib-cage from the front and around his heart and lungs; it is a very intricate and traumatic operation.

The problem is that the cancer is out of control. The tumour in the spine means there could be more tumours in Joe's bones. To deal with one may be useless in the long run, but it may save

Joe from imminent paralysis. Bone tumours are the most difficult to treat. This is almost certainly a death sentence for Joe, but the operation might make what is left of his life more bearable. The decision is urgent. He is considering doing the operation tonight, or tomorrow morning at the latest.

Alex and I must decide immediately, but we don't need to discuss it. We are both willing to agree to the operation. Grateful may be a more appropriate word. We are overwhelmed by Mr Richards's unqualified willingness to do such demanding surgery for what in cold reality is a short-term prospect.

He seems pleased by our decision. 'It's what I'd do if it were my child,' he says. He understands that we will try anything to save Joe. But there is one other possibility. The consultant radiologist, Dr Howard, is coming to look at Joe's X-ray. If he thinks radiotherapy can help, it will be much easier on Joe, and it can be started tomorrow. In the meantime, Joe is to start taking steroids which will reduce the pressure on the spinal cord a little.

Alex and I are stunned. Though we have known for so long that Joe's cancer is not thought to be treatable, it has responded so dramatically to chemo that we have persuaded ourselves that Joe is going to be the exception, the one who survives. We have always been aware that the cancer could take over again, but we have convinced ourselves that it won't. The news that it is back, more aggressively and uncontrollably than before, is more devastating than hearing that he had cancer the first time. Then there seemed to be some options open for him. Now we know there is no hope. Luckily Joe is tired and sleeps, so we don't have to make any effort to be cheerful.

ALEX The conversation with Mr Richards is like any other conversation, except that my mind is screaming inside, 'Don't let this happen. Let this not be true.' He seems like a very competent, committed man. He makes us feel that everything possible will be done for Joe, but we all know that what we are discussing is like a choice between hanging and the electric chair.

We are put in a room and begin to realize that whereas we

thought we were coming to Charing Cross for a few hours, or perhaps for a single night, in fact we may be here for days or even weeks. Immediately we miss St Stephen's – all our friends among the staff, the way that Kenneth Grahame Ward always seemed so relaxed that we almost felt at home.

*A*NN At some point, a staff nurse comes to our room to tell us that we will be transferred to the general ward the next day. We are astonished and say so. Though the same nurse was present during our conversation with Mr Richards, she is surprised at our reaction; she says that as Joe is neither neutropaenic nor has an infectious disease, there is no reason for him to have a room of his own.

We are distressed at the thought of having to live and sleep on a ward with other families while we grapple with the prospect of Joe's death. It seems a monstrously insensitive moment to suggest it. How can we relate to other parents, how can we cope with our emotions among the intrusion of noise and conversation? The nurse seems to think we have been terribly spoilt at St Stephen's and says it will be better for us to be on the ward, it is more normal. 'More normal than what?' I wonder. If your child has some short-term illness, then living on a ward for a few days is a small price to pay for the enormous benefits of the NHS. But it can't be normal for anyone who doesn't actually live in a commune. And for us it means an invasion of whatever time we have left, a destruction of the privacy we need.

The room we are in now is minute, but most of our possessions including the TV and video, are still at St Stephen's. We rely heavily on the video to keep Joe occupied when he is bored – we always watch his cartoons and talk about them with him, so that it is not just passive viewing. Now that he cannot sit up, it is more essential than ever, so Alex takes a taxi back to St Stephen's to get the car and pick up our things.

While he is gone, Dr Sinclair appears in our room at Charing Cross. He looks subdued and doesn't say much. He wishes me good luck and asks me to keep him informed. We shake hands and say goodbye. I feel as if we have been discharged by him. In the ambulance, my thoughts had raged against him and Lilias. Neither one of them had advanced the most obvious explanation, that the pain originated in Joe's spine. They had let Joe lie while they waited for a CT scan that could have been done days earlier in Brighton and was not, anyway, the most appropriate test.

While I speak to Dr Sinclair I feel constrained, I don't care if we are saying goodbye for ever. Yet I realize that though he is the consultant, reasonably or not, I blame Lilias more. She has been responsible for Joe's day-to-day care and yet in our view she let the situation drift on. No doctor can know everything, it is far more important to recognize his or her own limitations and ask an expert. If Lilias had consulted a more experienced doctor, like Dr Phillips, on the first Tuesday we took Joe to her with the shoulder pain, his problem might have been identified then. After our conversation with Mr Richards, and later, as the extent of the damage to Joe becomes clear, I am to feel this even more acutely. If Joe had been diagnosed even four days earlier, he need never have been crippled so badly that April.

I blame myself too. It is like a repeat of my conflict the year before. Why hadn't I made more fuss? Why hadn't I guessed it was a problem in his spine? It seems so obvious now. But two doctors hadn't suggested it, and I wasn't a doctor.

ALEX I feel miserable in the taxi going back to St Stephen's, and even more so in our room on Kenneth Grahame Ward as I pack up. Sister Sharon Bell is on duty and comes in to talk to me. Everyone on the ward knows how bad the news is, and I think we cry together. She tells me that Dr Sinclair was almost in tears earlier over Joe. I know that Ann feels hostile towards him and towards St Stephen's at the moment for what she sees as their failure to spot the tumour on Joe's spine, but I just feel grateful for all the love Joe has been shown. My anger does come, but it comes weeks later and it is always tempered by the gratitude I feel.

Finally, at about 11.30 p.m., feeling shocked and exhausted, I drive back to Charing Cross and make several trips up to Plymouth Ward with the TV, video and our clothes. I think Joe is still sleeping when I come in. I feel a rush of emotion when I see him – intense love mixed with the dread that, now, inevitably, at some point he will die. Today is Friday, 15 April 1988. Last year on this day Joe's cancerous left kidney was removed and after the strain of waiting for Joe to come back from surgery, we felt some small hope that he might recover. Now there is none, though we desperately try to block that fact from our minds.

On Saturday morning Joe has his first radiotherapy treatment. Dr Howard has decided that Joe's tumour should respond to intensive radiotherapy, and we are relieved that Joe may not have to undergo massive surgery.

To avoid moving Joe any more than is necessary, we wheel his whole bed down to the radiotherapy room. This is quite an operation, involving navigating sharp corners and fitting the bed, the porters, a nurse and Ann and me into a lift. We reassure Joe that radiotherapy will be all right, but really we don't know. We have been warned that it may make him sick and may cause localized 'sunburn' to the skin around his spine where it is given, but that it will certainly not be as bad as chemotherapy.

In the radiotherapy room it is decided that Joe can be treated on his bed, and we position it next to the equipment, which is as large and imposing as a CT scanner. The radiotherapy treatment is not much different from having an X-ray. Joe has to lie still, supported awkwardly on his side by foam cushions, while the radiotherapy unit moves round to direct its rays through a kind of funnel at his back. Radiotherapy uses radiation – normally either X-rays (though in far higher doses than are used for diagnostic X-rays) or gamma rays – to attack the tumour. The targeting of the radiation is critical, so that as little damage as possible is done to surrounding healthy tissue.

The worst part about it is that Joe has to be alone in the treatment room while the equipment is operating. Apart from when he has been sedated for a CT scan or during surgery, either Ann or I have always been with him. Now, we will be able to watch him through a protective glass window from outside the room, and to hear him via an intercom, but he will be on his own.

Joe is not especially happy about this, but we settle him and leave. We watch through the window for the three minutes or so it takes to give him the radiation dose, pleased that he is lying still, but wondering what thoughts are in his mind as he lies there alone. He looks so resigned, so accepting of his fate, and so isolated, that we wish we could hug him.

When it is over, we go back in and make him comfortable. He seems relieved that this is all radiotherapy entails, and rather cautiously we ask him, 'Isn't radiotherapy better than chemotherapy?' We certainly hope so, because he will be having it daily for the next fourteen days.

ANN That morning, when we realize they are serious about moving us to the ward, we resist the suggestion vehemently. A sister begs us to consider it. They have far fewer individual rooms than Kenneth Grahame, and there is the recurring problem that any child under one year old must be in a room of its own. With a sympathy that was lacking the night before, she asks us to try it for twenty-four hours and, when she promises to move us back into a room if we are unhappy, we feel bound to agree.

We move on to the small ward, only six beds, and at first it doesn't seem too bad. The other families are nice, Joe finds the activity around him quite interesting, and he is gratified by the other children's enthusiasm to watch his tapes, which are new to them, on the communal video.

It all proceeds smoothly till bedtime. Unfortunately, although Joe is a late-night person, the other children are not, and he is very put out when the ward lights are dimmed at about eight o'clock. It is impossible to read or talk or play without disturbing the others. We all feel depressed. Joe is often at his most delightful in the evening, and Alex and I feel as if this time is being stolen from us.

ALEX While the other children try to sleep, we sit with Joe with a curtain pulled round the bed and talk to him quietly. He is in a very active frame of mind, seemingly happy but sensing our despair too, I think. It is difficult not to overwhelm him with our love – we just want to hold him and touch him and kiss him and know that he's alive.

He manages to play with a pocket-sized skittles set I have bought him, the skittles on a tray, Joe propped up in bed on pillows, his legs bent because it is painful to straighten them. He seems particularly creative tonight, making us feel even more deeply how much we will miss his intelligence, his unique view of the world. He draws a number of pictures, including two of an 'elephant submarine', with a trunk at the front and a fin and a propeller, and several of a snake and an Egyptian mummy from a dream he says he had a couple of days ago. The dream sounds very disturbing, its element of death suggesting that Joe is as anxious as we are, though he tells us the mummy had a happy face:

JOE'S SNAKE/MUMMY DREAM

Joe is in The Train Shop [Harrods] with us. What happens next is unclear, but there is something about a rope turning into a huge snake and an Egyptian mummy which takes a very long time to come out of its box. 'It had red eyes and was smiling – but I think this was a frightening dream.'

Told to us on Plymouth Ward in Charing Cross Hospital on
16 April 1988

When Joe draws the snake, he says it is friendly, but it has three heads and big claws. 'One of the heads, the bottom one, is really crazy, its mouth wide open.'

Joe's mood is not as dark as this might suggest – when he gets tired of drawing himself, he asks me to draw funny pictures such as an elephant fish with a trunk and four feet, a catfish with a real cat's head, and 3-Girl-SuperTed smiling, with her legs bent like Joe's.

Ann and I feel dispirited, though, by the darkness of the ward and the need to whisper. Much earlier than usual, and before Joe is properly tired, we make our beds on mattresses on the floor beside him and try to sleep.

On Sunday, we explain our feeling that we are being deprived o precious time together and, true to her word, the sister we had spoken to arranges for us to be moved into a room that day. Possibly the effect on the ward of a child who is lively until at least midnight influences her decision.

Joe has radiotherapy again in the morning, and to our relief seems to be suffering no side effects at the moment. As far as he is concerned, it is a soft option compared to chemotherapy.

In the afternoon my parents visit and play cheerfully with Joe, my father making the paper aeroplanes which Joe loves and which I never seem to get right. They are obviously upset by the extent of Joe's paralysis – he is now unable to move either leg, nor wiggle his toes voluntarily – and by what the tumour on the spine implies. As always, they kindly offer to come up and babysit whenever Ann and I need a break – a two-hour drive each way for them from Bexhill.

In the evening, I am struck by feelings of intense depression. For the first time, I believe Joe's situation is truly hopeless. I hate the idea of him dying before us. I cannot conceive of life simply ending – just as when he was born, I could not accept that he had simply begun – so I feel that he will be entering some new realm of being, and I hate the thought of him going alone. I know that my love for him is the most satisfying and complete experience of my life, and I feel that I would like to die with Joe and Ann, the three of us together, holding hands.

Lying on our mattresses on the floor, which we have squeezed into our small room, I think seriously about suicide – and, in Joe's case, murder – for the first time in my life. I quietly tell Ann, 'I wish we could all die together now.' Joe is sleeping and somehow the thought seems clear and beautiful – certainly more beautiful than of him dying alone.

Ann shares my mood, but thinks that something would go wrong, that we would wind up dead with Joe still alive, left with cancer and no parents to help him through it. In any case, I can think of no reliable and achievable way of killing ourselves; the dread of something going wrong – for Joe, more than either of us – would scare me shitless. Perhaps I would not have the guts to kill myself whatever the circumstances, but it would be plain fear and not the result of any moral qualms.

*A*NN Though I understand how Alexander feels, my instinct is to carry on fighting, to let our fate run its course. I think about how, over the past year, we have fantasized about the sacrifices we would make if only we could keep Joe well. Our financial problems were already oppressive, but we would happily have been broke for ever, would have done any kind of work, would have given up our comparative freedom as free-lancers; it meant nothing if Joe would not be there.

Now I wonder, if you can bargain with fate, how would you know a deal had been done? Is it possible that the strain of our financial pressures, the wrench of Alex working away from home every day, when we were used to being together, was some kind of unknowing trade-off? If so, we had accepted it without gratitude. There is no satisfaction in paying a ransom unless you know what it's for.

I think about this unlikely aspect of fate that night because there were two incidents in Joe's life when he might have been seriously hurt or even killed, but came to no harm.

One happened soon after Joe's first birthday. I had taken him to see his friend Alice, and we were in her mother Mary's car, driving down a country lane on our way to lunch, when a car drove into us. I was sitting in the back with Joe on my lap because Alice was using the child-seat, and I was hurled out of my seat, hitting my head on the door handle. I must have lost consciousness for a split second because I have no memory of the impact, only of finding myself on the floor still holding Joe. He was crying, and I was terrified to see that blood was coming from a cut on the back of his ear.

At the hospital I was given an interesting explanation of this unlikely injury. Children's skin is very delicate and tears easily. As we had fallen, his ear had dragged against my jacket and the friction had caused the skin to rip. We had to stay in hospital overnight so the ear could be stitched, but he adjusted well to the situation and did not seem troubled by the accident. Later, some of the insurance money he received in compensation allowed him to pay for his first bicycle himself.

The second incident occurred when Joe was two and a half. Again it involved a car, this time with Alexander driving, on our trip to Spain. One afternoon we had driven around a remote and picturesque valley looking for a particular house that interested us, but had finally given up the search because we were due at the airport. Alex is an excellent driver and has had a lot of experience driving unfamiliar hire cars abroad, which makes it all the stranger that this was the only time in his life when he pulled out of a concealed side turning and headed the car into the wrong lane. We were in a deserted part of Spain, on the wrong side of a road which fell away sharply to the valley floor below, and suddenly coming straight towards us were two artic- ulated lorries. With no time to do anything other than react, Alex swerved straight across them, off the road and on to an incredibly fortuitously placed small ledge.

The lorries had braked when they saw us, and they both stopped. The point where they halted was way past where our car had been. If Alex hadn't got us out of their path – and if the ledge hadn't been precisely where it was – we would all have been dead. Similarly, if the cars in the Surrey accident had not both been going at a sedate pace, our injuries would have been far worse.

Remembering these incidents, I ask myself if they could rep- resent some element of borrowed time. Perhaps life after them was some kind of trade, a deal that had to be paid off? If so, there were times during Joe's illness, especially during this period in Charing Cross, when we might have wished we had all died together in Spain instead. But at the time it happened, 18 April 1986, Joe had almost exactly a year of good health left.

ALEX On Monday morning, 18 April 1988, Joe has his third radiotherapy treatment and, as we wheel him in his bed back on to Plymouth Ward, it is suggested that he might like to spend some time with the other children in the playroom. We push his bed in there, and the playworkers – who are extremely inventive and considerate in their efforts to occupy and stimulate their patients – immediately involve Joe in the painting, board games and other activities that are going on.

It is while Ann and Joe are in the playroom that he tells her of a dream which seems so moving and significant, it makes her cry. When she asks him to tell me about it a little later, I find I am actually scared by the clarity of the imagery, though I may be misinterpreting its meaning:

JOE'S SEAGULL DREAM

Joe opens the door of 'our new house in Brighton' and there are seagulls flying outside. One of the seagulls flies into his open arms and rests its head on his shoulder. The seagull's feathers tickle Joe as he hugs it. The seagull is very friendly.

'This is a very happy dream.' Joe smiles when he talks about the seagull resting its head on his shoulder.

[Later, on 18 May 1988, at the Royal Alexandra Hospital in Brighton, Joe talks about this dream again and grins as he does so: 'Every time I got the seagull's head on my shoulder, I had to fast get the head off my shoulder because it was tickling me!']

Charing Cross Hospital, 18 April 1988

Talking about this away from Joe, Ann and I interpret the seagull as representing Joe accepting death; Ann feels that at least the fact that the feathers tickled him means that he isn't ready to go yet. When our friend, Teri Gower, visits Joe later in the day and we tell her about the dream, she sees it more as a dream of freedom, of hope.

Whether it is about death, or hope, or both, it is at least a beautiful dream, and Joe's happiness and lack of fear are of some comfort. It is we who are afraid.

*A*NN Mr Richards continues to keep an eye on Joe, still ready to perform an operation at short notice if any crisis should occur. Most days he comes down personally, which impresses us enormously. He could easily delegate this task, and he has enormous responsibilities.

At this time Joe has no power over his legs, and making him comfortable, especially when he has to lie on his side for radiotherapy, is difficult. It is very important to establish that he still has his reflexes; if they disappear, the paralysis will be irre versible. Sometimes neither we nor the nurses can get a reaction when we scratch the soles of Joe's feet to make them jerk. On these occasions Mr Richards scrapes them desperately with a key; once, he even draws blood. We are horrified, but the smallest twitch in Joe's leg, and his reproachful voice saying, 'Oh, my poor little foot,' justifies the assault. It is what we all want – a sign of continuing life.

Originally, Joe had taken only Calpol for his pain, switching to a stronger, codeine-based pain-killer the day he moved to Charing Cross. Now we get the feeling that he is a little more comfortable, the radiotherapy is helping. But he is still taking steroids and these are beginning to have an unfortunate effect.

We have worked hard at keeping life as comfortable and bearable as possible for Joe, and even when he was really ill he managed to remain an affectionate, witty, serene little boy. But suddenly he is turning into a monster – cross, demanding, hard to please, shouting at us, hitting us, unloving. We are crushed by the sudden withdrawal of his love. Perhaps it has been less natural that he has remained so contented for so long. Why should a child in his situation be happy? One of the nursing sisters explains that it is undoubtedly the steroids which are causing this personality change, it is very common. She asks Dr Howard's permission to reduce the dose a little, and though he agrees, it doesn't improve Joe's disposition.

Another side effect of the drug is that it dramatically increases Joe's appetite. Suddenly he is hungry all the time. Luckily, like Kenneth Grahame, the Charing Cross ward acknowledges that children may not like the hospital food provided, and there are cooking facilities available for parents who want to prepare food for their children or themselves. I begin to feel like a galley slave, catering to Joe's whims: beefburgers, eggs, cheese on toast, baked beans. One day I make him prawn crackers, bought at Joe's request in Chinatown, deep-frying them in a tiny saucepan. I decide that I may be the only person ever to attempt this in a hospital kitchen.

At first I am delighted that Joe is eating so well. He has become very thin, and I already anticipate that new treatments or his general condition may make him thin again in the future. Putting some weight on him now, so that he can afford to lose some should the time come, seems an excellent idea. But his eating is compulsive and, if I suggest he wait for food, he rages at me until I give in. Because during this time he is lying almost flat, constipation becomes a problem. One day his stomach swells so dramatically that he is X-rayed – only to reveal a tummy full of ill-digested food. An evening of throwing up is followed by a spectacular night when his bowels seem to explode, releasing the remains of his bingeing in a dreadful, odorous mess.

I realize I will have to get tougher, even it it means distressing contests of wills and Joe's rejecting anger. I start insisting he has some fibre such as Weetabix or Shredded Wheat every morning before I will even consider cooking anything substantial and, by playing for time, manage to reduce his intake of food considerably. Nevertheless he is putting on weight visibly and his normally fine features have become bloated. Some of the podginess is caused by overeating, some by the steroids. It is frivolous to worry about his appearance, but I find I mind terribly that Joe, whom I consider to be the most beautiful child in the world, has become moon-faced and greedy.

Far worse than that, with the possibility of Joe's death returned so devastatingly to our minds, is the fear that, if he has to take the steroids for a long time, he might die as a cross, unloving child. In my more pessimistic moments I weep at the possibility that my last memories of him could be as this angry, voracious boy. How hateful it would be to have to push miserable images of this period aside to find the real Joe who was always so loving and cheerful.

Fortunately, it is decided that Joe can discontinue the steroids, and his dose is reduced a little every day until he has stopped them altogether. The change in him is magical. As the dose decreases, his disposition gradually improves and he is his old self again, smiling, joking, hugging. It is such a relief and, for Alex and me, a tremendous boost to our morale.

ALEX At a different level, life goes on. I am excited, though not nearly so excited as I would be under other circumstances, to receive a call from David Gernert at Doubleday in New York, who has just bought *The War Zone* for publication in America.

I talk to him one evening for about forty minutes on the Plymouth Ward pay phone, and feel charged up by his incredible enthusiasm for the book. When I wrote it, I had no idea whether it would be suitable for America. I thought its theme, incest, and uncompromising language and use of British slang might prove unacceptable in the States, though I hoped the force of its emotions might translate anywhere.

Now, sitting in a hospital corridor outside a children's ward, I listen to this man the other side of the Atlantic telling me he thinks it is one of the five or six most important books he has read. I am wary at first of American hyperbole, but David has already called the ward the week before and enthused to Ann about the book, and his grasp of it now and ability to quote chunks of it to me rather better than I could, convinces me of his sincerity – not that I have any wish to doubt it.

I hang up the phone at about 11.00 p.m., practically glowing from all the praise that has been heaped upon me, but wishing desperately that Joe were well enough for me to enjoy it fully. The irony is that after almost four years of struggle and financial hardship, slowly things seem to be turning around for me: in addition to the American sale of *The War Zone*, Christopher Sinclair-Stevenson at Hamish Hamilton has just offered a two-book deal for my next two novels. I would be feeling on top of the world if there were a chance that Joe might recover – or, better yet, if he had never been ill. As it is, I would trade everything for his health.

*A*NN From Joe's first Monday at Charing Cross, he has been having physiotherapy. At first this involves gently flexing his feet and legs. Lorraine and Mrs Beevis, the physiotherapists, have taught us how to exercise his limbs, and we repeat the routine several times a day. Then Mr Richards, who continues to show an interest in Joe although it is now unlikely he will be needing surgery, suggests getting him on to his feet.

Making Joe attempt to use his legs himself seems too demanding, even unrealistic, to us, but Lorraine and Mrs Beevis decide to give it a try. Joe is horrified at the idea of leaving the safety of his bed and weeps and protests, but we all insist. The smallest

movement will satisfy us, the straightening of a knee, the twitch
of a foot. Mrs Beevis and Lorraine hold Joe upright over a
thickly-padded sheet on the floor. Did he move his legs or not?
No one is sure, but just getting him to stand, however it is done,
is a breakthrough.

When Joe is tucked back into his bed, he is a different child.
He may have protested and complained while the physio was
happening, but the achievement has transformed him. He is
happy, with that wonderful elation and rediscovered confidence
that comes from crossing a fear barrier. He has been more
scared than we know. Now he has hope again.

We are relieved that this breakthrough has made him confront
his problem at last. Several times Alex has tried to discuss the
fact that his legs aren't working, wanting to encourage him to
talk about how he feels. But Joe has refused to deal with it,
furiously shouting, 'Be quiet!' or, 'Shut up!'

His attitude has even affected his relationship with Melissa
and Cookie, and in Charing Cross Joe has rejected them for the
first time ever, telling me to put them away in our holdall. I had
assumed that he would need them during this frightening time
and am surprised by his decision.

Occasionally I ask him if he wants Melissa and Cookie yet,
but each time he says no. He doesn't offer an explanation, but
have the feeling that he doesn't want them to see him at such a
disadvantage.

One day, when the physiotherapy is beginning to show small
signs of improvement, a Get Well card arrives from the staff a
the Royal Alexandra. Joe has received several other cards and
presents, but this seems to please him especially. Suddenly he
asks me to get Melissa and Cookie, because he wants to show
them the card. They are reinstated. Melissa, voiced by me
remarks that she hasn't seen Joe for several days, and Joe says
'I know, Melissa. I haven't been well.'

Every time Joe grumbles about physio, I tell him, 'You're no
just going to get out of bed and walk one day, you know. You've
been in bed for so long, your legs are very weak. The exercise
may be boring, but they are to help make them strong. You may

have to learn to walk all over again – we're all going to have to work very hard at it.'

Now the new exercises must suggest to him that he really is going to walk again, because suddenly he is enthusiastic. He asks when Mrs Beevis is coming. If she walks past our room, he is disappointed if she is visiting another patient. He is keen to get on.

But the truth is that no one knows how much of a recovery Joe will make. His spinal cord is badly bruised but not destroyed. Radiotherapy has dramatically reduced the size of the tumour. Eventually sensation and movement will return, but no one knows how completely, and it is partly up to Joe. There is no question of suggesting to Joe that he might not walk properly again. We have to keep him motivated; his will-power and belief in himself are going to be his greatest assets. If he is going to be disabled, we will only find out gradually, and we will tell him gradually, as he seems able to deal with it.

ALEX Our determination to help Joe regain the use of his legs, if he can, helps in some small way to push thoughts of his general treatment to the back of our minds, but we know that ultimately there is little that can be done about his cancer.

Chemotherapy has obviously failed, since the tumour developed on his spine while he was having the drugs. The tumour on his lung could probably still be removed surgically, but that would do nothing to prevent the spread of more tumours in Joe's bones or anywhere else. The tumour on his spine has responded very encouragingly to radiotherapy, but again that treats only a specific site and does not prevent the development of tumours elsewhere.

It does not take much intelligence to recognize that Joe's condition is desperate and that we are running out of medical options, yet somehow Ann and I cling to the hope that there may be some new medical discovery around the corner that will save Joe.

While we are at Charing Cross, we think for a day or two that it may exist. There is a report in a newspaper of a new cancer treatment which has saved two terminal patients who had failed to respond to chemotherapy and radiotherapy. It consists of an injection of monoclonal antibodies, which carry cell-killing radioactive iodine directly to the tumours in the body.

Wary but hopeful, I call Dr Phillips at Westminster General to ask if he knows of this new treatment. Since the earliest days at St Stephen's, we have been aware of the pooling of research into cancer, of the way in which chemotherapy and radiotherapy regimes are monitored internationally for their effectiveness. No doubt professional rivalry and commercial competition do exist in the fight against cancer, but there is also – particularly with a child – a sense that anything that can be done anywhere to help will be done.

The telephone conversation with Dr Phillips is depressing. He knows of monoclonal antibodies, but thinks there is no real chance of the new treatment helping Joe. So far, the successes have been in the treatment of brain tumours. The antibodies have to be laboratory-designed to home in on particular cancer cells. Even if the work had been done in the field of Wilms tumours, which it has not, the fact that Joe's tumour cell type is so rare would probably make it ineffective.

I ask Dr Phillips if there is any hope for Joe. I sense his pain when he tells me there is virtually none, but he does not completely pull the rug out from under us. I think he, too, must have some faith in miracles.

ANN Daily, Joe's condition improves. He can keep his legs straighter, sit up more; he begins riding around in a wheelchair and doing more ambitious physio exercises. After two and a half weeks, his course of radiotherapy ends and it is time to move on. Joe isn't ready to go home, but he no longer needs the radiotherapy that has kept him at Charing Cross. Everyone assumes that we will go back to St Stephen's in a few days' time, but we are not so sure.

While we are at Charing Cross there are frequent calls from St Stephen's; many of the nursing staff phone to ask how Joe is. Their concern is heartening. Toni, Nisha and Anna actually come and visit us – a busman's holiday on an off-duty evening.

One day Lilias calls and it is probably fortunate that Alex, who is less angry with her than me, takes the call. His account of their conversation angers me. 'It all happened so suddenly,' she says to Alex. My retort would have been that it was a gradual and measurable deterioration that she had not reacted to.

Now, though I long to be back at Kenneth Grahame among the warmth and affection of all the nurses who love Joe, I have no intention of delivering him back into Lilias's charge. I am disappointed in Dr Sinclair, but my lack of confidence still rests chiefly with her.

Alex has phoned Karen Bravery in Brighton a couple of times to report on Joe's progress, and she has told him of her conversations with the staff at the Royal Alexandra, and Dr Cree's readiness to help. Now Alex asks if Dr Cree will consider taking over Joe's care, in collaboration with Dr Phillips, if we discharge him from St Stephen's. When we hear on Monday that Dr Cree has agreed to this, and Dr Phillips is willing to discuss Joe's treatment with her, we ask Charing Cross if they can arrange an ambulance to Brighton instead of St Stephen's, and it is scheduled for Wednesday, 11 May 1988.

Joe and I leave London in the ambulance. Alex is going to follow in the car. I sit in the ambulance feeling as if we are making some kind of escape. I feel guilty and self-righteous at the same time. It is the end of my love affair with St Stephen's. They have been so wonderful, so supportive, so ready to try anything that could possibly help Joe – yet, in those crucial days, I believe they have failed us.

Back in Brighton the ambulance parks outside the entrance to Cawthorne Ward at the Royal Alexandra, and the attendant ambulanceman goes into the ward to announce our arrival. The rear doors open to let us out, and Karen and Sister Sharp are already there to welcome us. I hug them both and burst into tears.

15 *The Royal Alexandra*

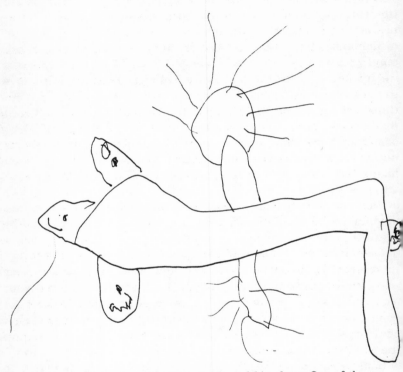

'A friendly snake, with three heads and big claws. One of the heads, the bottom one, is really crazy, its mouth wide open.' The snake from Joe's dream, drawn by Joe Buffalo, aged four years eight months, on Plymouth Ward, Charing Cross Hospital, on 16 April 1988

*A*NN The Royal Alexandra was a friendly haven after Charing Cross. Though Joe had had the attention of the consultants there, on Plymouth Ward we had never felt at home; we were like squatters, we didn't belong to them, and, what's more, in insisting on what we felt was right for Joe and us – the matter of the room – we had made ourselves unpopular. But if I had to choose between being liked and getting the best for Joe, he would always come first.

We seemed to be marking time now. Joe had finished his radiotherapy. No one had X-rayed his spine, so we didn't know if the tumour had gone or simply been reduced to a size where it wasn't harming him. It was academic really.

Our spirits rallied with the improvement in Joe, and once more we were adjusting to a positive mode. There was no point in continuing with the old chemotherapy regime, but there had to be something they could try, we couldn't just stand back and let the cancer take over. We felt sure that Dr Phillips would have some ideas; we desperately needed to have a sense that something was happening, to invent some hope. But first Joe needed a rest after the radiotherapy, and it was almost a relief to put our anxieties and feelings of urgency on hold for a few days.

For now, physiotherapy was the most important treatment for Joe. Though he had made such encouraging progress at Charing Cross, and some movement was coming back into his feet, he had a long way to go. When we had told Mrs Beevis and Lorraine that we were going home to Brighton and the Royal Alexandra, their reaction was mixed. They were obviously anticipating a big improvement in Joe's powers and looking forward to helping him achieve it, but they were very approving of the Royal Alexandra. They told us it had an enviably equipped physio department and the staff had an excellent reputation. It would be the ideal place for Joe.

Their prediction was absolutely right. On our first afternoon we were introduced to Linda Williams, who was to take charge of Joe's physiotherapy. The arrival of Linda into Joe's life was a huge milestone. Not only did she prove to be brilliant at her job, but she had the authority to make Joe work when he didn't really want to. She was like the best teacher in the world, sympathetic and kind, but firm and determined to keep the upper hand. The interesting thing was that Joe, who was very good at controlling people, loved it, and he loved her.

LINDA WILLIAMS It was Wednesday, 11 May 1988, when the referral came through to the physiotherapy department. I'd only been at the Royal Alexandra a week and a half, and as yet hadn't acquired a large patient care load. It seemed obvious that I should take on this new patient, transferred down from Charing Cross: Joe Buffalo Stuart.

My first meeting with Joe will always remain a vivid memory. Joe was half-lying, half-sitting up in bed, surrounded by videos, mountains of Lego, various other toys, pillows, spare mattresses, an assortment of food cartons, and medical paraphernalia, looking like the Infant Emperor of Cawthorne Ward!

Joe had an air of authority and turn of phrase that in a four-year-old hit you as precocious to say the least, until you got to know him. Having found him a suitable wheelchair, wheedled and cajoled him, he still refused point blank to even try it. I didn't relish the times ahead. I anticipated a battle of wills which I somehow had to win early on if we were going to work together, and yet I instinctively knew that Joe had such a vitality and determination that we would make it work.

Joe had spent much of his time with adults in hospital, and during this period had become very familiar with nursing procedures and medical terms. I had to adopt a very honest and in some respects direct approach in explaining to Joe how and why we were going to play the games and exercises over the next few weeks. He always wanted to know how things worked and had an amazing grasp of three-dimensional concepts from Lego instructions and video games.

On that Wednesday, Joe was virtually paralysed from the waist down but was beginning to make some recovery – small movements of his toes. From that point on, Joe was always excited when he came to see me because he had something new to demonstrate. All these things combined to ensure we were to become firm friends.

ALEX On the first weekend we were at the Royal Alexandra, it was agreed that Joe was well enough to go out in a wheelchair. He had barely been outside for a month, other than when we had wheeled him from Charing Cross Hospital to the

River Thames – a short trip of about a quarter of a mile, which seemed to cause him some discomfort.

Asked where he would like to go, Joe rather predictably said, 'The pier!' So, on Saturday afternoon, we drove to the seafront, began what was to become a familiar ritual of getting the wheelchair out of the boot, unfolding it and fitting Joe's cushion, then walked him along the Palace Pier, stopping to gaze down between the wooden boards and let the Sea – which we had brought back with us from Charing Cross – enjoy its homecoming.

'We're back again, Sea!' Joe announced.

'It's good to be home,' the Sea replied. And then, because I found voicing the Sea a useful way of trying to get Joe to talk about his problems, it asked, 'What's that you're in, Joe? That sort of seat with wheels? Is it a car?'

'It's a wheelchair,' Joe explained, in his 'serious' voice. He seemed at least accepting of the situation, if not a little proud. 'My legs aren't working at the moment.'

'I'm sorry to hear that, Joe,' the Sea said. 'I hope they'll be better soon.'

In one of the video arcades, we met Suzanne, who worked there and who had befriended Joe when he first became a regular on the pier in late 1987. Out of Joe's earshot, she admitted that she had not recognized him at first, partly because he was now in a wheelchair, but also because his face was still quite bloated by the steroids, even though he was no longer taking them.

It was only when my attention was drawn like this to how Joe looked, that I realized how blinkered Ann's and my vision was at times. We saw Joe with love and, mostly, with optimism; our image of him was always informed by the memory of how lively he could be when he was well. If he was momentarily sad, we knew how happy he was normally. We compensated for the damage caused by both his cancer and the various treatments, so that even though we knew he could look very ill sometimes, we tended to see him as we'd always seen him – as Joe.

I remembered when I had taken him to Hyde Park, during the first intensive period of chemotherapy, and Joe had played in the sand at Rotten Row (which had caused me a good deal of concern, since his immune system was low and Rotten Row was a regular dumping ground for the horses that were ridden there). An American had walked by, taken one look at Joe, a gaunt little boy with thinning hair, and had said, 'Someone's been very sick,' in a voice of such understanding and sympathy that it made me quite tearful.

Now I realized that the wheelchair was almost a cover for Joe's cancer – he simply looked disabled, not necessarily like a child who might die – and I wasn't sure how I felt about this. On one hand, it meant that he was immediately recognized as needing a certain amount of space, if nothing else, and that reduced the risk of his Hickman line, under his right armpit, being knocked accidentally, which had always been a slight worry. On the other, we didn't want Joe to regard himself as being too sick or too different from other children; we still hoped that his own will-power and positive outlook might help him conquer his disease.

I also wasn't entirely clear about how I felt about Joe's disability. I know that on the occasions when my sister, Lynne, had been forced to use a wheelchair as a result of her multiple sclerosis, I had felt sad for her, because I knew how hard she had fought to keep walking. At this point, I think both Ann and I viewed Joe's paralysis as temporary. We believed he would walk again, and I think the strength of my belief came from watching Lynne fight back with incredible courage from multiple sclerosis and her stroke. I had seen her lying in a coma for three weeks. I had realized both how fragile and how strong the body can be: one minute, she was relatively well; the next, she was unconscious and incapable of voluntary movement; then, more extraordinary than that, she was learning to walk again and regaining the ability to talk, almost as if her brain had not undergone a massive trauma. Her determination then helped me to respond positively to Joe's problems now.

LINDA WILLIAMS I saw Joe daily and, after establishing our boundaries, had a great deal of fun. I decided that for my sanity and Joe's temperament, it would be better if we had part of each session on our own. I also felt very strongly that it was

vital for Ann and Alex to have some time together – however
short. Talking about Joe (or anything else for that matter) was
virtually impossible: one or other parent was always within his
vision and Joe could be extremely demanding if he thought he
was excluded from a discussion. His favourite comment, quietly
to begin with, was 'Could I just say something?', increasing in
volume until you acknowledged him and allowed him his say.
Privacy was difficult.

*A*NN We swiftly realized that Joe's physio sessions really
were a teacher/pupil situation, that Linda needed to be in
sole charge. After a couple of days, she tactfully suggested that
her sessions with Joe might make the opportunity for a break for
us. We started off disappearing for fifteen or twenty minutes, but
Joe was so relaxed with her that he decided himself that he
didn't want us there at all. Alex and I were delighted. We had
already developed total faith in her, and this sign that Joe
shared our approval, and was happy without us, was a sign that
his own confidence was returning.

*L*INDA WILLIAMS The sessions evolved whereby Ann or
Alex would bring Joe up in his wheelchair and Joe would
toot the horn to let me know he'd arrived. He was always
accompanied by his friends, Melissa the raccoon, Cookie Monster and Leglin the badger.

He would practise old skills and try and find something new
each time to show to Mummy and Daddy when they came back.
Joe had such a wonderful imagination that I had to struggle to
keep up with his games, and I began to wonder if we really did
have a family of ducklings in the department. The ducklings were
Joe's imaginary friends, who lived under a bed we used in Physio.
They tended to make a lot of noise and provided a reason for Joe
to start moving on the floor and chase them out of his way.

The highlight of these days had to be when Joe took his first
tottering steps along the parallel bars. Ann was there to see it
and, normally so in control, we both had silent tears trickling
down our faces.

For the next few weeks, walking became our prime objective and Joe worked so hard to perfect the ultimate skill, moving from bars to rollator (a metal frame on wheels which gave him support as he pushed it along) to sticks, improvising at home with an exercise frame made from his Gymbo construction kit and chasing those naughty ducklings round the department! Progress was crucial for Ann and Alex as well as Joe, and despite knowing the odds were stacked against him, Joe showed such determination that he gave us all that glimmer of hope.

ANN Seeing Joe walk was wonderful. Joe, wearing gaiters to strengthen his legs and leaning for support on waist-high parallel bars, managed to haul himself, one foot slowly in front of the other, a distance of about six feet. This was his first approach to real walking, and the cost in physical effort and determination must have been exorbitant.

Alexander and I would be close to tears as we watched him. No parents could have been prouder of their child's accomplishments, or taken more pleasure in sharing his excitement at his marvellous achievement. This was a time of repetitive hard work for Joe, but his tiny daily triumphs were building. He began to see what was possible. Though he was still disabled, and his slow progress exhausted him, he was happy and optimistic. His paralysis was the lowest point in his illness so far, but this recovery from it was one of the most rewarding – a maturing, character-forming experience for all of us.

ALEX The importance of believing that he might walk again was evident in a dream he had in mid-May 1988, while we were still at the Royal Alexandra:

JOE'S DREAM ABOUT WALKING

ANN: Can Daddy hear your dream?

JOE: After I have the money to pay for them.

ALEX: Pay for the dreams?

JOE: Yes, because all my dreams are ones which I have to pay for. [Alex laughs]

ANN: You don't have to pay for dreams. All right, Daddy's going to go away then. All right, tell me about your dream, the one that's about you.

JOE: [Very excited] It was about me, when my legs weren't working and I suddenly got up and walked!

ANN: Oh, Joe, what a wonderful dream.

JOE: And I walked on my own! But just for a minute, mean I was a bit wobbly!

ANN: Yes, that's how you walked when you first walked when you were a baby. You used to get up and stand. You used to sit, and then you'd pull yourself into a standing position, and then you couldn't put your feet forward, so you'd just sit down again. And one day, you stood up and you did put a foot forward.

JOE: Well, Mum, my two feet were going, but then I was going round in a circle! [Ann laughs] And I finished going round in a circle, so I sitted down.

ANN: I think that's how it might happen, because if one foot was stronger than the other, then you might just go round in a circle, I suppose. That might be how it is when you walk again. But then you'd get stronger and stronger.

JOE'S TOY ROBOTS DREAM

ANN: Do you want to tell me the other dream before you eat your Frosties? You don't mind if they go a bit soggy?

JOE: My nother dream was about toy robots, and they had buttons to make them move.

ANN: Ah. Was there anything special about them?

JOE: Well, they don't do somersaults.

ANN: No.

JOE: They just carry hair-driers. [Ann laughs] They carry toy hair-driers, not real hair-driers, toys.

ANN: Why would robots need hair-driers, because they don't have hair, do they?

JOE: Well, they have them for real people.

ANN: So a toy robot could have dried my hair for me?

JOE: Yes, but they just give it into people's hands.

ANN: I see. It carries things around for people – like it might

have brought me a cup of tea, do you think? Or something
I needed? You just saw them, did you, moving about?

JOE: But I need a pee.

ANN: Oh, dear. Have you got anything to pee in? I'm going to
have to run down and get you a bottle, is that all right?

*A*NN A day or so after we arrived at the Royal Alexandra,
we had a discussion with Dr Cree about Joe's condition. She
ran through all the facts, and hearing them again made us cry,
even though she was only telling us what we already knew. All
she could say was that she wouldn't let Joe be in pain. It seemed
a feeble response. Until a few weeks before, we had never thought
in terms of Joe being in pain. Now the tumour on his spine had
shrunk, he was comfortable again; the only pain he got was from
his efforts to crank his legs back into life.

But if there were more tumours in his bones, there would be
pain again in the future. We were eager to have some tests run
on Joe: a CT scan maybe, or some X-rays. There was no point in
this, Dr Cree said. It was inevitable that there were more
tumours, and that others might form, but as there was no
question of giving Joe radiotherapy again unless they became a
real problem, there was no reason to locate them. Alex and I were
dismayed at this. We had a strong desire to know the exact
extent of the damage. Although it was completely illogical, we
would feel happier if we knew, and more hopeful if there were
not very many tumours.

Dr Cree had not yet made contact with Dr Phillips, but she
expected to talk to him very soon. We left her feeling vaguely
worried at her apparent lack of drive; she obviously didn't feel
anything was going to help Joe, but we needed the illusion that
something was happening, and hoped that Dr Phillips would
have some ideas. Only a miracle could save Joe, but for us,
perpetually struggling for something to pin our hopes on, that
miracle might lie in some new trial drug. Somewhere out there
might be the cure, as yet unproven, and maybe Joe would be the
patient who made the breakthrough. But the breakthrough
wouldn't come unless we kept on trying.

Having to confront facts we had already assimilated once left us feeling tense and miserable. Staff Nurse Karen Bravery offered to play with Joe for a while so Alex and I could go home together and talk, and we accepted gratefully. It was a relief just to collapse and give in to our feelings of panic and despair, but there seemed little left to say. We went to bed and made love; it seemed the most positive thing we could do.

Since Joe had wanted to sleep with us all the time during his illness, we had used his rather claustrophobic bunk bed for sex once he was asleep; having our own bed to ourselves was a luxury. But even that simple comfort was also a reminder of how much time there would be without Joe in the future.

A few days later Dr Cree surprised us with news of a drug she had discovered. She and Dr Phillips had already agreed that Joe should try a new chemotherapy drug, carboplatin, which was currently on trial. Only patients with very specific conditions were eligible, but Joe was qualified. Thankfully we agreed to go ahead.

Some information we were shown about carboplatin, written for doctors rather than anxious parents, underlined the situation. This was a trial for terminal patients. The drug might encourage a holding pattern. In other words, there was no suggestion that the carboplatin could cure Joe, only that it might control the tumours and extend his life. We learnt that when the drug was effective it achieved results after only two doses. Joe would be X-rayed before the treatment started. It would be given as before at three-weekly intervals. After two doses he would be X-rayed again. If there was an improvement, he would proceed with the treatment. If not, it would be abandoned.

The tone of the literature was detached, even ruthless, but it did not deter us. We had some hope to grab on to. If carboplatin was still on trial, that meant no one was sure of exactly what it could accomplish. Maybe it could do more than hold the cancer, maybe it could cure it in some patients, but the right patient hadn't tried it yet. Maybe Joe would be that patient.

We were hopeful again. The most important thing for us was that something was constantly happening, that there was always something to cling to, some faint possibility of a reprieve.

Although the rational part of us accepted that Joe wasn't going to get better, we couldn't think in terms of the word 'terminal'. For now, he was comparatively well and full of enthusiasm for his returning movement. His efforts and optimism were so uplifting and life-affirming that we could not possibly picture him dying. And even if he were going to die, when would it be? He could go into a rapid decline tomorrow and be dead in a few weeks, or he could continue as he was for months, even a year, if the tumours were dormant. And time was the vital factor. The longer we could keep him alive, the more hope there was that the drug that could save him would be discovered.

In order to monitor the possible side effects from the carboplatin, Joe had a kidney-function test and a hearing test, as well as the X-rays. Less than a week after we first heard about the drug, and a few days after we moved Joe home to the house, he had his first dose. We had been told it was much gentler than normal chemotherapy, and this certainly seemed true for the first treatment on 26 May 1988, when Joe was slightly sick for just a couple of hours. The second time, on 16 June, he reacted more violently, but he still recovered by the next day and was fine for my birthday the day after that.

I was forty-four, and we celebrated quietly with a trip to the beach with our friend Teri Gower. As part of my birthday present, Alexander had had two mementoes framed for me. He gave me the original drawing for Joe's birth announcement card, by our old neighbour Gray Jolliffe, with Joe's name already printed on it before his actual birth. Joe gave me a slim, oblong package that contained a framed cutting from *Variety*, the American showbusiness trade paper, announcing his birth. It was an extraordinary feeling to look at it, and contemplate his death.

ALEX We spent about ten days in all staying at the Royal Alexandra. The hospital was only five minutes' walk from our house, which made life a good deal easier after a month or more at Charing Cross, with trips home and back to London with laundry, to collect the mail, etc. Once the carboplatin treatment had been decided on, there was no reason for keeping

Joe in hospital, as his only other regular treatment was physiotherapy, and we could take him there for that, or Linda could
come to us.

Early in the year, I had written some pages to read to Joe at
night, based on his friendship with the Sea. I told him I thought
we should write a story together about it and our first discussion
was over the name the boy in the story would have. Joe wanted
to call him 'Joe', but I pointed out that I had already used that
name in a children's book I had written for him, called *Joe, Jo-
Jo and the Monkey Masks*, which was due to be published at the
end of May. 'I can't call every character in every book "Joe",' I
said.

So we thought about it and after some discussion settled on
'Henry', which was the name of one of our favourite house
officers at St Stephen's.

At first I wrote only a page or so, starting with a paragraph
drawing on everything Joe liked most about the Palace Pier and
using his own expressions, such as 'bone people' (skeletons) and
'blood people' (monsters):

> When Henry went to live by the sea, everyone said it was for
> his health. Which it was. Henry had never seen a healthier
> place: video games on the pier; hot dogs and fish and chips
> and hamburgers and sticks of rock and candy floss; healthy
> outdoor sports like riding the ghost train past bone people
> and blood people and worse. There was even a site of histor-
> ical healthy importance – an old Victorian sewage pipe
> which at low tide filled the air with a rich and possibly
> historical stench.
>
> From *Henry and the Sea*

I read this to Joe and found that he was both amused by it and
also very serious about what would happen next. In the story,
the Sea was rather affronted at Henry's complete failure to
notice that it was there, so it talked to him, 'in a low, rumbling,
almost sloshing voice which said: "Ah-hm, I am here, you
know."'

Joe immediately got involved in deciding what else the Se
would say to Henry, and what Henry would reply. When the Se
asked Henry, 'Aren't you a little young to come on your own?',
had Henry saying, 'My dad is right here beside me. Didn't yo
notice? He doesn't say a lot. He's too busy writing this down.' T
which Joe added: 'And carrying my bicycle.'

When the Sea asked Henry if he would come back and tal
tomorrow, Joe and I decided Henry would tell it he had to go t
London: 'We go there quite a lot. I have to go and stay i
hospital quite a bit. In St Stephen's. It's only for a few days, the
I'll be back.'

When the Sea caused a big wave to splash over Henry and hi
parents, and I had Henry's mother removing an eel from he
hair, Joe insisted that Henry's dad would have a crab pinchin
his nose. 'A crab is going to pinch *your* nose!' Joe added, squee
ing my nose between his forefinger and thumb, and laughing.

Working occasionally in the evenings on this, we wrote abou
eight pages by early March, but when, later in the month, Jo
started suffering the pains in his back, it no longer seemed suc
a fun thing to do. April was entirely taken up by the onset o
Joe's paralysis and the dreadful tension and fear at Charin
Cross, but now, in mid-May, back home in Brighton, I felt a hug
need to try and create something whole with Joe.

The possibility of his death, which now seemed more a questio
of when and how than anything, made me determined to turn th
story of Henry – whose central idea of talking to the Sea wa
entirely Joe's invention – into a children's book which woul
have Joe's name on the jacket. I re-read to him the pages we ha
written, and together we worked out a plot in which Henry too
the Sea to London, leaving the sea-bed all over the world drie
up.

Writing the book was a marvellous experience, because Jo
had started to appreciate structure (at the end of June, h
actually had a dream which he said was in three chapters – se
below) and was quite adamant about what he wanted. 'No, n
you've got it wrong,' he would tell me if I wrote something h
didn't agree with. 'That's not what the Sea would do,' or, 'That
not what the Sea would say.'

By the end of May, we had pretty well finished the book. I read it through to Joe several times, noting his comments and tightening up any passages which seemed to lose his interest. Then I retyped it and sent it off to Charles, who passed it on to Hamish Hamilton. Children's books are among the hardest things to judge, and I wasn't sure if perhaps *Henry and the Sea* might be too personal to work for other people, so I was delighted when, on Wednesday, 20 July 1988, Charles rang to say that Hamish Hamilton wanted to take it. Whatever else happened, Joe would be a published author.

JOE'S THREE CHAPTERS DREAM

Chapter One: Silly Dream Fred and me were having a bath. [ALEX: 'Was this in the Knightsbridge flat?' JOE: 'Yes, but you're not supposed to write down the flat.' ALEX: 'Oh, sorry.' JOE: 'You *did* write it down!' ALEX: 'I put that in brackets, OK?'] I needed a pee and so I had a pee in a pee bottle and Fred throwed away my bubble [bath] hippopotamus, and I had to get it out of the loo with my clean hands, and it didn't get flushed, and then I washed my hands in the bath.

And I said, 'Silly Fred.'

Chapter Two: Present I was at home in Brighton home with Mummy and Daddy and I got a present from them which was a elephant and a plane. And it had teeny teeny tiny bullets for the plane to put in the nose – you know about that – the nose opens up so people can put the bullets in.

I didn't have time to do all the nother words, because I suddenly cutted off that bit of dream.

Chapter Three: Bozzie's [*Fozzie's*] *Throwing Tomatoes Dream* The Muppet Babies were at millions of baker's shops and they were throwing tomatoes, and I came to the baker's and helped them throw tomatoes on all the bakers' face.

All of the bakers had the same nose. They were like crimimals! [ALEX: 'Were they like the bakers in (Maurice Sendak's book) *In the Night Kitchen*?' JOE: 'No, they didn't

have the sort of noses in *In the Night Kitchen*, they had very
pointy noses.']

Dictated at breakneck speed by Joe on 30 June 1988 at home
in Brighton

Joe dictated his 'Three Chapters Dream' to me on a Thursday
evening, shortly after Ann had come home from a rare day alone
spent shopping in London. This was the Thursday of a relatively
hopeful week. We had now been living at home for over a month
and despite what we knew about Joe's condition, we had been
encouraged on Sunday when our friend Rosemary Reid had
visited and we had got Joe out of his wheelchair and into a
child-sized dodgem car on the seafront. He had driven like a
maniac, trying to run us all down as we darted about the
otherwise deserted dodgem floor.

The following day, Monday, 27 June, Joe had managed his
first unaided steps since his paralysis – about forty steps in four
goes, a huge achievement for someone who, little more than a
month ago, had no sensation in or control over his legs at all.

Thursday, 30 June 1988, seemed especially significant, though
not in an entirely positive way. While Ann was in London, I had
taken Joe in his wheelchair to have his hair cut, and then spent
the afternoon on the beach with him, enjoying the sunshine and
playing with a new plastic boat we had bought. Towards the end
of the afternoon we had settled next to each other in deck-chairs
and I had started reading him Antoine de Saint-Exupéry's poignant story, *The Little Prince*.

Whether it was some quality of the book or simply the mood
created by the lengthening sun and the seagulls flying overhead, I
don't know, but completely unprompted, Joe turned and said to
me, 'When I die, I want to die and fly like a seagull.'

Joe may have been responding to the plane accident at the
start of *The Little Prince* and the narrator's reference to it being
a question of life or death for him in the middle of the Sahara
Desert. He may have asked me again what death was, though I
don't recall him doing so. I got the impression that Joe was
thinking in terms of *whenever* he died – when he died in the
future – rather than of the fact that he might die soon, but
whatever the case, it was a beautiful and moving image. It

eemed to connect clearly with the seagull dream he had had in Charing Cross (which he talked about often), and suggested an acceptance on his part which sadly was lacking on ours.

Perhaps, and I hope it does not seem too sentimental to suggest this, Joe himself was giving us a symbol to help us cope with the prospect of his death. I never finished reading him *The Little Prince*.

ANN We had to wait three weeks after the second carboplatin treatment, to give it the maximum time to work, before Joe's progress was monitored with X-rays. These were done on Monday, 4 July, and we were told that we would hear the results the next day, when Dr Cree had had an opportunity to examine them closely with the radiologist.

On Tuesday morning, we didn't discuss the tension we felt. We didn't know when we would hear, we assumed we would have a phone call at some point. Around midday, Alex decided to have a break from work and take his lunch down to the beach and maybe have a swim. I didn't say, 'Don't stay out too long,' but I knew he wouldn't.

At about two o'clock, Karen rang and asked if we could come in to talk to Dr Cree. I knew that if the X-rays showed an improvement, she would have just told me when Joe was to have his next carboplatin injection. 'That must mean there's bad news,' I whispered so Joe wouldn't hear. 'Good and bad,' she said, non-committally. I never did find out what the good news was.

ALEX I could write now in controlled language about sitting in Dr Cree's office at the Royal Alexandra Hospital and hearing that the carboplatin trial had failed, but it would not reflect the true extent of my feelings then. I made notes during Joe's illness, but only on two or three occasions did I sit down at the typewriter and let loose with my emotions, and each time I did so, I made myself weep. We saw Dr Cree on Tuesday, 5 July 1988; two days later, I wrote the following:

What's life? Lynne has m.s. and now Joe has tumours all over.

We saw the X-rays of his lungs on Tuesday. I had been on t
beach, coated in Ambre Solaire, keeping out the wind, leering
two girls next to me sunbathing topless. The wind was cold, t
sea was rough as it's been for the last few days (July is cra
now) and I wanted to canoe, but by the time I went to rent one
was ten past two and when I got back Ann had heard from t
hospital an hour before that things were not good.

We went round there and I sat in my shorts, smelling of su
oil, looking at X-rays of Joe's lungs which showed two lesions
they call them (the language is cool, but is cancer any more re
or tumours, what words can do justice to those fucking litt
cells?) getting larger despite the carboplatin. And then shado
on his spine where the cells are taking over the bone.

It was unreal. I think I entered a place I have been ju
outside for so long – 14 months now – denying all the time. No
it seems inevitable, and I know we should fight it but I feel
would be kinder to Joe to stay calm, to keep our lives sane, n
to rush off to Bristol or Liverpool [specialist cancer treatme
centres] or Disneyland (Ann was very much against this, she h
such a solid base of honest good sense) but go on here.

This is the hardest part to write, but I think there's a part
me that wants it to happen now, to be over, and yet eve
moment I'm with Joe I want it to last for ever. Life never sta
properly, it always feels like the start is just round the corne
then suddenly you realize it's passing. Every moment with Joe
a miracle, but it's a miracle clouded with shit because I know
will end unnaturally (though is cancer unnatural? it's just a
other system fucking ours up) and much sooner than it shoul
I'm getting waves of hate again, but that's the problem at t
moment, that was the problem last night – everything comes
waves, I can't stay with any one feeling for any length of time.

I'm getting away from the strength of what I wanted to p
down. I don't know what I wanted to put down. I haven't sa
even the first millionth of what I wanted to say about Joe, b
no words can capture him, he will live in my mind for as long
I'm alive, as he does now – he is downstairs, I can pick up t
phone or press our intercom and talk to him, but that's the on
difference between him being alive now or dead.

I cannot imagine the pain once he is dead of being here and wanting to pick up the intercom and talk to him and not being able to. I cannot imagine the pain of no one calling me Daddy. I cannot imagine the pain of not being able to smell him, touch him, hold him, feel his warmth, look into his eyes, hear his voice, hear him do his 3-Girl-SuperTed voice, hear him laugh, make jokes, say 'Are you joking? Are you having a joke?', kiss me, lick me, touch his hair, feel the firmness of his little belly (which was once so misshapen and then sunken when his kidney was removed). I cannot imagine the pain for Ann of him not being here. He is life to both of us and I don't know what comes next. I cannot imagine the pain, yet I know I'm going to have to, I'm going to live through a fucking awful experience and have to try and survive. I love Joe Buffalo Stuart more than the world, more than life, more than anything or anyone I've ever known and life is a cunt for taking him. I love him.

Extracted from pages written on 7 July 1988

16 *A Summer of Extremes*

'Joe's Hum About Everything Which Flies', dictated and drawn
by Joe Buffalo, aged five years, on 27 August 1988

*A*LEX It would be less than honest at this point simply to
continue with the events of 1988 as if Ann and I were in
control of either our emotions or the material. The strain of
writing the last few chapters has been immense, and we feel we
have suffered a large degree of emotional damage as a
result.

Dealing with the period at Charing Cross, in particular, has
prompted intense hostility on my part towards Ann and, presumably, towards the memory of Joe's paralysis. Simply reading through the chapter to check for mistakes left me with an
appalling headache and a feeling of anger. Transcribing the
pages I had written on 7 July 1988 for the end of the last
chapter had me sitting at my desk not simply crying, but wail-
ing – moaning quite loudly, in my room, alone. Yesterday,
while I was upstairs working, I heard a scream from Ann and
went down to find her crying at her typewriter, staring at her
own notes and feeling unable to go on.

In July 1988, when Joe was still alive, I had written: 'I can't
scream or cry enough to express the pain inside my head, my
body. There is a wail of grief that is universal.' These past few
weeks, I think we have both felt that pain more forcefully
than ever, and in the last day or so have actually doubted our
ability to finish this book.

We will finish it, not because we have a publishing contract to
fulfil, but because, along with the pain of working on it goes a
compulsion to complete it, to work through the memories and
somehow get as much of the horror behind us so that we can
concentrate on remembering the happiness. How we finish it is
another matter. Our perspective on the last five months of Joe's
life may not be as acute as it could be. We may feel extremely
emotional, but that emotion may not translate to the page. We
will not destroy ourselves utterly in a vain attempt to communicate what in any case can only be hinted at: the chasm created by
the loss of a child. [28 September 1989]

If life for all of us during Joe's illness had been unpredictable,
summer 1988 was to prove more extreme and desperate and
changeable than anything we had known. A moment of happiness
could be dashed by Joe's sudden announcement that he was

feeling pain. The enormous and inspiring progress he was making with walking could be overshadowed by any reminder that his 'recovery' was short-term: we tended now not to think in the long-term.

Despite this, somehow – perhaps through a form of protective stupidity – we managed to remain remarkably happy for much of the time. For all of us, Joe's battle to regain the use of his legs actually helped, in that it gave us something physical to focus on and get involved with. Ann and I had both had our own exercise regimes at various times, and Joe had enjoyed coming to the gym with me when we lived in London (he particularly liked tumbling head-over-heels on the mats and playing basketball with a full-sized ball and a lowered basket), so now physiotherapy became Joe's daily exercises.

One of the strangest aspects of this period was that he looked so well. His hair had slowly started to grow back towards the end of his chemotherapy regime, and now that he was to have no more chemotherapy at all, he soon had a full head of hair again, which in itself made a remarkable difference. He was also quite solid, largely as a result of the steroids he had taken in April and his steroid-induced appetite (which had lessened with the cessation of steroids in early May, but was still better than it had been for much of his illness). I liked his rather chubby look; Ann did not.

Whereas a year before, in summer 1987, Joe had looked like a child with cancer – thin, balding and with his vincristine-accentuated squint – now, in summer 1988, he could seem much like any other healthy, cheeky four-year-old, except for the fact that he was in a wheelchair. Then, in 1987, we had held on to a powerful hope that he might live; now, in 1988, we might hope, we might argue forcefully that Joe still might survive, but in our hearts I think we knew the truth.

A few days, even a few hours, could make so much difference to our mood. Less than a week after Dr Cree had told us that the carboplatin trial had failed, on Monday, 11 July 1988, we spent an afternoon with Joe at Chessington Zoo. Although we were living at home virtually all the time now, the trip to Chessington felt like an escape from hospital and thoughts of hospitals

Ann and I had somehow managed to rationalize the failure of medicine to offer Joe any further options with a kind of relief that we no longer need place much faith in the doctors we had to deal with (in particular Dr Cree, whose method of expressing her attitude we found so depressing).

Chessington, with its adventure rides, must have seemed to Joe like a wonderful mix of the Palace Pier and London Zoo, which he had always loved. Despite being lifted in and out of his wheelchair a great many times, he clearly enjoyed himself, liking best of all a space-theme ride involving attacking robots. On the way into this, he was given a pair of punky, X-ray spex-type sunglasses which he wore with pride; a couple of nights later, at home, he posed for a photograph in them, impressing us with his improving ability to balance standing up.

By the Friday of that week, Joe was walking quite well down on the seafront, his concentration focused more on steering his remote-controlled toy Porsche along the path than on the effort his legs were making. Our friend Annette Motley (who had given Joe his raccoon and badger Fluppets, Melissa and Leglin) was visiting from Ireland and was as delighted as us to see Joe in such fighting form, but only two days later, on Sunday, 17 July 1988, I wrote in my diary: 'Joe's legs starting to hurt in last couple of days.'

As a result of this pain, Dr Cree prescribed codeine tablets for Joe, which we could supplement with Calpol if necessary. Aside from the problem of getting Joe, who still would not swallow pills, to take them (we succeeded by crushing them and mixing them in chocolate chip ice-cream), we were horrified by what seemed to us the awful significance of this development. Other than Calpol itself, or when we first arrived at Charing Cross, Joe had never needed pain-killers before, and the fact that he was starting on them now – even a drug as familiar as codeine – truly did seem like the beginning of the end.

*A*NN That week, we started asking the Royal Alexandra for help for Joe. When Alex telephoned the ward to report that Joe was in pain again, he assumed that Joe would be X-rayed to find out the source of the trouble. 'What's the point?' was the response of the staff nurse he spoke to. Her attitude made us tense and uneasy. We had been told by Dr Cree during our initial conversation that Joe would have more radiotherapy if he needed it, and an X-ray would be the first step towards this.

Later we spoke to Dr Cree about investigating the pain and she was cautious. She said that radiotherapy was dangerous, which was true, and that it could only be used as a very last resort. Joe's experience of radiotherapy so far had been good, and we certainly viewed its use against the possibility of paralysis returning as a last resort. When we talked about his increasing pain, Dr Cree suggested stronger drugs; she advised morphine. This was a drug I viewed with mistrust, partly because such a strong drug seemed so final, a drug to die on; and partly because my father, who died of cancer, had undergone a disturbing personality change when he had taken morphine. For us, treating the tumour, if it could be identified, seemed a much better solution. Joe had not, so far, suffered from any of the side effects associated with radiotherapy, so our attitude towards it was very positive.

Dr Cree said that we must wait and see, that she couldn't take action yet. I never understood this line of thought. If Joe was in pain from a growing tumour, the pain and his disability were going to grow. It seemed more logical to treat the tumour while it was relatively small and spare Joe prolonged pain and disability. Waiting to see what happened seemed like madness – we all knew it wasn't going to get smaller again.

Dr Cree's attitude, which seemed to us to consist of letting Joe get to the brink of paralysis before any action was taken, combined with the nurse's remark, made us very dissatisfied and insecure. Suddenly we began to feel as if Joe were some laboratory specimen they were watching. The atmosphere was becoming less sympathetic, as if Joe had been written off.

During the next few days this feeling was reinforced a couple of times. Once, when I rang to ask for more codeine for Joe, which was always prescribed by Dr Cree and obtained from the hospital pharmacy, the staff nurse I spoke to asked in a very offhand way why I couldn't get it from Joe's GP. As our GP had no involvement in his treatment, and getting prescriptions from her would be a good deal more complicated and time-consuming,

I viewed this remark with some mistrust. It seemed like another sign of dismissal.

In the same period, when I had taken Joe to the hospital with me to collect a prescription, I mentioned to another staff nurse the possibility of an X-ray for Joe as he was still in pain. In front of Joe she said coolly, 'What's the point?' This phrase was becoming too familiar and once more I felt the chill of abandonment. 'Dr Cree did say Joe might have some radiotherapy if his pain got worse,' I told her firmly. To her credit, when she heard this, the nurse immediately went to speak to Dr Cree and came back and offered to look after Joe while I saw her.

I went into Dr Cree's office and told her how desperate we were, how the pain seemed to be getting worse, and our greatest fear was that Joe would be paralysed again. She explained that the tumour was in a completely different site and that, though it could be incapacitating, its effect would not be as dramatic as the first tumour last April. There was a shred of reassurance in this, but it still seemed to me in my demoralized state a harsh and over-clinical response. The wait-and-see policy still stood.

I began to think that the Royal Alexandra was a very bad place for Joe. I felt he was surrounded by people infected by a brutal, and to us incomprehensible, attitude. Perhaps by failing to get well he had become unimportant – the idea of throwing more pain-killers at him, while tumours which might be controlled were destroying him, seemed to us wilful and cruel. Radiotherapy seemed the better option to us, and yet our opinion was not being considered and we had no direct contact with any radiologist in Brighton.

The void that was left by the failure of the carboplatin was the worst that we had encountered so far. Before, there had always been some fragile prospect to cling to – mostly the possibility that some new drug might appear in time. Now Dr Cree had told us that there was nothing left to try. We felt cut off, hopeless, fearfully waiting to see exactly how Joe, who ironically was very lively and happy at this time, would deteriorate.

I began to think nostalgically of St Stephen's. Though I had been disillusioned when we left, I felt that no one there would have admitted defeat – they would at least have maintained an illusion of moving forward. Maybe another hospital would help? But committing Joe to the possibility of long stays in hospitals miles from home didn't seem practical or kind at this point.

One night, lying beside Joe as he slept, and almost at screaming point with the need for some calming protection from my fears, I realized that if there were to be any hope again, we had to create it for ourselves. My thoughts were racing, desperately searching for an idea, and having tried the scientific and the logical, I wondered about spiritual healing. I began to see that just taking the step of seeing someone like a healer would be a way of getting some control over the situation. I suggested it to Alex, not at all sure how he would react, and he agreed that it was worth a try. We needed a sense that something, anything, was happening.

Only days later, we saw a local healer. I had been worried at first that there might be something mystical or frightening about the sessions, but I made sure in advance that nothing would happen that could disturb Joe. The concept of spiritual healing seemed a difficult one to explain to a four-year-old, so we told him we were taking him to a new sort of doctor who didn't use medicine or operations, but would just touch him.

When we mentioned our decision to friends, several said that they had been tempted to suggest it, and our conversations resulted in two recommendations that we decided to follow up. One was Phil Edwardes, a prominent healer who lives in Sussex, the other was Matthew Manning, generally considered to be Britain's most powerful healer, and a man who had recorded successes with terminal cancer patients.

On our first visit to Phil Edwardes – a large, reassuring figure in his fifties – he sat and talked with the three of us before he treated Joe. Though Joe's presence inhibited our conversation, he was very comforting, talking about our feelings and encouraging a positive attitude, a bit like an undemanding psychotherapist. When he was ready to lay his hands on Joe, he asked me to sit him on my lap. As I held Joe I felt a charge through my body, although Phil was not touching me. Joe seemed quite unmoved by it all, just glad there was no more than touching involved.

Joe enjoyed his trips to Phil chiefly because Phil's youngest son had a pet rabbit in the garden which Joe liked to watch, and which influenced his wish to have his own rabbit for his birthday. On the first visit, Phil and I spoke for a few minutes while Alex and Joe inspected the rabbit. He told me that miracles could happen but, more pointedly, he said that he thought the parting of death was insignificant, he felt that in the scale of infinity our lives were very brief, and that any parting would be over in the blink of an eye. He seemed to believe in a form of reunion after death, an idea I desperately wanted to share, though it was a difficult concept for me.

When we drove back from Phil Edwardes's after that first visit, we all felt happier. Joe hadn't undergone any miraculous change, but he was more cheerful, and I felt calmer, less oppressed by worry than I had before. Phil may have been trying to tell me he didn't really think he could save Joe, but if his healing spared Joe any pain, or slowed down his deterioration, or maybe controlled some of his tumours even if it couldn't control them all, that might help prevent some suffering, or extend his life. The decision to see a healer had satisfied my requirements: it had restored a kind of hope.

During the next few weeks we saw Phil and Matthew Manning several times. We had been concerned at first about the etiquette of consulting two healers at once. We had applied to see them both, not expecting that both would agree to see Joe so quickly. But apparently it is quite common to visit more than one healer.

Matthew Manning, we knew, was a famous healer, the subject of books and television programmes and newspaper articles. We had learnt that he had a year's waiting list, but that he would always give priority to children, so on Friday, 22 July 1988, Alex wrote him a long letter. He explained the background to Joe's illness and its various stages, sketched his character and our love for him, and asked if Matthew could see him as soon as possible. His response was remarkable. The next Monday we had a phone call from Matthew's office, and the next Friday, only a week after writing to him, Joe had an appointment with him.

We knew Matthew was very young, only in his early thirties, but we were half expecting an imposing figure, as his gifts had

made him famous when he was only a teenager. In fact he turned
out to be a self-effacing man who inspired a mood of serenity.
His reaction was very much like Phil's. He described treating
Joe's cancer as being like trying to stop a runaway train; he
would have to get control and slow it down before he could
attempt to stop it.

It is impossible to say if the healing did any good. Though
there was no dramatic change in Joe, it's possible that Matthew
or Phil's influence did somehow slow things down or prevent
some even worse deterioration. Certainly there were psychological benefits for Alex and me, and Joe was affected in
some way by his encounters with both of them, even though his
concept of what they were doing was a little hazy and his
expectations couldn't have been the same as ours. We had told
him that Matthew was a very powerful man, more powerful than
any wizard he had seen on TV, in the hope that this would make
the visits more interesting for him. He always seemed in better
spirits after he had seen them, and on one particular occasion
with Matthew, he had the most extraordinary charge of energy.
He had been in some pain, and though he could still walk, he
had not wanted to for some days because it was difficult. After
seeing Matthew that afternoon, we decided to have tea in a
nearby hotel and Joe thrilled us by spending almost an hour on
his feet, walking around rather unsteadily but without discomfort and looking very happy. Moments like that were very
heartening for us even though neither of the healers had made
any promises. Even a few minutes of optimism, seeing Joe look so
happy and confident again, made the trips worthwhile.

Soon after that, Joe began to find travelling so uncomfortable
that we had to stop the visits. Though we desperately wanted
him to see Matthew again, it just didn't seem fair to impose the
long journey on him. For a while we continued to see Phil, who
was based much closer to Brighton, but in the end even the trips
to him became too tiring.

Although the idea of going to a spiritual healer at all had
been mine, it was an uncharacteristic step for me. I had finally
decided that if the healing involved religious belief, it was
theirs, not mine, that was important. In fact, healers seem to

have varying philosophies. Though Phil Edwardes's convictions were fairly unconventional, he did believe his gifts were God-given; whereas Matthew Manning was more interested in the idea that some people retain primitive, intuitive abilities which have mostly been bred out of us by centuries of relative civilization.

ALEX Early August 1988 had an intensity that had much to do with the approach of Joe's fifth birthday, on the 15th, and the pain he was experiencing in his back and legs.

We tried hard to make life fun for him, and to make the fact that he could no longer run around or ride his bike matter as little as possible. We bought him an inflatable dinghy, in which I would tow him up and down on a pool on the seafront. After a year of being unable to swim, due to the need to keep his Hickman line site sterile, it was marvellous to see Joe close to water again.

The dinghy proved its worth in a single day when we visited our friend Rosemary Reid at her parents' house in Chobham, where they had a swimming pool. Just as our evening at Chobham in 1987 had been one of the warmest nights of the year, this weekend – Saturday, 6 August 1988 – was incredibly hot, and because of the dinghy, Joe was able to spend virtually the whole day on the pool, sharing his dinghy with everyone and being very much a part of the action.

My own response at this time to Joe's worsening condition was to try to find an outlet for the anger and frustration I felt. Early in Joe's illness, I had channelled much of my energy into writing *The War Zone*, but now that I was trying to start a new novel, *Tribes*, I just felt distracted and unfocused. Before, during the months of chemotherapy, although there was a huge shadow over the future, our day to day lives followed a line that was clear and almost hopeful. Now, Joe was frequently in pain and nothing was predictable.

I had always liked running and swimming, and now if I swam in the sea, I tried to push myself further, to swim out as far as I could – I wanted an element of danger, to test myself, maybe to scare myself. I also saw the sea as a kind of magnificent force in a sense, as a physical representation of God or the power of the universe – and, whether I was swimming or canoeing, would talk to it, asking it to save Joe, to let him live.

I took up springboard diving, and found a coach who brought me close to achieving front and back somersaults, before I lost confidence or commitment and stopped going to the sessions. More than anything, I wanted the impact of the water on my skull fifty or sixty times an hour – I felt like banging my head against a wall, but the water was a softer option.

I also started going regularly to that summer's acid house parties. My friends, Spike and Neville, had run warehouse parties and clubs for a number of years and I had gone from time to time, but now it became far more of an obsession and release. I went mostly to our local Brighton club, the Zap, leaving Ann and Joe settling down to sleep for the night, and found the music, the dancing and the intense, friendly atmosphere the perfect way of shutting my mind down for a few hours. As with the diving, I wanted to stop thinking, to stop feeling – because when I thought or felt about Joe, it hurt.

As Joe's birthday grew closer, we desperately wanted him to have some radiotherapy so that he might at least feel better for the day itself. Finally, in the week before, we were given an appointment to attend the radiotherapy unit at the Sussex County Hospital. Recent X-rays had shown more tumours developing on Joe's spine; we felt it significant that, after Dr Cree's seeming reluctance for Joe to have radiotherapy, when we got to Sussex County there was no hesitation about giving him treatment straight away, and he had three radiotherapy treatments that week, ending on Friday, 12 August 1988, three days before his birthday.

This was the first radiotherapy Joe had had since Charing Cross, but he was remarkably relaxed about it. Again, we had to leave him in the treatment room on his own while the radiotherapy was given, but this time we could watch him via a closed circuit television system, and I think Joe was intrigued by the red light on the camera and the knowledge that we could see him on a TV screen. As before, though, I found myself wondering what thoughts were in his mind. His life had such a strange pattern now, and even though he had little experience of anything more normal, he was certainly aware that not every child lived an existence like this.

The preparations for Joe's birthday, plus the fact that the week of radiotherapy seemed to have an immediate effect in terms of improving Joe's comfort, made this a relatively happy time. Joe was a regular viewer of daytime children's television, and Ann and I decided he might enjoy the surprise of having a card shown on TV on his birthday.

A couple of weeks before the date, I worked in the evenings, making a card combining a photograph of Joe with a drawing of Snoopy in a yellow dinghy on the sea. We sent it off to the BBC, with a message from us and from all of Joe's 'friends' – Cookie, Melissa, Leglin, Snoopy, Woodstock, the Sea – wishing him a happy birthday and wishing him well. We included a note explaining that Joe had cancer (but asking for this not to be mentioned on the air), in the hope that this would guarantee his card being read out.

We had had some contact with Rosemary Davies at BBC Children's Television, who had sent Joe a video tape of the final episode of his favourite cartoon series, *Around the World with Willy Fogg*, which he had missed while he was in hospital, and she very kindly telephoned, a few days before Joe's birthday, to say that his card would definitely be on, so we knew we could settle him in front of the TV on Monday morning with confidence.

The Saturday before Joe's birthday was a marvellous day, sunny, hot and relaxed because Joe had had his radiotherapy and was not in pain. While Ann and I were out shopping with Joe, I took him into Brighton's Virgin Megastore and, on an impulse, lifted him out of his wheelchair and into the store's colour photo booth. The resulting strip of four pictures, of Joe and me laughing as Cookie, Melissa and Leglin tried to muscle into the frame, are among the happiest pictures we have of Joe, and captured his excitement at the prospect of my parents coming over to buy him a pet rabbit for his birthday.

At lunchtime, Gran and Fred arrived and we all drove across Brighton to a pet shop which we had already checked had young rabbits for sale (there was apparently a shortage of baby rabbits that summer). I carried Joe round the shop as he inspected the animals, but choosing was not difficult as, when we opened a cage containing two white rabbits, one of them virtually leapt into Joe's arms. He quickly decided that this was his rabbit, to be given the name he had already chosen for his bunny: Cabbage.

Back home, on the patio, my father put together the hutch he had built for Joe's rabbit, and Joe sat on his child-sized blue chair as Cabbage emerged from the cardboard box in which we had transported him from the pet shop. Joe's joy and pride at having his first pet were obvious, and Ann and I, as well as my parents, felt tearful, not least because we all knew it was quite probable that Cabbage would outlive his owner.

As Joe sat, a little later, with Cabbage on his lap, we took what I think is probably my favourite picture of Joe – beaming with pleasure, his hair fully grown again, his face and body solid; a picture in which he looks so happy and contented, and so much healthier than the year before, despite the fact that cancer was eating away his body from within and, two days later, on his birthday, he would walk virtually the last steps of his life.

*A*NN We wanted Joe to have a birthday party, but we had to be sure he would be able to enjoy it before we made any plans. So, once more, Joe's party was a last-minute affair. I made up a guest list, old friends from London and new ones from Brighton – quite a lot of names, but with such short notice especially as August was the holiday season, I didn't expect everyone to be available. To our delight, almost every child was able to come, and Joe had a total of fourteen guests, including a few baby brothers and sisters.

As well as working on the card for the television show, Alex had an idea for decorating a plain wall in the basement family room where we would be having the party. This couldn't be a complete surprise, as Joe spent so much time there. He saw Alex sketch in the huge picture of Snoopy (as his alter ego, Joe Cool) lounging against his dog house with his friend, Woodstock, but he didn't see the finished work until the morning. Alex stayed up very late painting in all the details – the grass, the red roof on the dog house, a large sun with a number five on it, four more birds to make five in all, and the words, 'Happy Birthday, Joe Buffalo'. It was a wonderful picture, about four feet by five, which we liked so much that we kept it on the wall for some months after Joe died.

When he was carried downstairs on his birthday morning, Joe was delighted with Alex's work. We settled him on the sofa to watch children's TV and when the presenter started to read out the birthday messages, Joe – usually Joe Cool himself – was astonished to hear his name and see his photograph on the card. 'Hey, I'm on TV,' he said incredulously.

Alex and I collaborated on the birthday cake as usual. Joe threw us by telling us sternly that he didn't want a number cake this year, he wanted a Woodstock cake. So I made a big round chocolate cake and Alex, at the last minute as always, decorated it with a large Woodstock which he cut out of rolled marzipan.

There was quite a crowd at the party, since all the guests brought at least one parent, and friends looked in, including Linda, who had given Joe a day off physiotherapy, and Teri, who brought another beautiful cake she had decorated with a brightly coloured dragon made from Smarties.

Joe had a great many presents, but the best of all was unquestionably Cabbage. I was afraid the stress of being surrounded by so many children would be too much for a baby rabbit, but Cabbage took it all very calmly, and Joe looked radiant and so proud and grown up as he carried him around. He was full of energy, moving about unsteadily but quite confidently, even having a sword-fight with his friend Statten out on the patio. The excitement of the occasion must have given him a boost of adrenalin, because that was almost the last time we saw him walk unaided.

Though the party was a success, I regretted afterwards that I had spent too much of the day organizing it, and not enough time relaxing with Joe. 'Next year, maybe we should have your party the day after your birthday,' I suggested, 'so the three of us can just be together and concentrate on you on the day.'

Joe's last birthday had left us wondering whether he'd survive another year, and here we were, Joe was five, but things were looking much worse. It made me feel good for a moment to look ahead, but I had very little confidence that Joe would live to be six.

ALEX On Wednesday, 17 August 1988, two days after Joe's birthday, I had what remains one of the most wonderful days of that year. I had decided to take Joe to London on the train as a post-birthday treat which would also give Ann a day off. Since Joe had been in his wheelchair, I had always taken him out in the car, and in fact realized that I had not travelled on the train with him since he was a baby. He liked trains, and the whole day seemed like a great adventure.

In London, we walked in brilliant sunshine from Victoria Station to The Train Shop (Harrods), our first stop and one of the few things Joe seemed to miss about living in London. For a couple of hours I wheeled him round the toy department, buying a few small toys and stopping to watch a magic show, after which Joe bought his first magic trick. We then got some lunch from the food halls to take with us and headed for Hyde Park, our old haunt, where we hired a skiff to take out on the Serpentine.

We left Joe's wheelchair on the jetty, and for an hour or so could almost pretend life was as it was before his illness. Joe managed to sit quite comfortably in the boat and we rowed under our favourite tree – the willow which had figured in our games as dense jungle foliage. We ate our lunch, fed the ducks and wondered what Ann was getting up to back home. I asked Joe if he would like to visit his old friends at St Stephen's, and when he said he would, we took a taxi from the park to the Fulham Road. Sadly, there was virtually no one we knew on duty on Kenneth Grahame Ward, but Joe enjoyed demonstrating how fast his wheelchair could move and playing with a tiny highly-charged toy racing-car he had bought.

Early in the evening, we took the train back from Victoria and Joe enchanted everyone in our carriage with his newly learnt magic trick, involving a series of cups and disappearing fluff balls, which he would announce quite confidently with the words: 'Listen, my friends, now let me show you my magic trick.'

We arrived home, having bought some flowers for Ann at the station, and what had already been a magical day with Joe seemed even more special when I opened a letter which had arrived for me. It was from Anthony Burgess in Switzerland, whom I had written to asking for a cover quote for *The War Zone*. The novel was not to be published for another six months, but David Gernert at Doubleday, my American publishers, had suggested it would help to have a quote from a respected author.

Charles, my agent, had made a comparison early on with the energy of Burgess's *A Clockwork Orange*, which I had found not only flattering but enormously helpful in writing the book, so I was unbelievably thrilled – and amused – now to read Anthony Burgess's own response:

Dear Mr Stuart

I apologise for being so late with a comment on *The War Zone*, but, as you can guess, I've been busy with other things and reserved reading your book till night when, tortured by mosquitoes and gnats, I wouldn't get much sleep anyway. The book certainly kept me awake apart from those. I don't know what kind of a comment your US publishers want, and I may, of course, have misunderstood the work entirely, but try this:

This is a pungent shocking book, superbly written (sharp, sensuous, bitter), which, from the viewpoint of one of the more intelligent adolescents of Thatcher's England, presents the theme of incest not as a device of sexual titillation but as a symbol of social breakdown. I was horrified but seduced from first to last. The writing is remarkable.

Something like that, anyway. Congratulations and every good wish from

Sincerely

Anthony Burgess

Switzerland, 11 August 1988

I was over the moon. My book had been read by very few people as yet, and while the early response from Charles and Christopher

Sinclair-Stevenson and David Gernert had been incredibly encouraging, I now felt as if I were a real writer. I felt as if I had joined the club!

But there was another aspect to the letter which, perhaps illogically, encouraged me. Early in Joe's illness, I had remembered reading, years before, that Anthony Burgess had at one time been diagnosed as having some kind of a tumour and had been given six months to live. He had immediately set about writing three books, one of which was *A Clockwork Orange*, in order to provide for his then wife after his death. In one of life's ironic twists, she had died and not him, and here he was, twenty or thirty years later, writing to me. The fact that he had disproved the doctors gave me hope for Joe – that Joe might also be the exception to the rule, might somehow defy fate.

In retrospect, the day in London seems perfectly timed, in that it was almost the last occasion on which Joe was well enough to enjoy such a tiring day out. A week later, as he sat in his wheelchair on the seafront, I noticed a bump on the back of his neck, just below the skull, which I knew could only be a secondary tumour. I had always had a dread of Joe's cancer spreading to his brain; now that dread seemed real.

That night, Wednesday, 24 August, he scared us immensely when he appeared not simply in pain from his back, but almost delirious. Ann and I by this point had lost all patience with Dr Cree, who seemed reluctant to do anything for Joe other than prescribe MST (morphine sulphate) tablets to stop the pain, which in any case they did not effectively do.

We woke early on Thursday, determined to call the radiotherapy department at Sussex County directly, if need be, and ask for more treatment for Joe. I was so tense that I went for an early morning run down to the sea. I arrived on the beach at about 8.30 a.m. to find a group of nuns praying at the water's edge, like a scene out of a Fellini movie. It seemed so symbolic, so much an extension of what I was thinking and fearing, that I knelt by the water myself and wept.

'Haunted House' by Joe Buffalo, aged five years four months,
December 1988

ALEX September 1988 was without doubt the worst month of
Joe's illness. Although his physical condition was to deteriorate further towards Christmas, September is the month I
remember with the most horror. More so than at any other

point during the nineteen months of Joe's cancer, it was then that he was most visibly and most consistently in pain.

By the second week of the month, his condition had altered so radically that he could not only no longer walk, but could not even sit comfortably in his wheelchair for any length of time. During the day, he would lie on the sofa and whimper and cry. He was miserable and obviously suffering, and Ann and I found it very difficult to stay positive in any way. We didn't want to scare Joe, but when he cried, we felt like crying. The situation seemed increasingly hopeless, and together with the fear that Joe might die came the fear that he might die like this – unhappy and in pain.

ANN During this period, Joe's pain became so great that he finally started taking morphine. This proved to be far from satisfactory, as the form available was in a time-release tablet, MST (morphine sulphate). Joe, like many children, could not swallow pills and this caused a major problem. He could only take them crushed and disguised in a mouthful of ice-cream, but to retain some of the slow-release qualities of the MST, I couldn't grind the tablet to a fine powder as usual, but had to break it into coarse chunks which made it very unpleasant to take.

It also meant that the effectiveness of the pill was impaired. Discussing it at the hospital, we found that this was a recurring problem among the younger patients, but no solution, such as a more easily administered drug, had been found. The morphine worked well most of the time, but it was released into the body so unevenly that sometimes what was called breakthrough pain would occur.

Dr Cree's reaction to any complaint of pain was to increase the dose, which may have been the appropriate medical response, but when I told her that heavier doses didn't eliminate the breakthrough pain, she had no answer. We particularly hated Joe having high doses of MST because it made him quite depressed. I asked if there wasn't some other pain-killer he could take, but Dr Cree's only suggestion was that she could prescribe valium for the depression if necessary. I wondered what she would prescribe if he had side effects from the valium, picturing

Joe taking a chain of drugs, each designed to counter some
aspect of another, and refused her offer.

ALEX I felt increasingly angry and hostile at this time,
particularly towards Dr Cree, whom both Ann and I found
immensely depressing to deal with – far more so than other
doctors, who had been no more hopeful in their prognosis, but
had approached our situation from a different perspective.

It was largely a problem of our simply not responding well to
her personality, but sadly she was the only oncologist at the
hospital and there was now no question of transferring Joe's
care back to St Stephen's – he was no longer well enough to
travel back and forth to London. As a result of this, the last
months of Joe's life were more difficult for us to cope with than
might otherwise have been the case.

A major part of our difficulty in dealing with her was due to
the influence we felt her strong Christian beliefs played in her
thinking. I would not for a moment suggest that she talked
about Christianity in her daily work, but Ann and I felt very
aware of her faith and enormously hostile towards it, because
we feared that it affected her general attitude.

It seemed to us as if she saw Joe's cancer as ordained by
God, and that his death would be merciful, since Joe would
pass on to some wonderfully benign afterlife. While this could
have been her attempt to help us to come to terms with our
situation, because of our own beliefs we did not find it helpful.
Unlike all the other doctors we had dealt with, she constantly
advised us to tell Joe he was dying, an issue we had hardly
ducked, since our original request at St Stephen's for family
counselling had been largely to explore how we might explain
Joe's cancer to him and whether we should talk to him about
death.

It was only when Ann explained to Dr Cree how we had
encouraged in Joe a sense of reincarnation, and that Joe had
decided he wanted to be a seagull when he died, that we suspected
what Dr Cree actually wanted was for us to tell Joe about the
Christian concept of heaven. She seemed shocked by the rather
looser interpretation we put on things, and Ann was convinced

that Dr Cree's approach to Joe was best summed up by the phrase, 'Jesus wants him for a sunbeam.'

Ann's agnosticism and my own sense of a vast, arbitrary, beautiful but by no means painless universe meant that we did not share this enthusiasm for eternity and we felt increasingly desperate as we repeatedly raised with Dr Cree the prospect of more radiotherapy for Joe. She warned us that there was a limit to how much radiotherapy the body could take, but our feeling was that she saw it as pointless, since he was going to die anyway; that more morphine was the answer to relieving Joe's pain. We felt that the radiotherapy had an immediate and powerful effect in improving Joe's comfort – something the MST tablets did not seem to do effectively – and that if the argument against radiotherapy was its attendant risks, then that was itself negated by her own argument that Joe was going to die in any case.

We were well aware of our own general, unfocused anger at the helplessness and injustice of Joe's situation – what Dr Cree would later refer to as our 'displaced anger at God' – but resented the implication that we could not at the same time have a specific and, as we saw it, justified argument against a course of treatment recommended by a particular doctor.

It was very difficult to express our anger to Dr Cree. I have always found it hard to vent my anger in any case, and the situation was compounded by the fact that she was really the only doctor we could deal with and, for Joe's sake, we didn't want to add to the tension we already felt at visiting the Royal Alexandra.

I could sense the hostility within me in a way I never had before. Earlier in Joe's illness, I had channelled much of it into the writing of *The War Zone*, but now I was finding it impossible to concentrate adequately on *Tribes*, and in any case the anger felt more physical.

I became aware of how close to the surface it was when someone I had met diving phoned to ask if he could borrow some money. He came to the house, my intention being to lecture him on how, with my son ill with cancer and possibly facing death, I didn't need to have to consider for a moment whether I could trust him or not. When he arrived at the door, I just exploded, screaming at him, 'I am fucking angry!' over and over again and pounding the wall so hard I could hear the plaster falling off the lathes.

If I had hit him, I would have wanted to kill him. As it was, my throat was hoarse for twelve hours, but I felt as if I had released something inside me – I had literally felt something physical coming up from my stomach as I yelled. I knew that the person I was shouting at didn't matter in the least to me; I only wished I could have let go so freely with Dr Cree. But, ultimately, of course, she was not a worthy target either.

The next morning, Friday, 9 September 1988, we took Joe to the Royal Alexandra to see Linda Williams and to try and persuade Dr Cree that Joe needed more radiotherapy. While we were there I could barely speak, my throat was so sore from shouting the night before; back home, I sat at the typewriter and tried to work through my anger, typing the words I had screamed and noting Joe's condition that day:

> Joe suddenly in pain, his back hurting, his shoulder – this after the morphine to try and stop it. Him crying for mother, saying, 'Get closer,' then sleeping, thankfully, sleeping.
>
> His sweat, the smell of his hair, an unhealthy smell but beautiful, the shine of his cheeks. Playing baseball with an inflatable bat and ping-pong balls.

Joe was X-rayed that Friday and we were relieved to be given an appointment to see Dr Rodriguez in the radiotherapy department at Sussex County, the following Monday. Joe then had a course of four radiotherapy treatments in the space of eight days, and for a while at least his pain was reduced.

*A*NN The school year started in September and, though I had had doubts about Joe's condition in the preceding weeks, it seemed best for everyone's morale to continue as if he were going. In the summer term Linda had been to inspect St Paul's, and had established that the single-storey building was very suitable for Joe's wheelchair. The staff were willing to let

him attend in it if necessary, though at that time we had anticipated Joe walking into school on his first day.

The only real preparation involved was buying his school
uniform. It wasn't compulsory, but at least 95 per cent of the
children wore it and, as Joe's wheelchair would make him feel
conspicuous already, it seemed especially important for him to
conform in this matter. The uniform needed only minor adapta-
tions to make it suitable for Joe. Woven fabrics could rub and
feel stiff to someone sitting in one position for long periods, but
ordinary shirts and trousers could easily be replaced by similar
items in soft, stretchy cotton jersey. The only difficulty was
finding plain grey tracksuit trousers instead of regulation grey
flannels, a problem I still hadn't solved when it became obvious
that Joe simply wasn't comfortable enough in his wheelchair to
cope with even the part-time schooling we had planned.

Tuesday, 6 September 1988, was to have been Joe's first day at
school, and Alex and I were disappointed at missing this important milestone in our child's life, though we still held out hope
that if he had more radiotherapy he would be able to go later on.
We realized that school was probably a short-term prospect, but
felt it might have provided some interesting stimulation. Joe,
who just didn't feel up to any new challenges, was obviously
relieved; even if he had been well, going to school would have
been a wrench for him at first. When we had planned his
uniform, which he'd enjoyed, he had told me, 'I wish I could go to
a school where mummies go too.'

In the end, Joe almost got his wish. When it was obvious he
wouldn't be going to school in the foreseeable future, we applied
for him to have a home tutor. At his age he was only entitled to
four hours a week, which would be divided into three or four
sessions, and we felt that these short periods would provide a
shape to Joe's days and an opportunity to learn without the
stress of going to school. By a happy coincidence we discovered
that our neighbour Rosemary Machin, whom we knew was a
teacher, did home tuition; and with some intervention from her,
she was appointed Joe's teacher. This was an excellent arrangement all round, as Joe and Rosemary were already friends, and
she and I were able to negotiate her teaching hours to suit ourselves.

As Rosemary preferred to have Joe to herself during their lessons, she didn't mind if I sprinted down to the shops while she was with him, but mostly I was somewhere in the house, a fact Joe liked. Occasionally Rosemary brought in her grandson Daniel. He was a year younger than Joe, but exceptionally bright and imaginative; the two boys already knew each other well, so it was a treat for both of them to share a lesson with Rosemary.

Linda was still coming four times a week to give Joe physiotherapy, so his days were quite full; sometimes it was a struggle to fit in meals and medicine if their sessions were close together. It was almost a relief that neither of them could come on Thursdays, which we came to regard as our day off.

If there was a reason for Joe to be paralysed in April, which I felt could have been avoided, it was to get him, and us, through the next phase of his illness. He had been completely paralysed and had walked again, and that had taught us to hope. Now we desperately looked to radiotherapy to pull off the miracle again.

Writing about early autumn 1988 brings back the feelings of fear and insecurity, the impression that our efforts to persuade Dr Cree to refer Joe to a radiologist took an eternity. It felt like months; in fact, it was about three weeks, not such a long time, except that it was three weeks of slow deterioration – and even three minutes of what we were all feeling was too much. If the pain had been caused by something static, we could have addressed more readily the idea of merely controlling it with drugs. But the constant thought, every minute, of the tumour growing and causing more pain, more disability, was unbearable.

The relief after Joe's first course of radiotherapy at Sussex County was enormous. He felt better, he applied himself to walking again, but it didn't last and the nagging pains came back. On Thursday, 25 August, only a couple of weeks after finishing the first course, Joe was back at Sussex County having more radiotherapy. This time there was some indecision as to the source of Joe's pain, and on 12 September he started a third course of radiotherapy on another tumour site.

*

This was a very bad period for me, arousing all sorts of guilt and anxiety, though Joe actually survived it quite well. Nigel Andrews had given me plenty of notice that he would like me to cover for him on the *Financial Times* in September. At the time I agreed to do it, I had been confident that Joe would be feeling all right, though I had told Nigel I would prefer to do the minimum amount of work, two weeks instead of the usual three. This must have created more work for him, but as the time approached I became more and more alarmed that I wouldn't feel able to leave Joe at all. A week before I was due to start, I called Nigel, intending to ask if he could possibly find someone else to do the column, and discovered that he was about to put his suitcase in his car, ready to leave, when he answered the phone.

I must have been very scared for Joe at this point. The column only involved three days' work a week, one of which was spent writing at home, and I only did it rarely. I remember saying to Nigel that I couldn't bear the idea of my child dying while I was off somewhere watching a movie. I was being melodramatic and in the circumstances, having left Nigel with no time to make other arrangements, I had to go on.

When my first week's work began on Monday, 12 September, Joe was due to have radiotherapy that day. Apart from blood tests and other routine visits that he could take in his stride, I had never let Joe go to hospital without me. Although Alex would be with him, I felt a total failure for going off to London and leaving him. I got home that night to learn that Joe had been perfectly all right without me.

The Wednesday, when he had his second session, was actually worse for me. I was at home, but didn't dare take the time to go with him because I had copy to finish that night. In this period Joe was going to hospital by ambulance because it was more comfortable for him, and it was difficult for Alex to manoeuvre him in and out of the car safely without my help. I went out to the ambulance with Joe and Alex, feeling like the world's worst mother, and kissed them goodbye. When he came back, Joe was tired but all right, not cross with me.

Usually when I was writing, Joe would come in to see me from time to time, sit on my lap and play with my typewriter a bit, trying to distract me. I had missed that since he stopped walking. Now he would lie downstairs with Alex and every so often a little voice would call out, 'Mum, I've got a kiss for you,' and I would go downstairs to get my kiss, sometimes a bit impatient if I had been in the middle of a thought, but always grateful for his affection.

Now when I sit in my room typing, I still hear his voice in my head, 'I've got a kiss for you.' I have photographs and video tapes and audio tapes of Joe, but there was no way of preserving those kisses and hugs.

ALEX I find it very hard to fix on how Joe himself was during autumn 1988. I have very few notes about him for the period between late September and late November, and few drawings. We made no tapes at this time. Even my memory seems blocked in some way. This certainly reflects the anxiety Ann and I were feeling then, and the fact that Joe was often in lower spirits than he had been before, but it would be a mistake to regard the whole period as depressing – in the space of a few hours, he could go from crying with pain to laughing at a cartoon on the video, feeding Cabbage on his lap, or playing some quite active game.

As Joe became increasingly bed-bound, we found that the sofa was no longer such a good place for him to spend his days and so bought him a metal-framed garden recliner, which we padded with a duvet folded in two as an extra mattress. Joe was not comfortable in his wheelchair, and the recliner at least allowed us to carry him outside on the patio to see Cabbage or to enjoy the fine weather in September and early October. The recliner also made lifting Joe and setting him down a good deal easier, because it meant that we could approach him from either side, or even stand right over him.

Joe was by now a solid five-year-old and Ann had great difficulty lifting him. She could manage to haul him from the recliner on to the rather smart new commode which Linda had provided for our basement room, the nearest loo being at the top of the stairs on the ground floor. But when we woke in the mornings or went to bed at night – or if we wanted to take Joe

out of the house – I had to carry him, and I grew to like the pull
of his arms round my neck and even the strain on my back. It
gave me a reason to hold Joe at least twice every day, and I
think, more than anything, I needed reassurance by touch that
he was still very much alive and with us.

The video recorder became more important than ever to Joe
during this time, and we all spent hours watching children's
programmes together – often episodes of shows such as The
Flintstones and Top Cat which I remembered seeing from my
childhood. It seemed remarkable how poignant even these innocuous cartoons could be on occasion: Top Cat more than once
featured some sort of misunderstanding in which T.C. or Officer
Dibble were believed to be dying, with everyone rallying round.

Joe became very keen on a series called Knightmare, which
was a sort of television version of a Dungeons and Dragons-type
computer game, involving real children interacting with video
monsters. We would tape the programme and Joe would watch it
several times, often asking us to get closer to him for a particularly frightening bit, and obviously enjoying being scared.
It interested us that he seemed equally scared each time he
watched, even though he knew what was coming. We had our
own fears, accentuated by the constant images of death on the
screen – swinging pendulum blades, gargoyles thundering the
word 'DOOM!', skull-creatures with spider-like, bony legs.

At the end of September, Joe had a dream which seemed strongly
influenced by watching a tape of a children's natural history
programme called The Really Wild Show directly before going to
bed. The show featured microscopic film of ticks feeding on the
blood of animals, but while that might explain the content of the
dream, it must also have reflected Joe's anxieties at the time,
although he claimed that it did not trouble him too much:

JOE'S FRIGHTENING DREAM

Mummy slid open the top of a box (Daddy was upstairs
working) and all these things which sucked blood out
of people came out and kept landing on Joe's head and
sucked blood out of him. When they were in Mummy's

jumper, they were really tiny – Joe only saw these tiny dots – they sucked the wool off of Mummy's jumper and it was really delicious. Joe saw Mummy slide the box open and then he felt these things on his head. They were smaller when they were on Mummy, but they were as big as wood beetles when they were flying, when Joe saw them. But it was only a dream.

30 September 1988

At some point around this time, I made a note which reflects both how happy we all could be and how precarious that happiness was:

Last night Joe said he wanted a 'proper daddy' if he could have three wishes (the other two were a dolphin and a hippopotamus – on the patio!). It made me laugh a lot – he said he didn't like the look of my face. When I mentioned it again a little later, he seemed a little defensive and said it was a joke, 'a thousand times a joke.'

I said that if I could have a wish (or if Mummy and Daddy could have one between them), I knew what it would be: that Joe could be completely well again. He said that he liked his illness and that was why he was so perky this evening.

He is on morphine, and sometimes he seems a little stoned, but not that much different from normal. Better happy and stoned than in pain. I love him.

ANN It seemed as if this time the radiotherapy wasn't going to work for Joe. He was still taking MST, still getting breakthrough pain, and still not able to sit up comfortably, let alone contemplate trying to walk.

On Friday, 7 October 1988, we took Joe to see Dr Rodriguez, the radiologist, yet again. He didn't feel that there were any more options. Though Joe had tolerated it well, he had had a great deal of radiotherapy now, which hadn't been beneficial for any length of time. Alex took him aside and stressed how desperate we were to get Joe out of pain. He pointed out that with

Joe's life expectation so poor, long-term side effects were not going to worry us, and asked again if there were anything Dr Rodriguez could do.

ALEX While Ann kept Joe occupied, I saw Dr Rodriguez alone in his office. We were desperate, and I know he sensed that, but I also felt that he was more sympathetic to our need to do something than Dr Cree was. I asked Dr Rodriguez a question which had scared the hell out of me whenever I thought about it: 'One of my biggest fears,' I said, 'is that the tumours on Joe's lungs will kill him, and that he'll die coughing up blood and be frightened. But what if the lung tumours don't kill him, what if somehow they stabilize and the tumours in his spine get worse? How can the bone tumours kill him? I can see how they can cause him immense pain – but how can they kill him?'

I sat watching Dr Rodriguez, partly because I thought I knew the answer. I knew the answer was horrible, but I wanted him to think about that horror – though it is only my presumption that he wasn't thinking about it anyway, since he knew far more than I ever would about the effects of cancer. I liked Dr Rodriguez and trusted him. He had young children himself, and both Ann and I felt more able to relate to doctors who were also parents; we felt that those parent–doctors showed a sympathy and an empathy that went beyond medical or even humanitarian concerns.

I hoped that facing up to this question, and the almost tangible gloom it seemed to throw over both of us in the room, might help persuade Dr Rodriguez to try anything, even a long shot, to help Joe.

Dr Rodriguez looked at me from behind his desk. 'The tumours might simply weaken Joe's spine to the point where it might snap, severing his spinal cord,' he said.

We stared at each other for a moment. This was a thought which had gone through my mind every time I had picked Joe up since his paralysis. I had a dread of actually causing him damage – or at the very least precipitating it. I tried to visualize what it might be like: me picking Joe up, his neck falling back or his spine collapsing beneath my grasp, Joe in an agony of pain, both of us terrified.

'Our main concern at the moment,' I said, 'is to find some way of reducing Joe's pain now. I think Ann and I know he's going to die, even if we block it all the time. But the drugs don't seem to work, and, in the short term, radiotherapy has helped him so much.'

Dr Rodriguez told me that there was one more possibility, a single session on something called a linear accelerator, which was more powerful than the normal radiotherapy equipment and which would irradiate the whole of Joe's thoracic region – below the neck and above the abdomen. One of the problems with Joe's continuing pain was that it was very difficult to isolate the source or sources. This high dose of radiation would hopefully hit the developing tumours wherever they were. It would mean that Joe's lungs would be irradiated, which could slightly impair his breathing, but this risk seemed outweighed by the possible benefits in terms of Joe's comfort.

*A*NN Dr Rodriguez seemed to think that the linear accelerator might finally deal with Joe's pain, though it involved such a strong dose of radiation that Joe would have to spend a night in the Royal Alexandra on a drip, to prevent dehydration. He also warned that Joe would be very tired for some time afterwards. As the alternative was for Joe to be rendered almost comatose by higher doses of morphine, which we didn't believe would ever be completely effective, we accepted Dr Rodriguez's suggestion, and a week later Joe was back in hospital for twenty-four hours.

Again the session went well. At Sussex County, Joe had to be left alone in the room containing the rather daunting linear accelerator. This was so powerful that we couldn't even wait directly outside, as the approach area was restricted by warning signs while the equipment was operating. Joe took this all calmly and the next day he was home again. He was very tired and slept a great deal for several days afterwards.

From the day he was on the linear accelerator, Joe didn't mention pain again. At that time he was taking 50mg of MST three times a day. In order to avoid the possibility of further breakthrough pain, but chiefly because morphine is highly addictive, Dr Cree advised me to wait a couple of days for the radiotherapy to take effect, and then reduce the MST by 5mg and continue to reduce it very slightly about every four days as long as Joe remained comfortable. In this way we eventually got Joe off MST completely, but it took eight weeks.

In this period I also started giving Joe a great many vitamins and minerals in an attempt to build up his immune system. Chemotherapy and radiotherapy were miraculous when they worked, but they both affected the immune system very dramatically, so that, whether or not they benefited the patient, they left him debilitated and his body unable to protect itself.

I was giving Joe vitamin E, B complexes, zinc, dolomite, vitamin C and selenium, all of which I either ground up myself or purchased in powder form, and mixed with ice-cream. He did not enjoy these potions, but it was significant that he was now mature enough to take them – when he was first ill, I had decided against any kind of vitamin therapy simply because knew Joe would never cope with the tablets in any form. Even now, there were all sorts of rituals we had to observe. Different tablets went with different flavoured ice-cream, some with chocolate, some with vanilla. Sometimes he needed a mouthful of plain ice-cream or a drink of juice before or after taking the tablet. When he needed to take MST in the night, I had to take ice-cream up to bed in a thermos flask so he could have everything to his liking.

It is impossible to say how much the supplements helped, but when his eating was erratic they seemed a good idea. I did have evidence that the dolomite (a combination of magnesium and calcium, good for bones but also known for its relaxing properties) had a short-term usefulness: there were several occasions when Joe was able to sleep after I'd given it to him because he was restless with pain.

I never failed to be impressed by how heroically Joe took the nasty-tasting mixtures every day, and to encourage him I introduced a system of prizes. Officially, these were awarded once a week, but in practice they tended to be given at intervals of between four and ten days, according to the size of the prize. Deciding what his next prize would be – a Lego or a car, some kind of space toy picked out in the toy shop or from a catalogue – and negotiating how many days it would take to earn it, seemed to make a great deal of difference to Joe's morale.

It was during our negotiations that Joe told me, 'Only toys are presents, not books or videos.' I was sorry to hear this, as I enjoyed choosing books with him, and a pre-recorded video tape was an excellent investment if he enjoyed it, because he would watch it over and over again. I suppose he regarded these items as educational and therefore to be given unconditionally, not earnt. This was a shame, as some of the toys he chose were rather poor value, but the system was pointless unless he got something he really wanted; it was worth the expense to provide him with an incentive he considered worthwhile.

When deciding on which vitamins and minerals to give Joe, I had been greatly helped by my late husband's daughter, Christine Hampson. She in turn had got much of her information from her mother, Betty Logan, who was convinced of the value of food supplements and had studied the subject for some years. On Joe's behalf, Betty followed up encouraging references to a substance known as Green Barley Essence or Green Magma, a powdered concentrate of barley exceptionally rich in vitamins, minerals, enzymes, amino acids and chlorophyll. It was extremely nourishing and there was anecdotal evidence that the boost it gave to the immune system was enormously beneficial to cancer patients.

The Green Barley was so expensive that Christine, apprehensive of pressuring us into purchasing something Joe might refuse to take, gave us his first jar as a gift. She had been warned that it had an unpleasant taste and Betty, knowing Joe was an *Asterix* fan, suggested that we told him it was the Magic Potion. Though I was usually quite straightforward with Joe about what he was taking – pills to stop pain, pills to make him stronger – he was going to need some incentive if it really tasted foul. Betty's idea would certainly appeal to his imagination, and I decided to try it.

I took some of the Green Barley myself, so I would know what Joe had to contend with, and discovered that it was quite tolerable, like very strong greens water, no worse than anything else he took. I gave Joe a small dose mixed in some orange juice and he washed it down with more juice quite cheerfully. Asterix's Magic Potion has much the same effect as spinach on Popeye, and a few minutes later Joe was doing some mock weight-lifting to show us how strong it had made him. He was supposed to have a small dose, which I would gradually increase, twice daily, but a couple of hours later he was saying, 'I think the Magic Potion's wearing off, I'd better have some more.'

This brilliant green drink was certainly the supplement that Joe found most interesting and, I'm convinced, the one that did him the most good. Even in the final stages of his illness, when he was barely eating, Joe continued to take the Green Barley, and his complexion was clear and pink, and his eyes bright, right up to his death.

Around this time we were also recommended a homoeopathic doctor in London who had done a good deal of work with cancer patients. Though he sent Joe some drops to help build his strength, Joe was never well enough to travel to London to see him. If I have any regrets about turning to alternative medicine, it is that we didn't do it earlier when Joe was in better condition, so that it could have been a complement to conventional medicine instead of an afterthought. But at the beginning of Joe's illness we didn't consider other options, and Joe might have been too young to deal with them.

The supplements, the healers and the homoeopathy represented the socially acceptable side of fringe medicine, but by this time Alex and I had agreed that we would try any treatment we came across that we thought Joe could cope with. Discussing it with Linda confirmed our decision. She had worked a good deal with terminal patients and said that a recurring regret among bereaved parents was that they might not have tried all the alternatives available, that their child might have lived if only they had been more open-minded. We felt better for making this decision; though, because Joe became increasingly house-bound, we did not pursue it. But at least we had tried everything that was practical.

There is a common fear that by going outside conventional medicine, people are vulnerable to exploitation. This may

happen, but it was not our experience. All the healers we consulted asked for the most modest fees, far less than a plumber,
which they would waive in cases of hardship; the Green Barley
did cost about £2 a day when Joe was taking high doses, but was
visibly worth the money; and the homoeopath never sent us a bill.

ALEX Looking at the regularity with which we sought and
Joe received radiotherapy, a fairly consistent decline in his
condition is identifiable, but it did not seem so to us at the time.
Particularly after the wider-ranging radiotherapy to Joe's chest
on the linear accelerator on 14 October, we had the illusion that
he had recovered to some degree.

There were high spots in October and November – relaxed,
enjoyable moments, such as an indoor 'picnic' at his friend
James Ryan's house, which Joe attended on his recliner; or
hollowing out the face Joe had drawn on a Hallowe'en pumpkin,
and then darkening the basement room (where we now spent
almost all our time) to get the full effect of the candle inside.

When Rosemary Reid visited one weekend, we even managed
to carry Joe, tucked up like a prince in his bedclothes on his
recliner, the length of the Palace Pier. For the first time in what
must have seemed to Joe like an eternity, he was back inside the
Pleasuredome, or 'Circus,' his favourite video arcade, where we
held him as close to the familiar screens as we could get him and
let him shout 'diructions' as we steered three-dimensional Pac-
Man through the maze, or karate-chopped video opponents atop
a moving train.

On 5 November, Joe didn't feel up to going outside for fire-
works, so we had some of the indoor variety, but the next evening
he was brighter, and we were joined by his friend, Daniel,
Daniel's mother Lindsey, and Rosemary (Joe's teacher), for fire-
works on the patio – which culminated in Lindsey and me running
and ducking as a rogue rocket ricocheted from wall to wall.

But there were low points too, and one of the worst came on
Monday, 24 October, when Joe seemed very listless and feverish.
Dr Cree was away, but we called the Royal Alexandra in any
case to ask if a doctor could come to the house to examine Joe,

as we did not wish to move him unnecessarily. We were told that Dr Reid, the registrar, would not be available for some time, and were advised to call our G P.

We did so, but unfortunately our own G P, Dr Jane Roderic Evans, was not on call that day, and instead one of her partners Dr Sacks, came to visit. He had never seen Joe before and, in his defence, was obviously inexperienced with childhood cancer, but he put us through the most agonizing few hours we had ever suffered when he told us that he thought Joe might be in the first stages of death.

Our shock and disbelief that Joe might have started so suddenly to die was equalled only by our immense relief at the complete rejection of this prognosis by Dr Reid at the Royal Alexandra, where, after Dr Sacks had left the house, we immediately took Joe in a state of utter fear and panic. Five days later, I had recovered sufficiently to write an extremely angry letter to Dr Sacks, expressing the pain he had caused us:

Dear Dr Sacks

I am writing because I feel strongly that I must complain about your manner and the psychology behind your advice and comments to me when you visited our son Joseph last Monday, 24 October . . .

. . . I am going to say this in very plain terms, terms you will no doubt attribute to a heightened emotional state under our very trying conditions. How dare you come into my house, having never met me, Ann or Joe, and on the basis of a ten minute examination give me to believe that my son was dying there and then? I can understand – I think – how, seeing Joe for the first time very briefly on Monday, he may have seemed to be close to the final stages of his illness, but do you not think you should have been a little more cautious and considerate before practically intoning the last rites?

Dr Reid, when we took Joe round to the Royal Alexandra Hospital, did not bear out your observation. He is experienced in oncology, I understand, and he seemed to think that, given the circumstances, Joe seemed quite well. He also did not think Joe needed the enema you seemed to feel was so desperately required ...

... Joe, since Monday, has generally improved without the help of an antibiotic. All the cultures proved negative. He is waking better and has been playing and watching his videos on TV. He has been sitting in his wheelchair for brief periods of time for his physiotherapist. His MST has been further reduced from 30mg three times a day to 25mg, without any mention of discomfort. None of this proves anything, I know. He may be very sick again within hours or days. My only point is that you made last Monday afternoon a painful, untimely and unwelcome rehearsal for Joe's death – and did so, I feel, unnecessarily.

Extracted from a letter to Dr Sacks,
dated 29 October 1988

A more significant climax to the anger and frustration we had been feeling came as a result of a telephone call on Tuesday, 1 November 1988. Our friend, Mozafar Aminian, phoned from London to ask how we all were and to tell us that his nineteen-year-old cousin, who had cancer, was responding well to an experimental treatment being pioneered by the Hammersmith and Queen Charlotte's Hospital.

Although the treatment, called Contracan, had initially involved painful injections, it was now being tried in suppository form and had no apparent side effects, beyond causing constipation. Mozafar thought we might like to investigate further and find out if it might help Joe, and he gave me the contact number of the consultant surgeon, Mr Wood, who was overseeing the trial.

Ann and I hardly dared to let ourselves get excited, but we had always held on to the possibility that some new cure or treatment might be developed that would save or prolong Joe's life, and this sounded too good to be true – a treatment which was proving effective, could be administered painlessly and which had no serious side effects.

Somewhat nervously, I called Mr Wood at Hammersmith and Queen Charlotte's, to find out more about Contracan and whether there was any possibility of trying it for Joe. Given what we saw as a breakdown in communications with Dr Cree, it was refreshing to talk to a consultant who sounded so positive and unpatronizing. He was obviously excited about this new drug, and while he admitted it sounded unlikely that it could save Joe, he was prepared to meet me to discuss it further.

On Friday, 11 November, I took the train to London and went to Hammersmith and Queen Charlotte's. The entry in my diary for the day before records: 'Very negative day – exhausted, arguing with Ann.' This must have reflected the tension we were feeling, for we had very few rows during the course of Joe's illness.

Certainly, on the Friday, things seemed brighter. I met Mr Wood in his office at the hospital and explained, as thoroughly as I could, the stages of Joe's cancer. He, in turn, told me how he and his partners had developed Contracan as a result of research into the balance of saturated and unsaturated fat in the cells of cancer patients. He drew me a diagram and explained that this ratio had a direct bearing on cell death and the spread of cancer, and that clinical trials of Contracan to date had shown that it inhibited that spread, thus stabilizing the patient's condition.

He warned me that there was no evidence that it could do anything other than stabilize the cancer, but that several patients had reported greatly reduced pain and had been able to withdraw from morphine and other pain-killers. He emphasized again that he did not think Contracan could save Joe, but that it might help relieve his pain. Once Joe had had a 'base' X-ray from which his progress could be monitored, he was prepared to supply the suppositories, which we could administer ourselves at home, and there would be no charge for the treatment. He agreed that, if he were in my shoes, he would try anything that might help Joe, so long as it did not actually endanger him, and he felt that Contracan would not.

I had mentioned some of the difficulties we were having in dealing with Dr Cree, and Mr Wood stressed that I must talk to Ann and to Dr Cree before we went any further. Excited by even the remotest possibility that Contracan might help ease and prolong Joe's life – perhaps long enough that another treatment could be found – I called Ann from Queen Charlotte's and she agreed that I should call Dr Cree straight away.

I did so, from a pay phone in the Queen Charlotte's lobby, and was horrified by the total negativity of her response. She accused me of going behind her back, whereas before my meeting with Mr Wood I had known so little about Contracan that there would have been nothing to discuss. She said that she felt Mr Wood's behaviour – presumably, simply in meeting me – was unethical and made it clear that she felt any further trial for Joe was unwarranted and cruel. If we wanted to remove Joe from her care and place him under Mr Wood's (an impractical suggestion, as she well knew, given Joe's immobility now and our distance from London) then, fine, we could go ahead with Contracan, but she would not agree to it.

I asked her at least to think about the new treatment and to call Mr Wood, to which she responded that he could call her. I put the phone down, then immediately called Mr Wood and explained her reaction. He seemed unperturbed and was reassuring. He would talk to Dr Cree. I left the hospital and spent the afternoon in London in a foul temper, mentally cursing Dr Cree and feeling strongly that I would like to punch her.

My mood, certainly as far as Dr Cree was concerned, did not improve over the next few days, and was shared by Ann. We felt she had become a positive block to caring for Joe and we resented the fact that, whenever we talked to her, she sanctimoniously stressed that what was important was 'what's best for Joe', as if that was the furthest thing from our minds. No other doctor took this attitude, and we hoped that as parents we were sufficiently self-aware to weigh up our obvious, selfish wish that Joe should live and be with us, against the possibility that further treatment could actually impair the quality of what was left of his life.

We had particularly grown to resent Dr Cree's 'surprise visits', when she would pop round to the house unannounced to see how Joe was – and, it seemed to us, to remind us that he was dying. It was fortunate, therefore, that, having planned one of these for Tuesday afternoon, 15 November, she ran into Linda Williams in the Royal Alexandra car park and mentioned that she was thinking of seeing us. Linda, aware of our feelings, tactfully suggested that perhaps Dr Cree should telephone us first.

When Dr Cree did call, I answered the phone. When she said she was thinking of coming round, I said, 'No!' in no uncertain terms. I had never had an opportunity – or felt secure enough – to tell her a little of my feelings, but now seemed the time. I said that Ann and I were extremely angered by her reaction to the Contracan proposal, that we felt she was effectively exercising moral and emotional blackmail by suggesting that the only way we could proceed was by removing Joe from her care. I told her that we had grown increasingly unhappy about her attitude towards treating Joe, that we felt patronized by her, and that we were scared that her faith in God and Christian heaven meant that she was more willing to accept Joe's death than we were. 'We feel bludgeoned by your Christianity,' I said. I told her that we had no faith in her any more and did not wish to deal with her or for Joe to see her.

I was so angry by the time I finished speaking to her that I was flushed and shaking. I felt slightly guilty at the hurt I must have caused her and knew that she was probably not as terrible as we thought, but at the same time, for whatever reasons, she had caused us immense, unnecessary pain and anxiety simply through her failure to respond to our needs as desperate parents. I went downstairs and told Ann about our conversation. Above all, we felt relieved that our feelings were out in the open and that we would no longer have to deal with Dr Cree. We were not sure who would take charge of Joe's care now, but anything seemed better than the doubt and distrust we had been living with.

*A*NN By November, Joe had recovered from the tiring after-effects of the linear accelerator, his dose of MST had been reduced significantly, and he was much more cheerful. Linda decided that he should attempt sitting in his wheelchair again now that his back pain had been dealt with. At first this was exhausting and he could only sit for a minute or so before complaining. But gradually he was adjusting, and one Friday afternoon, when Linda wanted him to aim for five minutes, he did not want to get out of the chair. Suddenly he was enjoying sitting up again, and when Linda left, fifteen minutes later, he was still in the wheelchair, sternly instructed by her to rest soon.

This progress encouraged us to take Joe to the pier the next day. He had been there a few times since his back had troubled him, but only at quiet, mid-week times when it wasn't crowded and his recliner wasn't a nuisance. When he asked on Saturday afternoon, 19 November, if he could go, our first reaction was to say no. We were delighted that he wanted to go out, but the weekend was a busy time and we knew we couldn't ask to take the recliner into the Pleasuredome. Then, thinking about his improving comfort in the chair, Alex asked Joe if he could cope with being carried in Alex's arms along the pier, and sitting in his wheelchair if he got tired. Joe was sure he'd be all right, so we decided to try it.

We put Joe in the back seat of the car, propped up with quilts, and drove down to the Palace Pier. Then, while Alex carried Joe to his favourite spot at the very end of the pier, I followed with the wheelchair. Joe had his arms round Alex's neck, holding on, but his legs dangled uselessly, all the life gone from them now, his feet covered by two pairs of thick socks to keep them warm, because he couldn't flex them enough to wear his boots.

It was exhausting for Alex, supporting Joe in the video arcade, but thrilling to see him back on form; Joe was very good at video games and even had his name on some of the top scorers lists displayed on screen when the games finished. There had been one trip to the pier when he had stayed on his recliner, too weak to do anything but watch Alex play, only able to enjoy the games vicariously. But now he found the energy to sit on Alex's lap in the *Road Blaster*, a game with a car-shaped exterior in which the player sat and simulated driving a hair-raising course of obstacles, while all the time shooting at other vehicles. He went from level to level, scoring more than he ever had before – possibly because we were not concerned about the cost and must have put in almost five pounds to keep the action going for him before he was tired.

We had always been pleased by the effect the video games had on Joe's movement. Right at the beginning of his paralysis, when certain exercises were difficult, we had found that if a similar effort were required to operate a video game, Joe would find the will to perform really well. Now he had sat for at least twenty minutes, manoeuvring a steering wheel, pressing buttons and making split-second decisions.

Joe was tired, but Alex was exhausted; the effort of supporting Joe in a cramped position had been enormous. We sat Joe in his wheelchair and were pleased to see that he looked comfortable and happy. Alex had intended to carry him back to the car, but I decided to start pushing Joe in the chair and see how he reacted. I wheeled him on a circuit of the Pleasuredome, so that he could inspect the other games, then took him outside.

It was dusk by then, and beneath us the sea glittered darkly with the reflected lights from the pier and the town. A peaceful night, mild for November. A wooden walkway the length of the pier made for a very smooth ride, and wheeling Joe all the way back to the car was a small triumph. A short ride today could mean a longer one tomorrow. This could be the improvement we had wanted. For a moment the immediate future looked brighter, less confining, a place where Joe went for rides in his wheelchair.

18 *The End of the Year*

Cat by Joe Buffalo, aged five years four months, December 1988

ALEX If Saturday evening's walk on the pier felt quite magical at the time, it was to seem even more so in retrospect, for it was the last time Joe would ever visit the Palace Pier and, apart from a single trip to hospital two days later, his last time outside our house.

On Monday, 21 November 1988, we were still feeling encouraged by Joe's greatly increased comfort in his wheelchair. I realized that it was months since Joe had been able to spend any time in my workroom, but that the wheelchair might now make that possible. I knew he was fascinated by the computer I had recently bought but which he had not seen, so I suggested he might like to be carried up to play with the 'paintbox' programmes and computer games. Joe seemed very keen, so I set up his wheelchair in my room, then carried him up.

The computer must have seemed like another video game to Joe and he certainly enjoyed experimenting with the colour graphics. After about an hour I thought he had had enough, so I took him back down to the basement and settled him on his recliner, but as I did so I noticed an unusual swelling around his left thigh, clearly visible because Joe was wearing only a disposable nappy and a sweatshirt.

I stood over him on the recliner and tried to look relaxed, so as not to alarm Joe. I studied the shape of his body and legs, wanting to be wrong, and even doubting what I saw, but it was as if something was sticking out at the top of the thigh. Joe appeared happy and certainly not in pain. I called Ann down to come and look, experiencing the familiar sick feeling in my stomach that always signalled panic and fear. I hoped this was only a swelling caused by some inadvertent muscle sprain, but it didn't look like that. It looked more serious, and my recurrent dread that I might damage Joe's bones simply by moving him resurfaced with a vengeance.

Ann came down, looked at Joe, then popped upstairs with me for a moment, on some pretext, to get out of Joe's earshot. She quietly agreed that there was obviously something wrong with his leg. The anxiety this immediately created for both of us was accentuated by the fact that I had had my 'show-down' argument with Dr Cree on the telephone only the week before. We had no desire to call our GP because, while we had great faith in Jane Roderic-Evans, it might be Dr Sacks again who was on call, and neither of us wished to see him. We felt totally isolated.

ANN Joe's bad luck was compounded by the fact that Linda was not making her usual visit that day – we had had a call to say she was sick – when she was the person most likely to identify what was wrong. We called the Physiotherapy Department and explained that we were anxious about the unnatural appearance of Joe's thigh, and Linda's colleague, Judy, promised to come as soon as possible. The extraordinary part of all this was that though there was obviously something very wrong with Joe's leg, he was quite unaware of it. Presumably the complete insensitivity created by his paralysis eliminated any pain.

When Judy arrived, Alex and I were anxious but Joe was still quite serene. 'What seems to be the trouble?' she asked him. 'Well,' he said seriously, 'you know when you've got a really tight bogy? It's really hard to get out.' We were all a bit stunned at this answer, as Judy hadn't come to discuss Joe's nose-picking habits, but undeterred she looked at his thigh.

We had hoped the problem was a dislocation which a physiotherapist might be able to manipulate back into place, but Judy said right away that she thought it was a fracture, and Joe would have to go to the Royal Alexandra to be X-rayed. In the past we would have simply taken Joe straight to Cawthorne Ward and let Dr Cree deal with it, but now she was the last person we wanted to see. Judy said that there was no reason why Joe shouldn't be admitted to the hospital via the Casualty Department. After helping us get Joe upstairs and into our car, gently laid along the back seat on protective quilts, she went ahead to warn Casualty that they needed to book an X-ray for Joe.

In the hospital, Joe could be moved around on a trolley and we went easily from waiting room to X-ray to treatment room. We discovered that Joe had fractured his left femur (thigh bone), and that this had happened spontaneously because a tumour site in the bone had made it so fragile. Normally the treatment would involve putting the leg in traction for two or three weeks while the bones started to knit together. In Joe's case, this knitting would take much longer and, if the tumour were still active, might not be achieved at all. However, the only course available was to put Joe in traction and wait and see; the doctor estimated that it would take five or six weeks to get an idea of what was happening.

While Joe was in X-ray Dr Cree appeared, looking so lost that we felt a pang of guilt at the way we had overridden her. But the prospect of five or six weeks on Cawthorne Ward, where we imagined Joe would have to be in traction, renewed our determination to avoid her. We were told we had the option of having Joe in traction at home in the care of a paediatric community nurse and we immediately accepted. It was too late for the nurse to visit that day, but it was decided that we would take Joe home and make him comfortable until she came on duty in the morning.

Joe couldn't possibly sleep in our bed at the moment, or be moved around the house; the obvious place to base him was downstairs. Before we moved to Brighton we had lived in flats with tiny kitchens. The only piece of yuppie-dom I had ever craved was a home with a large family room/kitchen area where I could have easy contact with Joe while I was cooking. We had gained a room like this in the gutted basement of our house, and it had been invaluable while Joe was leading a sedentary life. Now that he was going to be completely immobilized for a spell, we could virtually live in the room and Joe need never be left alone.

This was going to involve some strenuous furniture-moving, getting the sofa out of the basement and dismantling Joe's bunks so that one of the beds could be taken downstairs for him. While Joe and I waited for an ambulance to take us home, Alex went ahead, hoping there would be a neighbour available to help him get the room ready before we arrived.

ALEX Even during the two- or three-minute drive back home alone, I was already experiencing a sense of guilt that I had fractured Joe's leg by moving him. I tried to rationalize this by telling myself that the bone was so fragile, it would have broken at some time soon in any case. I went over and over in my mind how I had lifted him, and knew I had handled him no differently than on the countless other occasions recently when I had had to carry him, but the guilt was inescapable.

I parked the car and immediately rang on the door of a neighbour, Hugh Clench, hoping that he would be home and be able to help me move the furniture. He was, and when he came to the house a few minutes later we set to, manoeuvring the sofa round an incredibly tight corner at the bottom of the stairs and moving Joe's top bunk bed down to the basement.

As we worked and chatted about Joe's condition, I realized just how bad the implications of this fracture were. The fact that Joe's femur had been weakened so much by a tumour did not augur well for his spine; I remembered the conversation with Dr Rodriguez about Joe's vertebrae simply collapsing and snapping his spinal cord. The deterioration of Joe's femur (where, so far as we knew, there had been no active tumour for the past year) suggested a further steady decline in Joe's overall condition.

In the improbable fantasy we still clung to, of Joe somehow being saved from cancer, there was now the problem that his bones would be damaged. Even if Joe didn't die – and we still, even in the face of this fracture, refused to accept that he would – it was unlikely that his bones could ever recover. Even if he lived, would his spine be strong enough to support him?

Hugh and I were in the last stages of assembling Joe's bunk when the ambulance arrived with Ann and Joe. We quickly finished tightening the bolts, put the mattress in place, and then the ambulancemen carried Joe downstairs into the basement.

He did not appear to be in a state of shock, perhaps because he was in no pain; his reaction to this latest development wouldn't really become apparent until the next morning. Ann and I tried to put a positive glaze on events by stressing how good it was to see Joe back in his bunk bed – he had slept in ours since his illness, so there was a kind of nostalgia about seeing him there.

Joe soon dozed. Ann and I managed some dinner, but we were exhausted, as much by the anxiety as any physical effort. I brought Joe's other bunk bed mattress down for Ann to sleep on, then went up to our room and lay in bed alone, aware that we had passed some new, negative milestone.

ANN When we woke up on Tuesday morning, we had entered a new phase in our lives. I had slept downstairs on a mattress on the floor and, while Joe was confined to the basement, Alex and I would take it in turns to sleep there with him.

There were two paediatric community nurses in Brighton, we discovered when they arrived together, Beryl and Anne. We had been very nervous of moving Joe and doing more damage to his leg, but they were soon showing us the most efficient way to wash him in bed and keep him comfortable. Though it took both nurses to set up Joe's traction and get us organized that first day, Joe was to be in Beryl Ruston's special care. It was very

reassuring to know that she would be visiting Joe every morning
to check his leg and help get him washed and dressed.

Beryl and Anne had quickly established that Joe's bed wasn't
suitable for traction; they needed a metal, high-framed hospital
bed. Alex had barely recovered from his furniture moving the
night before, when he had to reorganize beds once again.

Joe was obviously a popular figure at the Royal Alexandra, in
spite of his demanding parents, because not only did Sister
Sharp immediately agree to let Beryl borrow a bed from Cawthorne Ward, but the porters, knowing it would take at least
another day to arrange transport, offered to wheel it to the
house as we lived so close.

The two men arrived, hot and tired, with an hilarious account
of having almost lost control of the bed on the steep hill down to
our street. On the way they had met our neighbour Rosemary,
who had asked, 'Is it for Joe?' Mishearing her question as 'Is it a
joke?' and obviously feeling as if they were taking part in some
rag-week stunt, they had replied, 'No, it's serious.'

Getting the bed down the street turned out to be the soft
option; our narrow basement stairs were even more of a problem.
Watching Alex help them bring the dismantled bed down piece
by piece and reassemble it kept Joe interested, but he was not
happy with the new situation. Though he had taken events
calmly the day before, he was now showing signs of shock, he
was sleepy and depressed – and miserable, after the hopes
aroused by his outing on Saturday, at the prospect of being
house-bound till Christmas.

Beryl soon had as important a part in our lives as Linda.
Because of the extent of his paralysis, Joe was a dead weight to
move around, and the knowledge of how fragile his bones had
become had made us very nervous of moving him. Beryl's visits
gave us confidence and she was an immediate source of good
advice. We were extraordinarily lucky to have nursing help at
home, not just because it was another benefit of the NHS, but
because the paediatric community service, which does not operate in all parts of the country, had only been introduced to
Brighton that April.

After a few days Joe got over the first shock, and began to
adjust to his new situation. He took an instant liking to Beryl and

enjoyed seeing her every day. Life became even more hectic – people were coming and going all the time. Linda and Rosemary still visited Joe, and I had also become eligible for a home help, Jean, who called in a couple of times a week, mostly to help with shopping. This was invaluable now that Alex, who had more or less taken over major trips to the supermarket, had to spend more time helping me with Joe as well as trying to get on with some writing.

LINDA WILLIAMS I was away at the time Joe's leg broke and returned to find him in bed at home, all strung up in traction. Obviously very shocked, he was proud of the fact that his bed had been wheeled by the porters through the streets from the hospital to his house. Joe soon got back to his usual verbal self. His empire had become considerably smaller and was confined to one room, his subjects largely Ann, Alex, Beryl, his grandparents and me – but his authority barely wavered.

We would do arm exercises and I would move his legs. Joe played counting games while I held his legs straight, but given the chance, he preferred to continue playing with his video games. I tried not to give him the chance, and many bargains were struck! He had no feeling in his legs by this time and we had to make a plastic splint to rest his foot in. In true Joe style, he also wanted me to make one for his clockwork mouse's tail.

All through this period Joe's morale was high, despite some very grumpy days. He hadn't encountered a peer group to define his boundaries, so all areas of authority had to be experienced through the adults around him – this could be quite difficult for all concerned.

ALEX Joe had been effectively bed-bound since September, so traction simply tested our ingenuity further in terms of how we could keep him entertained. The fact that the hospital bed was on wheels meant that we could manoeuvre it – just about, given the size of it and the shape of our basement room – over to the telephone, so that Joe could make calls to Gran and Fred. We could still play baseball, using Joe's inflatable bat and ping-pong balls, which gave Joe the illusion of playing sports like Charlie Brown and Snoopy on his video tapes. And we invented other games, such as a form of hide-and-seek, with me crawling under the bed and trying to catch him out when I appeared from either side.

Joe adjusted to the traction as he had to everything else – remarkably well. It meant a new pattern to his days: not simply Beryl coming in to wash him and dress his leg, but the need throughout the day to move him regularly from side to side to avoid sores. Joe helped himself do this, using the 'monkey bar' over his pillow, with which he could pull himself up a little so that Ann or I could turn him.

The monkey bar also figured in the exercises Linda encouraged him to do, as much for motivation now as for any hope of recovery. She moulded a plastic support for Joe's left foot – the leg that was in traction – to retain at least some of its correct angle and flexibility, and we performed gentle manipulative exercises from time to time, which Joe seemed to enjoy.

Ann and I still refused to accept consciously that Joe was dying. We acted as if we believed his femur would repair itself, which was the only way we could deal with the situation. He was never in pain from the fracture – a sign of his creeping paralysis – and it could be argued that traction was unnecessary, even cruel, in terms of placing added restrictions on Joe's movement during the last weeks of his life; but, for him as well as for us, the sense of life carrying on positively and with a purpose was vital, and his state of mind during this period remained incredibly strong:

JOE: Ma!
ANN: Yes, Joe.
JOE: One whole thing.
ANN: What is it, darling?
JOE: Something I haven't told you about Melissa and Cookie Monster and Leglin. All of them three are on a diet.
ANN: Are they?
JOE: Yeah, mean, the things they are allowed to eat are crumpets, cake, hamburgers . . .
ANN: Well, that sounds like a nice diet: crumpets, cake and hamburgers.

JOE: . . . cream cheese sandwiches . . .

ANN: Gosh!

JOE: . . . cheese. And . . .

ANN: And?

JOE: . . . and fish and chips.

ANN: Fish and chips? I see. Well, that sounds like a good diet. Has it got a name, this diet?

JOE: It's just they're on a diet because they have been eating some things which are not good for them. But there's only two things they can only eat: cabbage and peanuts.

ANN: That sounds quite an interesting diet, a cabbage and peanut diet.

JOE: Yeah, but they eat all the kinds of things I eat.

ANN: They might be better off on cabbage and peanuts. It would be quite well-balanced, really, you'd get protein and starch and some sort of roughage, and green stuff. I don't think you'd like a diet of cabbage and peanuts, would you, darling?

JOE: No, I wouldn't! Cabbage isn't really food for people, it's food for rabbits. Only lettuce is for people.

ANN: No, people eat cabbage. Mummy and Daddy have cabbage sometimes. Sometimes we have white cabbage, which doesn't look the same. What Cabbage eats, we call 'greens' usually, because they're very green. Which reminds me that I must get some out – oh, there are some out. Did Daddy get them out?

JOE: That's because Dad hasn't – Cabbage hasn't been fed today.

ANN: Oh, Daddy fed him this afternoon.

JOE: Daddy realized he hadn't been fed and fed him.

ANN: I know. Well, I wouldn't feed him because he bit me yesterday, and I got upset.

JOE: Yeah, but unfortunately you will have to feed him quite a lot.

ANN: I know, but I don't like feeding him, because he bites me so often.

JOE: Yeah, I'm not going to let him!

Transcribed from a tape made while Joe was in traction, in early December 1988

*A*NN Being in traction gave Joe a new identity. Just as the wheelchair had made him seem like a disabled child who might have a full life ahead of him, so the traction made him look like an ordinary boy who had broken his leg. Once, when a delivery man, impressed by the sight of a hospital bed in our basement, asked what was wrong, I heard myself saying, 'Oh, he's broken his leg, so he's based down here for a while.' It wasn't that Joe's cancer was a secret, but it was nice for him not to be the object of explanations that always had to be made light of, and comforting for me to pretend for a moment that we had a normal, recoverable life ahead of us. That Joe was just a boy who had broken his leg.

At the start of Joe's illness, immediately after the operation to remove his kidney, when he was still in pain, I had hated not being able to hold him. I had thought then how miserable it would be if he died without having one last big, squashy hug.

Now the situation had returned. With bones that might break under too much pressure, and comfortable only lying propped up by many pillows (at one count, Joe had nine supporting his leg, back and shoulders), it was impossible to hold him really close, the way I wanted. It seemed an eternity since he had sat on my lap and I had been able to put my arms right around him. I was reduced to putting my arms along his front half and holding him gently, wishing I could crush him to me. Luckily Joe could still put his arms – which were very strong – round me, and he was generous with his hugs and kisses.

While he was in traction, he began to realize that Alex and I needed to rest. Often, before he went to sleep at night, he would keep asking for hugs. I would get up from the mattress and go over for a hug, settle down again, and ten minutes later Joe would be asking for another. But at some point he started understanding our exhaustion. One night, after getting me up, he kissed me and said, 'Now get some sleep,' and he didn't disturb me again that night. 'Now get some sleep' came to be a regular conclusion to his bedtime ritual, another sign of maturity.

ALEX If one new 'toy' helped to transform the time Joe spent in traction above anything else, it was the Nintendo video game system he bought with his half of the first advance from *Henry and the Sea*. We had told Joe that he would get 'quite a lot of money' – about £250 – for writing the book, and that he should decide how he wanted to spend it. The cheque had arrived a week or so before Joe's thigh bone fractured, and he had already made his decision, based on the endless children's commercials he saw on television.

The Nintendo system had made a big impression on him, with the various video games it advertised and, in particular, the battery-operated robot that came with the system and which interacted with the games on the TV screen. The whole package cost over £150 and initially we had thought about making Joe wait until Christmas for such an expensive toy, but we felt that the money was rightly his and that, in his condition, such self-discipline was hardly necessary or fair.

On the Saturday I bought the system for him, Joe was delighted. We set it up and played countless games of *Duck Hunt* and *Gyromite*, which came with the pack. A few days before Joe's fracture, Ann bought him a new game, *The Legend of Zelda*, far more complex than the others, and it was this game especially which made traction more bearable.

Zelda was a computer-animated, *Dungeons and Dragons*-type video game, which involved a quest through a vast overworld of forests and mountains, battling various monsters and trying to find the secret entrances to eight underworld mazes. In these the struggle was even greater, as you searched and fought for various magical possessions which would help you complete your quest. The game was storable so that you could return to it again and again, which was just as well, as it required razor-sharp reflexes to operate its remote controls, and involved a good deal of skill and thought, including the ability to read a map, something Joe learnt by playing it. We never did complete the quest, despite a total of more than a hundred hours' playing time.

Joe loved this game and, during traction, almost lived for it. We would play it in the mornings when he first woke up, and last thing at night before we went to sleep – which is not to say that we didn't play it throughout the day as well. The nature of the game was such that you could name the character undertaking your quest on screen, and could have three entirely independent games stored in the memory at any one time. Joe chose 'Warrior' as his protagonist, and this little video hero became a part of our lives.

As with the other video games Joe had played on the pier, we felt that *The Legend of Zelda* helped motivate him. It certainly kept him occupied, and if there was a negative side to all this, it was the accompanying electronic soundtrack, which at first had seemed a good deal more sophisticated than usual, but which took on the elements of Chinese water torture after a week or so.

A more surprising aspect to this video game obsession was that it resulted in Joe enjoying J. R. R. Tolkien's book, *The Hobbit*. I read often to Joe while he was in traction, especially at night – and by mid-December, both Ann and I were spending every night sleeping on mattresses on the floor beside him.

Before we settled down, usually around midnight, I would read Joe a story, or we would listen to a favourite tape of Maureen Lipman reading Jill Tomlinson's book, *The Owl who was Afraid of the Dark*. Joe particularly liked this tale of a young owl overcoming his fears, and it seemed very appropriate to us at this time. We would listen together in the dark, sometimes falling asleep as we did so, though on one occasion Joe asked for the lights to be put back on so he could make a drawing which he called, 'Hunter the Barn Owl'.

Partly because Joe seemed to appreciate the richness of the imagery in *'Twas the night before Christmas*, which I was also reading to him regularly (from the Peanuts card he had given me the previous Christmas), but largely because he seemed so excited by the video dragons, magic weapons and forests, mountains and caves in *The Legend of Zelda*, I thought he might enjoy *The Hobbit*, and presented the book to him as being like a story based on *Zelda*.

As I started reading it aloud to him one night, I wondered if I hadn't made a mistake. Joe was still only five, and perhaps *The Hobbit* was a bit too sophisticated. Certainly it was the densest text he had ever been read, but Tolkien seemed almost to have intended it to be read aloud. The rhythm of the words and the spell he wove with descriptions you could almost taste and smell, and subtle and not-so-subtle jokes and asides, worked their magic on Joe.

When I finished that first night, he wanted more. He wanted to know what happened next, what sort of a wizard Gandalf was, whether there were really hobbits, and whether there were going to be fierce dragons in the story. From then on, I think I read by candle-light to increase the atmosphere, and Joe and I had a marvellous time following the tale of Bilbo Baggins. Some may criticize video games as being essentially mindless or aggressive, but *The Legend of Zelda* had taken Joe to a new level of children's literature.

ANN We had been aware that Joe's bones were affected by tumours and that he should be handled gently for some time, but the fracturing of his leg was still a terrifying reminder of how fragile he was. Now our eternal optimism was strained to extraordinary limits. Not only was there the cancer to defeat, but his frail bones and the extent of his paralysis, which would mean a lifetime of severe handicap.

His recovery now would involve a series of three miracles. First the cancer would have to be banished from his body – and if that happened tomorrow, he would still be left with frail bones. We had been told that in the cases where bone cancer was cured, the bones would eventually repair themselves and strengthen, so perhaps that would take care of itself. But then there was the extent of Joe's paralysis. He still had an advantage over many disabled people in having excellent reflexes in his arms and hands, demonstrated by his skill with his Nintendo game, and his mind was very alert. But there was no chance of him having anything approaching a normal existence. Even if we could protect his happiness and self-esteem through childhood, what sort of adult life would he have?

In his present condition, if he kept the use of his arms and brain, he could have a wonderful intellectual life, but would that be enough? He would be dependent on us, or carers if we died; he was unlikely to marry; he would never enjoy sex or creating a family of his own. A miracle now would have to incorporate astounding advances in neurosurgery, so that Joe's useless spinal cord could be brought back to life. Without all these miracles, would he think his life was worthwhile?

Though Joe had kept control of his bladder for a remarkably long time, at some point before the fracture his lack of sensation had finally stopped him knowing when he needed to pee. After a couple of accidents I had suggested, as tactfully as I could, that Joe wear a disposable nappy for a while. Luckily he was a practical child and accepted this idea quite calmly. He never expressed any embarrassment or distress over reverting to nappies, but he did have a brief dream that revealed his unhappiness.

One morning just before he went into traction, he told me, 'Mum, I had a wonderful dream. I dreamt that I told you I wanted to pee, and you got a pee bottle, and I did pee!'

I agreed that this was a marvellous dream, and tried to look for a hopeful sign. Sometimes Joe did seem to know when he was actually urinating, though not sufficiently in advance to give me warning; maybe this was a sign of some returning sensation.

Now, in traction, the fact that he had no control over his bladder was a bigger problem. The frequent manoeuvring to change him was a hazard to his fractured thigh and his potentially breakable bones. At first we were nervous of moving him without Beryl's guidance, but we soon learnt the knack of changing him with the minimum of disruption.

We had resisted the suggestion of a catheter for him; though it had obvious advantages, we knew it would distress Joe. However, it soon became inevitable. The change in gravity caused by tilting his bed for traction made it very difficult for his bladder to empty. It would fill completely, bloating his tummy, and only drain when outside pressure from a hand was used. The appearance of a bedsore, caused by pressure but aggravated by wet nappies, was an extra complication, and at this point we agreed to the catheter.

For a day or so Joe was absolutely miserable, although the benefits gained in keeping him dry were enormous. A day after it was inserted, Joe told Alex that he was 'so sad' because of the tube in his penis, but luckily his spirits improved and a couple of days after that he was demonstrating to Rosemary the clever tube that helped him pee.

It was ironic that Joe had to be catheterized at this time, because it meant exchanging one tube for another. Since chemotherapy stopped, and his regular blood tests for neutropaenia became unnecessary, his Hickman line had been almost redundant. Alex and I had tried to persuade Joe that it would be a good idea to have it removed. The effort of maintaining it seemed a waste now, and we felt he would be better off without it, but Joe had been upset by the idea. A few days after he was put in traction, presumably strained by the extra lifting involved, Joe's Hickman line came out unaided, discovered by us when we undressed him for his morning wash. Joe was very upset, he obviously regarded the line as an old friend, but Alex and I were relieved. As always, Joe came to accept the situation and a few days later was as glad as we were that there would be no more dressing or flushing the line.

ALEX Despite the fact that Joe's fracture and traction made a base X-ray impossible, Mr Wood had provided a supply of Contracan suppositories at the end of November, and we had started to administer them. Joe had been given anti-emetics rectally once or twice during chemotherapy and had not liked the experience, but now, with virtually no sensation below his waist, he did not object.

I started to keep a detailed Contracan diary for Mr Wood, so that at least he would have some anecdotal evidence of Joe's response to the drug. It makes depressing reading, as it covers virtually the whole period of Joe's traction, including Christmas and the New Year, and focuses on his bowel and bladder activity, the drugs he was taking, his consumption of food and fluid, and the battle that developed to treat Joe's first bedsore.

Beryl had noticed at the end of November that the skin around Joe's anus was slightly discoloured and immediately suspected a developing sore. In early December, we started dressing it with Tegaderm, but its position meant that it was almost impossible to keep clean and dry. When Joe was catheterized, on 9 December 1988, it helped a little, but by the weekend before Christmas the sore was looking much worse, and Joe had developed terrible diarrhoea, which could only aggravate its condition.

Dealing with the diarrhoea was nothing as compared to dealing with the bedsore. I hated it. It was open and bleeding slightly, and bruised in the centre. I particularly hated this bruising: it looked black and rotten, like the first signs of death, and I hated the whole aspect of decay it seemed to signal. Ann, Beryl and I desperately tried to treat it, using ice-cubes to restore circulation to the spot and dressings impregnated with vitamin E oil to help the skin recover.

*A*NN It was very much in our minds that this would be Joe's last Christmas. We intended to have a huge tree, and I wanted it to look magnificent. Joe loved tree decorations, so I bought lots of new ones to add to his favourites, and put them away to surprise him when the tree arrived.

By the beginning of December it was up, crammed into a room already filled by the bed and the dining-table, with all the best decorations on the top half, as the base was obscured from Joe's view by his bed. I had bought a new angel, but Joe had indignantly insisted on the old one, a very modest figure made of gold paper, for the top of the tree as usual. We had the tree lights on all day, and the high frame that supported Joe's traction was hung with baubles.

I had meant to make Christmas puddings early in the year, but found myself making them in late November with no proper time for them to mature. Though he didn't like Christmas pudding, I tried to involve Joe, thinking he would enjoy seeing all the ingredients measured out. I arranged everything on the table by his bed so that he could help if he wanted, but Joe wasn't very interested. When it came to mixing it all together I couldn't persuade him to give the traditional help with the spoon. Even Linda, who arrived and took her turn, couldn't convince Joe that it was good luck for everyone in the house to stir the pudding and make a wish. I realized that I was beginning to seem obsessive. The batch I was making would last two or three years and, so strong was my feeling that this was Joe's last Christmas, that I desperately wanted the thought in the Christmases ahead that Joe had stirred the pudding we were eating. It was ridiculous of me, and Joe was beginning to wonder why I was so insistent, so I gave up the idea.

Though Joe couldn't go Christmas shopping, he took a keen interest in choosing presents. He was very clear about what he wanted to buy Alex: a wooden parrot to stand on his desk, and a mug with a seagull on it. I was to buy two of these so that he and Alex could have matching mugs. I loved his ideas, though I did talk him out of also getting Alex a water-pistol. Appealing to Joe's practical streak, I pointed out that the more I spent on Alex, the less I'd have to spend on Joe, and he immediately saw the point of rationing Alex's presents.

My mother, who was going away for Christmas, came on Thursday, 15 December, to see Joe and bring his Christmas presents. Knowing he was always more interested in the moment than the future, she brought him a couple of small gifts to have right away. These included a giant, three-foot Christmas cracker she had carried all the way from North London, which he loved. He was in such good form that day, bright and talkative – she could only stay a short while, but what were to be her last few hours with Joe were happy, lively ones.

ALEX The week leading up to Christmas was a strange and tense time. Joe recovered from the diarrhoea, but his condition varied enormously from day to day, and even from morning to night. We watched everything, worried if he wasn't drinking enough fluids, or if his appetite was poor, or if his mood was low. The entry in the Contracan diary for Wednesday, 21 December 1988, gives a fair indication of one of the better days:

Passed 450ml urine overnight. Woke up slightly ratty, then brighter – tennis with balloons, etc.

Much better day, seemed in far better spirits. Appetite good: one and a half fried eggs and one rasher of bacon for both lunch and dinner; slice of bread and toasted cheese crumpet at midnight.

Co-trimoxazole [antibiotic] given. Calpol given once or twice. Contracan given around 12.30 a.m.; no bowel move-ment. No diarrhoea during day.

External events intruded slightly on the week, in that Luc Herring at Doubleday in New York had asked if I could possibl read through the American proofs of *The War Zone* befor Christmas and courier them back to her, and I had agreed. I la alone in bed reading them, thinking about how the novel ha spanned the stages of Joe's illness.

This was also the week when our friend Teri Gower, who wa illustrating *Henry and the Sea*, brought round her pictures t show us, before sending them to Hamish Hamilton. Joe, unfortur ately, was in a bad temper when she arrived and did not respon well to the drawings, though he had earlier admired her jacke illustration for the book.

But most of our thoughts, of course, were given over to hov Joe might best enjoy Christmas. We had the tree, we had variou Christmas videos, including a *SuperTed* Christmas episode and *Yogi Bear* Christmas cartoon Joe loved, but we wanted to d something special. In previous years, we had always taken Jo to visit Santa Claus, either at Harrods or last year at Har ningtons in Brighton, and we were determined that somehov Joe would see Santa this year.

I looked through Yellow Pages and had little success in track ing down a Father Christmas who would make a house cal when it struck me that I should try Hanningtons itself. I was pu in contact with the store's publicist, Natalie Nortcliff, who wen far beyond any professional interest in arranging a visit fror Father Christmas to the house, a visit Hanningtons provide purely as a gesture of goodwill.

Natalie found a truly wonderful candidate for Father Christmas Alan Wright, a man who had never been a professional Fathe

Christmas, but who had recently retired and had expressed a wish to play Santa. At Natalie's suggestion, he phoned a few days before he was due to come, to ask about Joe, how he was feeling, what sort of attitude he had to his illness, and what he might like as a gift from Hanningtons.

On Friday, 23 December, at 4.00 p.m., the doorbell rang and Father Christmas arrived, accompanied by his 'helper', Natalie. Joe seemed genuinely amazed to see Father Christmas in the house and appeared completely convinced by Alan's explanation that he had come to check whether we had a chimney, or whether he should use the back door on Christmas Eve. Joe – usually so cool – was definitely thrilled and more than a little shy at the honour of having Father Christmas come to him.

Later, when Joe had died, we received the most wonderful letter from Alan Wright, which captured the magic of the situation – a magic Alan created by the consideration and integrity he brought to playing his role:

My dear Ann and Alexander,
... I'll write a little about Joe, if I may. A reasonable acquaintanceship was established during the brief time that Joe and Father Christmas had together. He was alert, attentive, full of enquiries and utterly likeable, and Father Christmas was delighted to meet him.

I thought you two were splendid as well: there was tremendous wit, Ann, in the way you asked Father Christmas why he was so grumpy as you all considered Raymond Briggs' biography of the great man, and I shall long remember the total reasonableness of your summary, Alexander, as we remembered the translations of 'waiter' – 'garcon' and 'camarero'. 'Father Christmas has to be able to speak all languages,' you noted, to Joe's complete satisfaction.

The energy, success and love with which you looked after your little son were heart-warming, and you gave him a full life. There was so much going on in his mind and in his growing experience of life that he seemed scarcely deprived by missing what would have been, I suppose, his first term at school. His imagination ranged over all fields of learning, and you provided appropriate opportunities for him. He must have missed friends, but then there were alternative friends: Charlie Brown, perhaps, and those who were responsible for what Natalie thought was an American accent. He was a delight.

I keep an occasional diary, and after Father Christmas' visit to you I wrote in it: 'The kindness and friendliness of the Stuarts lifts one's spirits, and I must write and tell them this.' With Christmas following so hastily on our meeting, I didn't write, which was neglectful. I hope the reminder, coming late, will nevertheless help to reinforce Joe's terrific qualities in your minds, and make you doubly aware of your imaginative and loving care.

> With love
> Alan Wright
> & Father Christmas
>
> From a letter of 10 January 1989

ANN On Christmas Eve, I put Santa's snack, chosen by Joe orange juice and cookies, with carrots as usual for th reindeer – on the kitchen counter and settled down. After hi conversation with Father Christmas, Joe was confident tha Santa would find him downstairs, but a bit worried in case h was put off by all the lights Joe liked left on.

As soon as Joe was asleep, we quickly filled his pillowcas with presents and put it in place. In the early hours, he wok and wanted to be moved. It was a sign of how blasé he was tha he didn't even mention his presents, though he was keen enoug to see them in the morning:

ANN: [as the voice of Leglin the badger] Joe, listen to me. I wa sitting all night by your bed and I think a burglar cam in. I can describe him, though. He had a red coat with hood and white fur stuff round it . . .

JOE: What do you mean? That was Father Christmas!

ANN: [as Leglin] Father Christmas? Oh, who's Father Christmas

JOE: The one who brought all of this.

ANN: [as Leglin] You mean he brought stuff, he didn't take i away?

JOE: Yes.

ANN: [as Leglin] Oh, thank goodness for that, I didn't know whether I should wake you up or . . .

ALEX: Is he a criminal, then, Leglin?

ANN: [as Leglin] Well, I'm not sure, but he broke into the house and he was over in the kitchen . . .

JOE: [laughing; emphatic] I think it was Father Christmas! You said he had a red coat and a red hood.

ANN: [as Leglin] I could hear him. I didn't dare go and look, but I could hear chewing and stuff, and jingling.

JOE: Dad! Could I have all this stuff moved and take a look at my *Manta Force*, I want to take a look at it?

ALEX: Are you pleased with your Christmas presents?

JOE: Yes, very pleased.

ALEX: Very nice, that's a lovely thing to say. And you've got more to come from Gran and Fred.

JOE: [perkily] I sure hope you're right!

From a tape made on Christmas Day 1988, while Joe was
still in traction

Our Christmas celebrations were very subdued. Joe was excited by his presents, which made us happy, and he was pleased to see Gran and Fred when they arrived mid-afternoon. We had an early Christmas dinner sitting awkwardly round the dining-table, which was rammed alongside Joe's bed. I was disappointed that he wouldn't even try the turkey, which he usually liked, but later he had one of his favourite meals, an egg-meat-burger.

The day was rather dominated by Joe's Nintendo system; both Gran and Fred and Teri Gower had given Joe new games, but it gave him great pleasure and seemed an excellent stimulant. When I tried it, I found my physical and mental co-ordination were no match for Joe's, and I admired his skill even more.

ALEX Although Joe was slightly disappointed with two of his presents – a large, plastic-cased ghost game which he liked but which was broken when we opened it, and a children's talking computer I had bought him, which seemed just too demanding for him in his current state – the opportunity of

replacing them permitted a little invention on our part. I wrote
him two letters from Father Christmas, one replacing the game,
the other to accompany the Lego kit he had asked for in place of
the toy computer, and Ann and I went through elaborate perform-
ances to create special deliveries at the front door, direct from
Father Christmas. The effort was well worth it; the presents
were carefully wrapped and had large, unusual stamps on them
from the North Pole, and Joe seemed thrilled at this extension of
Christmas.

Having actually met Father Christmas, he seemed quite
prepared to receive a letter from him such as this:

> Top o' the World
> North Pole
> Midnight, 30th December 1988

Dear Joe

My supplies arrived in the middle of a snowstorm tonight,
but I am pleased to say your Lego fire station did not get
stuck in a snowdrift! I hope you enjoy making it; I am sorry
you had to wait so long.

Perhaps I might suggest that next Christmas you make a
list of the presents you would like – not too long, please (the
sack gets heavier every year) – and send it to me in good
time. I can't promise everything on the list, but you know
I'll try my best.

My reindeer and I hope that you feel a little better than of
late. We think of you often – Comet, especially, sends his love.

As do we all,

> Father Christmas
> X X X X

In spite of this, it would be foolish to pretend that the week after
Christmas was magical and relaxed. After his pre-Christmas
diarrhoea, Joe now had acute constipation and was complaining
of pain in his arms and – more unusually – headaches. The
secondary tumour which had appeared on the back of his neck
in the summer, but which had responded excellently to radiotherapy, now increased in size again, renewing a deep-seated
fear we had of Joe's cancer spreading to his brain.

New Year's Eve 1988 was memorable mostly for the sense of negativity and doubt it inspired. A couple of hours before midnight, Joe's bowels started performing quite spectacularly, and though it may not have been the most obviously enjoyable way of welcoming the New Year, Ann and I coped with this with a feeling of relief – that Joe would be that much more comfortable.

We even managed to drink a bottle of champagne, but when I spoke to my brother-in-law Peter on the phone shortly after midnight, he asked a question which scared me with its bluntness:

'Are you ready for it to happen?' he said. 'Have you and Ann prepared yourselves?'

19 *One Week*

'Moonbuggy 5' by Joe Buffalo, aged five years four months,
December 1988

*A*NN As the New Year began, Joe's condition deteriorated
His appetite was becoming even more erratic, he would
have fancies for favourite meals but just eat a mouthful here and
there. We began to rely on feeding him milkshakes, boosted with
supplements like Caloreen and Buildup to keep him going, and
he was still taking the Magic Potion.

We had felt wretched when he began mentioning pains in his
arms, and we had started giving him MST regularly again, in
slowly increasing doses. On Sunday, 1 January 1989, Joe mentioned aches in his legs. He asked Alex to do some physio with
him, stretching his toes and bending his knees. It was the first
time he had mentioned any sensation in his legs since before his
fracture. The next day, Joe mentioned the ache again, and on
Tuesday he said he wanted to flex his toes and actually wiggled
the toes on his right foot.

If the general situation had been better, Alex and I would

have been trying to convince ourselves that the Contracan was having a dramatic and beneficial effect on Joe – and it may have been responsible for this change – but now instead of being thrilled, we were apprehensive. A return of sensation would inevitably mean a return of pain as well; at the moment Joe was better off without it.

On Wednesday, 4 January, Fred and Eileen came to sit with Joe for a couple of hours in the afternoon so Alex and I could go out together. I was going to the optician, and wanted Alex's opinion on new spectacle frames. Though it was very mundane, we enjoyed this rare outing together and were feeling in good spirits as we went home, but when we arrived, Eileen and Linda came upstairs to talk to us out of Joe's hearing.

Apparently Dr Jane Roderic-Evans had made an informal visit while we were out, and had remarked on how high Joe's entry point (the line on his body at which he began to feel sensation) was. This had crept from waist level to chest level since the autumn, and though this information had scared Eileen, it was nothing new.

However, the conversation turned to the implications of the pains in Joe's arms, and for the first time we asked Linda about the possibility of Joe losing their use. She admitted it could happen, and even though she didn't think it was imminent, this thought made us utterly miserable. If Joe couldn't use his hands for Lego or drawing or Nintendo games, he would be forced to be completely passive; his only options would be to watch television or listen to stories. He had adjusted to his growing disability so philosophically, but this would be a blow he couldn't bear.

The thought of his incomprehension and depression should this terrible thing happen – and our inability to rationalize it – made me want to scream, to break things. I felt so unequal to helping him accept the unacceptable.

LINDA WILLIAMS The Wednesday before the weekend of Joe's dramatic deterioration, he was in fine form: we played baseball, the ducklings came to visit, and we began to construct the latest Lego model Father Christmas had brought.

Alex's parents were 'Joe-sitting' that afternoon, and whereas Joe's morale had remained quite high, ours had plummeted on numerous occasions. That Wednesday did us all good, although the severity of Joe's condition remained with us.

ALEX I remember the first week of January 1989 as a depressing blur. There were times when Joe seemed brighter, but he was complaining increasingly of pain in his arms, and the conversation Ann and I had with Linda on Wednesday afternoon, about the possibility – or inevitability – of Joe's arms becoming paralysed, struck fear in my heart.

The previous night, Tuesday, at the suggestion of our friend Sevilla Delowski, I had called a doctor in Texas who had developed an experimental cancer treatment programme. I talked to Dr Burzynski for some time, but even as I explained Joe's condition, I think I realized how utterly hopeless the situation was. There was no way we could take Joe to Texas in the near future, and the near future seemed to be all we had.

On the Thursday and Friday of that week, Joe slept for much of the day. I escaped the house on Friday evening and drove to Spike and Neville's London club, MFI. This would hardly be worthy of mention, were it not for the fact that while I was there, talking to friends I hadn't seen for some time, I used the words, 'I think Joe is dying,' for the first time. I had never fully accepted this before, but on Friday night, I knew Joe's death was close.

ANN Friday, 6 January, was Twelfth Night, and though I knew Joe would miss it, I was eager to take down the tree. It had been in the house since early December and was so dry that a shower of needles fell off every time it was touched. Alex and I had intended to dismantle it during the day, but in the end he didn't have time before he left to go to Spike's club.

It was quite late, but Joe, who had been dozing during the day, was awake and interested in my decision to strip the tree so that we could move it quickly the next day. The tree was almost bald by the time I'd removed all the decorations, and Joe watched me pack them away.

When I took down the little angel from the top, I asked Joe if it was still his favourite; he said it was, and that he didn't want me to buy a new one. I had an enormous compulsion to establish this with him. As with the unsuccessful episode with the Christmas pudding, I was somehow trying to create a stake in the future for him. I wanted to feel his influence, even if he wasn't there.

Our determination not to deal with Dr Cree was a potential problem for Beryl, who would normally have referred all questions concerning Joe's treatment to her. Luckily we were all familiar with the sort of medication Joe needed, and Jane, our GP, or another doctor at the Royal Alexandra could write prescriptions. Questions concerning Joe's fractured leg could be dealt with by the orthopaedic consultant. But if there should be any new developments caused by the cancer, Dr Cree was the only oncologist.

Joe's bout of diarrhoea before Christmas had been followed by constipation, which had been dealt with fairly successfully with lactulose, senna or an enema. But during the first week of January, his breathing became slightly laboured and, on Friday, his stomach was bloated. We wondered if this could be caused by wind, aggravated by constipation (this had happened once before, in Charing Cross), but when Beryl saw him the next morning she was immediately concerned that it could be fluid on the peritoneum (the lining of the abdomen).

As it was a Saturday, a locum appeared in response to her call to Jane's surgery. He agreed with Beryl's diagnosis but felt that a specialist should be consulted. There was no alternative but to involve Dr Cree at this point, and Beryl went back to the Royal Alexandra to call her. Less than an hour later they returned together, and Dr Cree confirmed that there was fluid on Joe's peritoneum and also fluid or more tumour on his lung.

In a conversation which, given our relationship, was already tense and difficult, she told us that there was little to do except keep Joe comfortable, increasing his dose of MST to keep him relaxed until he died. An X-ray would confirm whether his breathing was impaired by fluid or growing tumours, but this was fairly academic, and moving him to the hospital would be traumatic. **Dr Cree told us that his breathing would be eased if the fluid were drained from his lung, but she didn't recommend it because again it would involve the disruption of going to hospital, and the improvement would only last two or three days.**

Though we had known that Joe was going to die, we had had no idea of when and how it would happen. Even though we had felt he was having his last Christmas, we had thought of it only in terms of the unlikelihood of him living another year, not with any concept of how much longer he might have. In spite of our acceptance that he would die, the fact that he was actually dying was still a shock. The moment had arrived.

The most likely course of Joe's death would be that his breathing would get more and more laboured and eventually the effort would cause his heart to fail. Since Alex's conversation with Dr Rodriguez, we had feared that Joe's death would be agonizing and frightening. We had no idea if the problem with his lungs would end with Joe fighting for each breath. We hoped it would bring a gentler death.

Saturday and Sunday drifted by. Alex and I felt miserable, but fairly calm. If Joe lived another three or four weeks, as Dr Cree predicted, we had to stay sane. On Sunday, the traction was taken down; Joe's feet had become slightly swollen from more fluid. He was very sleepy, dozing much of the time now.

*A*LEX On Sunday afternoon, 8 January 1989, I went upstairs to write while Joe slept. The conversation with Dr Cree on Saturday had simply confirmed what we already sensed – that Joe was entering a final decline – though still we argued desperately for another option, some way of draining the fluid on Joe's peritoneum, some way of saving him.

I sat in my room and wrote, trying to straighten out the way I had felt since Friday night at the club:

This has been a lousy 48 hours.
    Spike's club was useful on Friday. I needed a change, but just the drive to London seemed unreal. Lights on the

Downs, on the motorway, the fact that I've virtually not been outside the basement of the house for the past 6 weeks . . .

. . . It must be the only way I can deal with the situation of Joe dying. Did I know things were coming to a head on Friday? Driving back from the club, I went past St Stephen's, doubled back and drove into the hospital grounds – only to find that the gates beyond the automatic barrier on the way out were closed, which they've never been before.

A few hours later, after getting home, finding Joe awake, or having woken easily and seemed quite bright, having slept, finding that Joe's abdomen was so distended that we actually agreed to let Dr Cree come back and tell us he was dying. Soon.

Ann wants to fight on, every ounce of her body wants to fight on, prolong Joe's life, but I think for the first time, I don't, I think I want it to be over. Is that selfish – do I just want to get the pain over, or (hopefully) is it just that I don't want Joe to suffer? That is such a fucking cliché, I hate the words even as I write them, but I'm shit-scared of him having to face any more than he has to face.

He must know something is up – he was disturbed on Saturday by the way we all kept disappearing upstairs for private discussions. I want to zonk him out with drugs now, I want him to drift into some hopefully elated state, I don't want him to have any fear at the end – but does he have to? Maybe he can face it sober, maybe it's just the pain he must avoid, maybe he can face death more bravely than I can. Who knows?

I still don't know whether he will die without us telling him he is going to, but whatever Dr Cree may say, and I don't give a fuck what she might, the time has not been right to tell him yet and it may not come. If it does, I'm sure we'll know it. I want him to go out with courage, with confidence, feeling that we are with him, as we are and will be. He will not cease to exist; he exists and has always existed and will not be diminished by death.

Extracted from notes written on 8 January 1989

After I finished writing I made some phone calls. I talked to a friend in London, Lynda Myles, telling her how Joe had been and that I thought I had finally accepted that he was dying, but I started crying and had to hang up.

Then, just as I was about to go back downstairs, Ann buzzed up on the intercom to tell me that Joe had woken and said, 'Tell Daddy I sure miss him.' I cannot explain how that made me feel, the sense of love and loss and sorrow it created and creates now.

ANN That evening, he was alert enough to take some Magic Potion, as well as his MST and some senna for his continuing constipation. Joe had stopped eating solid food, and even sipping a milkshake was an effort, so the Magic Potion was more valuable than ever. I sat beside him and told him that it was Alex's birthday soon, and that maybe when he felt less tired he'd like to decide on a present for him. Joe said yes, and drifted off to sleep again. In my usual desperate way, I was hoping that Joe would let me know what he'd like to give Alex – even if he didn't live until Alex's birthday on 27 January.

ALEX I went back downstairs and sat with Joe and talked while we all watched TV together, but he was quite grumpy and complained of pain in his shoulder. We gave him more MST than usual and he became a little delirious later in the evening, but the dosage was still much lower than it had been in the autumn and his state of mind seemed more to reflect his general condition.

I read him some of *The Hobbit* as we settled down for bed, and he was definitely following the story, but he also said things like, 'I want to watch that again, can we watch that again?' when the TV had been turned off, or 'Mummy is washing between my toes and it feels funny!' – smiling, quite happy, though in fact Ann was upstairs in the bathroom.

We kissed Joe goodnight, and as I lay down on the floor, a gentle sense of light seemed to come into my mind. Joe's bunny night-light was just above me on an awkward, wooden bedside table borrowed from the hospital, but it was there every night as

I lay down and this feeling of light only happened once. It was as if Joe had entered my mind and was saying to me, 'It's all right, it's going to be all right. There will be other children.'

I drifted almost immediately to sleep – Ann and I were so tired for the whole period of traction that sleep came very fast. I certainly didn't think consciously that Joe might be starting to die there and then.

20 *Death*

'Hunter the Barn Owl' by Joe Buffalo, aged five years four months, December 1988

ANN At around 6.00 on Monday morning (9 January 1989), I heard Joe call out, 'Daddy.' I am a much lighter sleeper than Alex and I was relieved when I realized he had heard Joe and was getting up; I could stay in bed. My relief only lasted a few seconds. When Alex, who was sleeping on the floor alongside Joe's bed, got to his feet, he found him in a very changed state.

ALEX [My account of Joe's death in this chapter is taken directly from pages written in the week after he died.]

I went round to Joe and knew instantly, in my gut, that he was dying, it had started. His head had slipped down a little, his chin was resting on his chest, and he couldn't really speak, though he was saying something.

I tried to lift him up, to support his head. He wasn't in pain, he was quite calm, quiet, but he didn't look comfortable and I think also I knew he had had a bowel movement, a soggy! I tried lifting him, but he couldn't grip my neck with his arms, whereas only four hours earlier, when we had gone to sleep, he had been able to pull himself up on me, had even supported himself by hanging on to the monkey bar above the bed while we changed the pillows earlier in the evening.

So something had happened. I thought straight away he might have had a small stroke, because of seeing Lynne with hers. I just couldn't lift him, not even when Ann got out of bed and came to help and I climbed up on to Joe's bed and tried to get my arms round him – I could feel the bones in his spine clicking and I was shit-scared of precipitating something else, having his spine crumble on me and send a spasm of pain shooting through him.

ANN We went upstairs and hurriedly discussed what we should do. One of us said, 'It's happening, isn't it?' Beryl was not due at the hospital before 8.00 a.m., but she had told us to call her at home in an emergency. While I went back downstairs to Joe, Alex called her and reported the dramatic change.

Beryl's arrival made us feel better. She immediately moved Joe into a better position and arranged for him to be fitted with a syringe pump which could give him morphine subcutaneously, as he was in no condition to swallow drugs.

ALEX Beryl wanted Jane Roderic-Evans to fit the pump, but Jane wasn't there, so Dr Gayton came instead. He was lovely, he'd seen Joe once before, had four children of his own, but he obviously had difficulty in dealing with his emotions seeing Joe. He was a bit manic, talking a lot, actually talking about Joe dying, which we'd never done in front of Joe, though he used the word 'terminal', which wasn't in Joe's vocabulary.

*A*NN Joe's dying process had accelerated in an unexpected way, but there was little more to do except wait. We sat beside him all morning, holding his hands. He was not fully conscious, but we were sure he knew what we were saying. We told him we loved him, we told him to relax. His breathing was very laboured now, and sometimes he seemed agitated. We tried to calm him, just kept talking, saying we loved him.

Once, when Alex moved away to go up to the bathroom, Joe, with an enormous effort said, 'Come back.' It was just a whisper, I was barely sure that was what he said, but when I asked Alex to come back to Joe's side, he became much calmer. Later I'm fairly sure he said 'Ma', which he often called me. It was so faint, but he said something. I like to think it was 'Ma'.

Alex had said to Joe, 'We're not sure what's happening, Joe, but we think this might be the time when you become a seagull.' When he called Alex back, we wondered if he felt ready to die, but a little while later he didn't protest when Alex dashed upstairs.

During the morning, Joe seemed to be struggling to breathe. I was holding his hand, telling him to relax, be calm, breathe slowly. I had the strongest feeling that he was fading away. Joe had been born on a Monday at midday, and I wondered if he were going to die at the same time. But twelve o'clock passed and he was stable. Now I had no idea how long he would last.

*A*LEX We had agreed with Beryl and Dr Gayton that we would try and prevent Joe from regaining consciousness properly (if that were even possible, given the stroke) as he was obviously dying and there was no point in prolonging it. I remember feeling almost excited about the idea – definitely adrenalin running through my body – as if I knew I had to face this, now here it was, let's get through it with as little pain as possible, let's be courageous, go head first into it, not show fear.

I know how beautiful Joe looked, but also that you could see he was dying, there was a translucent quality to his flesh, a cool, almost marble-like quality to his face, and a greyness at times. I remember the greyness particularly around 11.00 a.m. on Monday, especially around Joe's lips, when I thought he might be about to die then.

We were constantly holding his hands during this time, telling him we loved him, that it was time to become a seagull:

'You know we talked about becoming a seagull, Joe, well maybe it's time now to think about flying, to think about being a seagull and soaring high over everything. Mummy and Daddy will be with you, we'll all be seagulls together.

'It's time to go on an adventure, Joe. Go through that door, just relax and go with it, don't fight it, just breathe gently and go with it. We're with you. We'll always be with you, Mummy and Daddy and Joe together. We love you. We love you very much, we'll always be together. Just relax, my darling. It's going to be all right.'

I know that, right at the start, about 9.00 a.m., around the time Dr Gayton fitted the syringe pump, I wanted to override it if necessary, I was quite prepared to give Joe a lot of morphine if he seemed in pain – enough to kill him. Beryl kept saying, 'While there's life, there's hope,' but I had asked about euthanasia once with Dr Cree and I knew now that if it came to it, I would be prepared to make that decision – certainly given this particular set of circumstances. I didn't give a shit what was legal or ethical: if I had felt it would help Joe to ease him out of consciousness and life into death, I would have done so, I would have pressed that button on the syringe pump until he died.

Thankfully, it wasn't necessary, and I think the feeling initially that Joe might suffer quickly passed. He seemed so comfortable, his breathing was a little laboured, but not a huge struggle, just shallow and a little difficult. He was not crying or murmuring with pain, he seemed quite peaceful, and, holding his hands and kissing him and telling him we loved him, the desire to end this stage quickly soon passed.

I think we entered into the moment and began to love him more than ever, and know that he would not be with us for more than a matter of a few more hours and those hours suddenly were extraordinary, special, unique, serene, an experience that was quite outside any kind of expectation you might have, outside so-called normal life. The sense of love was so intense, so beautiful – and Joe looked so beautiful, so wonderful lying there.

We knew we were losing him in some senses, but it wasn't a loss, more a parting, hopefully a temporary parting, whatever 'temporary' means. I knew the physical loss would be dreadful, would be unbearable – life without Joe – but during Monday and Monday night, that seemed far off, distant. We were totally wrapped up in what was happening now. I think I kept running around saying, 'This isn't as bad as I thought it was going to be.'

There was almost a sense of elation, like at a birth, a feeling that this was one of life's great moments, this was part of the huge cycle that we are part of, not some piddling little event dreamed up by us, something that was there to be experienced, to be lived.

ANN I don't remember eating or drinking during the day, but I suppose I did. Beryl stayed all day, I think she must have made sure we had something. All I remember is sitting beside Joe's bed, never letting go of his hand, and talking all the time. Joe seemed barely conscious, but if he had lost his faculties to such a large extent, maybe he was alert inside, unable to communicate. If we held his hand, and he heard our voices, he would know he wasn't alone.

I told him how much I loved him, how lucky I was to have such a gorgeous boy. In the background we were running his favourite story tapes, or music, or even a familiar video tape. It seemed important to have signs of life, a stimulus all the time, so he wouldn't feel alone.

ALEX At some point on Monday afternoon, Joe struggled to say the word, 'Treasure'. We think it was the last thing he said, his last word, and it was a huge achievement that he said anything, that he could speak – he had to fight through whatever was blocking his consciousness, whatever the stroke or simply the fact of dying was doing to him.

We puzzled over its meaning. I was reading him *The Hobbit* on Sunday night; perhaps it had something to do with the dwarves' treasure in that? Perhaps, as Charles later suggested, he had found it! Found the treasure! Or perhaps it was connected to *The Legend of Zelda*, though there was no particular reference to treasure in that, it was more about defeating various dragons and creatures and rescuing Princess Zelda, whom we had never seen.

*A*NN Alex and I were still calm. It was Joe who was dying, our job was to reassure him, help him go through it serenely; we would give in to our emotions later. Beryl went home to freshen up and then came back. She had been with us all day, and was insistent that she was going to stay – if she went off duty, another nurse would have to attend Joe during the night, and she knew we wouldn't want a stranger in the house.

Though she had dealt with so many terminal cases in her career, Beryl was not the sort of person to be desensitized. During the afternoon, as she sat at the table making notes, I had seen that she was crying. Now she wanted to stay the night.

Linda had been in a couple of times during the day and came back to the house after work. She immediately suggested that we move Joe so that we could lie with him, instead of sitting up all night. Carefully, we planned how we would organize it, lifting Joe off the bed on his Spenco mattress (a very light, undulating mattress designed to ease pressure and prevent bedsores), arranging the two bunk mattresses together, and placing Joe in the middle so that we could lie either side of him and hold him. The dismantled hospital bed we leant against the wall.

Jane Roderic-Evans arrived, she had heard the news and come, even though it was her day off. We sat quietly on the mattresses together for a while. Her presence was always very calming; knowing she was a Buddhist seemed to help in some way.

We were still holding Joe's hands, still talking to him gently.

Jane had told Beryl she thought Joe would die that evening, but later that night Beryl told us that, in her experience, Joe could last another twenty-four hours or more. She explained that children take longer to die than adults, because their hearts are so much stronger.

ALEX Joe was breathing quite steadily, he seemed to have settled into a pattern, his eyes were half open, more than half open, during all this time – all day and all night too, I think – so it wasn't exactly as if he were sleeping (though, like me, he used to sleep with his eyes part open), but he seemed very rested, very peaceful.

Monday evening was almost like Joe's birth, when I had wanted to play gentle, happy music to welcome him. Now I had an anxiety to create the right mood for Joe – play the right video tapes, the right music, as if you can control anything, even death, as if you should even try to.

We had had Joe's favourite video tapes on all day – his latest Christmas ones, especially the Christmas *PacMan* video he loved, and a cartoon version of *The Lion, the Witch and the Wardrobe*, and the *Troll* Christmas cartoon, and various bits and pieces.

In the evening, for a brief while, I tried finding suitable music, calm, relaxing, gentle music, but nothing seemed quite right. I played one of Matthew Manning's tapes, *Eastern Opus* (which was what we played at Joe's funeral), and some of Vangelis's *China*, which Joe had liked, and a little of Flora Purim's *Open Your Eyes You Can Fly* – because Joe loved the cover (a dove in flight) and it seemed appropriate, though the jazz was not quite relaxed enough for our mood.

ANN I do remember eating in the evening because Teri, who had come in to see Joe during the afternoon, came back with a pasta dish for us which we shared with Linda and Beryl. At midnight, Linda left, and Beryl was alone upstairs. She intended to doze on the sofa and refill the syringe pump when it was due. Alex and I were still awake, lying alongside Joe, reading stories, still encouraging him, playing a tape he liked that had seagulls on it.

ALEX During the evening, I think the later part, around 11.00 p.m. to midnight, I read to Joe. I asked him at one point if he would like me to read to him, and if he would like me to go on reading *The Hobbit*, and he definitely responded (earlier in the day, I had started playing *The Legend of Zelda*, thinking this would be familiar and might comfort him, but he definitely let me know that he didn't want it on, it was disturbing him).

I think I only read a few lines of *The Hobbit*; it didn't feel right, somehow, it was a bit too involved. Then I read *Amos and Boris*, our all-time favourite story for Joe, which I had read to him in St Stephen's when he was first ill, during chemotherapy, often even while he was asleep, and I think we all found it comforting – Ann and me, especially. So I read that, and I think I started reading *Winnie-the-Pooh*, but he indicated he didn't want that, so I read *Red Fox and his Canoe*, and then, *Joe, Jo-Jo and the Monkey Masks*, and finally, probably around midnight, I read him *Amos and Boris* again – because I didn't want to end on our book, somehow it seemed a little too egocentric. I didn't read *Henry and the Sea*, I don't know why, but maybe it seemed too long, it didn't feel right anyway.

ANN By 2.00 or 3.00 a.m. I was very tired. Alex was half asleep beside Joe. I tried to get comfortable but, because of the way Joe was bolstered up on pillows, I couldn't lie down properly and stay close enough to him to hold his hand easily. I had held his hand all day, even eating and drinking with one hand so I could keep contact. But if I had to make it through perhaps another twenty-four hours, I had to rest.

I saw that Alex was still holding Joe's hand – he had that comfort, and I felt sure he would know I was near. I let go of Joe's hand, meaning to doze for a while. I must have been exhausted, because I slept through Beryl coming down a couple of times, and Alex reading to Joe at 5.00 in the morning.

ALEX We dozed, Ann and I actually slept for periods, both of us a little terrified that Joe might die while we were asleep, that we might miss that very special moment of parting, of peace. We felt we wouldn't – we were holding his hands, it seemed unlikely that he could die without us knowing, with our parents' radar at full blast. But you never know. I dreaded waking and finding him dead, that I had missed our last moments together, but it wasn't a huge dread, somehow I knew we'd wake.

At about 5.00 a.m. Tuesday (10 January), I woke. Maybe I changed the video – I'm not sure what had been on, but we had been sleeping with the video playing and I think it must have been an older tape, with lots of *Flintstones* and *Top Cat* cartoons, because I have some vague memory of those, drifting in and out of sleep with Fred and Barney's and Wilma's voices, or T.C.'s.

Anyway, I woke up and had a strong compulsion to read *Amos and Boris* to Joe again – I wanted him to know I was there, and also I think I knew this was my last chance ever to read to him. So I read it, on one elbow (it was hurting from leaning on it too much), with a slightly raspy, throaty voice. Even so, I loved doing Boris the whale's deep, rumbly voice and Amos the mouse's little one, and was incredibly moved by it all, but especially by the part where Amos almost drowns and wonders what it would feel like to die: 'Would it feel just awful? Would his soul go to heaven? Would there be other mice there?'

I think I had already put another video tape on (Joe used to like tapes to be playing even while I was reading to him) – the start of *The Lion, the Witch and the Wardrobe*, which I had loved as a book as a boy. Ann was sleeping quite soundly; I read to Joe, made sure he was comfortable – I held his hand throughout this – and no doubt kissed him again. Then I think I whispered in his ear:

'It's time to go on an adventure, soon. We're all going. We're all going to be seagulls and soar through the sky. Let's fly to the North Pole and see Father Christmas. We can do that. I love you, Joe Buffalo. I love you more than every star in the sky. There is no way to tell you how much I love you. Mummy and Daddy love you, absolutely, always. We'll always be with you, together. We'll all be seagulls together. And you can be whatever you want, whenever you want it. You can be a seagull, you can be a dolphin, you can be a little boy again. You can be whatever you want.'

*

And then, the next thing I knew was Beryl leaning over me at about 8.00 a.m., changing the syringe on Joe's syringe pump. I asked how Joe was and she said his pulse was a lot weaker – his breathing seemed very quiet, very shallow, but very peaceful.

I think I knew it was close, but not as close as it was. I thought about waking Ann, who looked shattered, and almost didn't – I wasn't sure Joe was that much different than he had been at 5.00 a.m. But I did touch her hand and wake her, and I'm so glad I did, because almost immediately the pattern, the rhythm of Joe's breathing seemed to change.

Ann struggled into consciousness herself, I think she may have wanted to go up to the loo, but we both realized it was really close. We each held Joe's hands, me on his left, Ann on his right, lying facing the kitchen. I know the *Sesame Street* movie was playing on TV – it was on the same tape as *The Lion, the Witch and the Wardrobe*. It was one of the sad songs, and this was Joe's special movie in a way (though by no means his favourite), because we had once arranged a preview of it at the Columbia preview theatre just for him, and he had been told he could invite his friends, and it had been Joe Buffalo's screening.

So, *Follow that Bird* was playing on TV, Ann and I were on either side, and Joe just looked exquisite – this was it, this was the moment of his death; we had been at the moment of his birth and this was part of the same flow. We had never loved him more. We held on to every breath, every pause. He was calm, peaceful, serene; there was no suggestion of fear, he just looked so delicate, so vulnerable, so quiet as he breathed more and more shallowly.

I had been terribly afraid that the end might come as a struggle, that at some point, not necessarily this late, the tumour on his lungs might cause him to cough up blood or something, which would frighten him – and us. But it was peaceful, it was as perfect as it could be. He breathed in, breathed out – like a little sigh. Ann and I held our breaths, as we wondered if that was it.

We whispered in each ear, 'I love you. I love you, Joe Buffalo. For ever and always. Mummy and Daddy love you and are with you.' He breathed again, very shallowly. Then there was a long pause and he didn't breathe any more.

ANN At eight o'clock, Alex woke me. Beryl had just been down and told him that Joe's pulse was much slower. The moment I woke I took Joe's hand, feeling guilty that I had left it for so long. My other hand held Alex's as we told him, 'Mummy's here, and Daddy's here, we love you.'

Joe was scarcely breathing now. He breathed in very slowly, we waited, he breathed out. His breath got slower, a long pause, another breath. He breathed in, we waited, after an eternity he breathed out. 'We love you, everything's all right, just relax.' He breathed in, a long pause. He breathed out.

At ten past eight, we knew Joe Buffalo was dead. We lay and held him and cried quietly. The real grief hadn't come yet.

ALEX The realization that someone is dead is not instant; it's like a creeping sensation, flowing into your mind slowly, informing you that there is no more contact in the immediate sense, you can touch that person and they are still warm, maybe even the heart is still beating, but they are not any more, they are not there as they were.

Joe lay there, still, beautiful, and I think we hugged him and kissed him and still spoke to him, and I think we cried, but not as powerfully as I might have expected – that came later, the shuddering, the heaving, though even then I think we had done a lot of the angry, shocked grieving long ago, when Joe was first ill.

I think I called Linda down – she was the only person in the house, Beryl had just gone to the hospital for a few minutes. Linda came down and I think she took Joe's pulse. He was dead. I'm not sure what happened then, maybe Ann and I hugged, maybe we just knelt over Joe and kissed him and hugged him.

ANN When Linda had arrived a few minutes earlier, Beryl had gone up to the hospital. After staying with us for so long, she hadn't been in the house when Joe died. We cried together when she got back. Then she left us to sit with Joe for a while before the next stage – life without Joe – began.

21 *The Funeral*

The first words of 'Pooh's Hum' by Joe Buffalo, aged four years
seven months, 16 March 1988

*A*NN Hardly an hour after Joe's death we were having to
make the decisions we had always avoided considering.
There would have to be a funeral, and that meant choosing an
undertaker and deciding on burial or cremation. Beryl, who had
had to help in these situations before, found a list of undertakers
which included Hanningtons. We had such pleasant associations
with the store because of their part in Father Christmas's visit,
that we immediately decided on them; and it was obvious that
cremation was best for a boy who wanted to be a seagull.

Though she was visibly distressed by Joe's death, Beryl continued to be a support to us, and made all the arrangements for

the undertakers to come to the house. We knew at once that we wanted to keep Joe at home until the funeral. We would never have sent him away to strangers while he was alive, and had no intention of doing so now. But even if he were to stay at the house, his body had to be prepared with some kind of preserving fluid, and he needed to be dressed. I gathered a selection of Joe's clothes and together Alex and I chose a shirt, his Mickey Mouse sweatshirt, his nicest tracksuit trousers, and the socks, decorated with bright red and yellow stars and stripes, that he liked best.

It was hard letting Joe go, it made his death seem very definite, but the undertakers were very considerate. They promised to bring him back very quickly and took him away in an ordinary car, wrapped in a blanket as if he were sleeping. It was a cold day and I remember, as I saw them off, trying to tuck Joe's bare feet into the blanket for warmth.

When he came back, we settled Joe on the sofa in my workroom on the ground floor. He was so beautiful, dressed in his favourite clothes now, resting on a pillow and covered with a duvet. It doesn't seem possible to describe him without resorting to clichés. He looked so relaxed and healthy, so serene; it is true that the dead look as if they are sleeping, an illusion that can be kind or cruel. It was nice to pretend for a moment that he might wake up again, appalling to realize that this really was the end.

The funeral was to be on the afternoon of Friday, 13 January, and we found that the days we had Joe in the house were invaluable. If he had simply been taken away that Tuesday, to return in a coffin on Friday, it would have been intolerable. Being able to look in on him, or sit with him, hold his hand, kiss him still, was a vital part of letting Joe go. It is hard to stop thinking like a parent, and we found ourselves reluctant to leave him in the house on his own even now he was dead. We went in to see him first thing every morning, we said hello and goodbye as we went in and out of the house – usually separately so he wouldn't be alone – we looked in the room every time we passed it, we said goodnight. He still looked so pink and peaceful and alive, but his hands and lips were so cold, and his skin felt so solid.

Friends and neighbours wanted to see Joe, and after Rosemary Machin had visited him, she told us that her grandson Daniel had asked if he could come too. Though it had not occurred to us that Joe's friends should see him, it seemed important that Daniel be allowed to do so if he wanted to.

The next day he arrived with his mother, Lindsey. I warned him that Joe felt very cold, thinking he might prefer not to touch him, but Daniel obviously didn't have any of the misgivings some adults feel in the presence of the dead. He stood quite calmly, looking at Joe for a while, and then he took Joe's hand and said, 'Thank you for being my friend.'

Daniel had brought a bunch of snowdrops and violets, and we added them to the flowers in the room. Kim Ryan had arrived on the afternoon Joe died with a huge white poinsettia, and flowers and plants had been arriving ever since. They surrounded Joe with a wonderful flowery smell, and with his toys around him, and a tape of *The Owl who was Afraid of the Dark* playing, the room was as happy and friendly as we could make it.

By the day of the funeral, Alex and I were as ready as possible to part with Joe. We had had long enough to say goodbye. We had thought the most appalling moment would be seeing him put into the little white coffin, but being allowed to help settle him made it easier. We decided immediately that Joe still needed Melissa and Cookie Monster and Leglin. They had been his constant companions and an invaluable support for him; it was impossible to separate them now. Without Joe they would become sad, shabby relics; with him they would keep their magic, the three faithful friends.

We tucked them around him, and added two blurry photographs he had taken of us, a postcard of a seagull Charles had sent him once, another with dolphins from Sevilla, and a drawing from James Ryan. Then the lid was secured in place. Joe was really dead.

The funeral seemed to pick up an irreversible momentum: the slow drive down our street behind the coffin, the ride to an unfamiliar part of Brighton, arriving with family and friends at the crematorium. Then more faces: Linda and Beryl; Jane Roderic-Evans; Santa's assistant, Natalie; more friends from Brighton and London; Sharon Doughty, Joe's first nurse at St Stephen's, who had come all the way from Bedford.

We had booked a tiny chapel, assuming there would be a small attendance. There was a kind of comfort in seeing the crowded chapel, no empty spaces, so many people who had also loved Joe.

Neither Alex nor I liked the idea of a stranger conducting some religious ceremony Joe wouldn't have understood and that we didn't relate to. When we planned the funeral, Alex had immediately asked if we could arrange the service in our own way, and been told that we could. I loved Alex's idea of doing the reading himself, from Joe's favourite stories, but I was concerned that he wouldn't be able to deal with speaking for so long when the time came. But Alex was determined to do it, and already knew which extracts he would use. My only contribution was to suggest the closing lines from *The House at Pooh Corner*, moving enough for any parent, and always very poignant for us.

ALEX As I lay next to Joe in the hour after he died, I promised him that I would be the one to speak at his funeral. I thought Ann wouldn't want to speak herself, and knew that neither of us wanted anyone else to do it. I had never been to a funeral before and had only depressing images from films to draw on in imagining what it would be like, but I was determined that Joe's would be different. I was certainly nervous about the idea of standing up in front of everyone and making myself heard – I thought I might just collapse into tears – but I told myself, 'If I can hold my son's hand while he dies, I can stand up at his funeral and say goodbye.'

What follows are the words I spoke on Friday afternoon, 13 January 1989, at the Downs Crematorium in Brighton:

First, I want to thank everybody for coming to say goodbye to Joe Buffalo.

We all loved him and each of us will have some personal, private thoughts they wish to send him, but before that I would like to say goodbye in the way I decided to on Tuesday, when Joe died – by reading a few brief passages from Joe's favourite books.

I want this to be as positive as it can possibly be – I want this to be something Joe would have liked and enjoyed. Which is why, also, Joe's three favourite puppet friends will be cremated with him: Cookie Monster, Melissa the raccoon and Leglin the badger.

As many of you will know, Joe asked about death in the way any four- or five-year-old might, with enormous curiosity – and we let him guide us in what he thought it was. We encouraged a sort of general belief in reincarnation and continuity: that he could be anything he wanted to be when he died. He wanted to be a seagull, and later perhaps a dolphin, which might explain a rather nautical emphasis to these readings.

The first is from a wonderful book called *Amos and Boris*, which we used to read to Joe before he was ill, and then found very beautiful and comforting when Joe was first in St Stephen's Hospital. The story is of a mouse called Amos, who builds a boat and sets sail, and then, as this passage reveals, falls overboard . . .

One night, in a phosphorescent sea, he marveled at the sight of some whales spouting luminous water; and later, lying on the deck of his boat gazing at the immense, starry sky, the tiny mouse Amos, a little speck of a living thing in the vast living universe, felt thoroughly akin to it all. Overwhelmed by the beauty and mystery of everything, he rolled over and over and right off the deck of his boat and into the sea.

Amos nearly drowns but is rescued by a whale called Boris and they become the closest possible friends. Later, Boris the whale is washed ashore by a hurricane and Amos has a chance to save Boris's life – by having two huge elephants push Boris back into the water. This is how the book ends:

He [Boris] looked back at Amos on the elephant's head. Tears were rolling down the great whale's cheeks. The tiny mouse had tears in his eyes too. 'Goodbye, dear friend,' squeaked Amos. 'Goodbye, dear friend,' rumbled Boris, and he disappeared in the waves. They knew they might never meet again. They knew they would never forget each other.

The next passage is from *Henry and the Sea*, the book Joe and I wrote together, which is published this July and is based entirely on the fact that Joe used to talk to the sea and take the sea with him invisibly to St Stephen's. In the book, a small boy, Henry, befriends the Sea and the Sea magics itself into a paper cup to be with him. This creates all sorts of unexpected problems, and Henry convinces the Sea it has to go back . . .

'I'm going to miss you,' Henry said.

'I'll be here,' the Sea told him. 'You can come and see me every day, like you always did.'

'Yes,' said Henry.

'And even when you're not here, you can think of me,' the Sea went on. 'Promise me this, that every night when you lie in that splendid wooden bunk of yours, you'll imagine you are on a boat sailing around the world under the stars. No need to worry about where you're going,' the Sea said. 'I'll guide you.'

'All right,' said Henry.

Then a seagull overhead startled them with a cry, saying: 'Don't worry, Henry. I'll stay in your home instead of the Sea. I'll keep you company.'

Almost finally, I'd like to read one very short passage from a Winnie-the-Pooh story – in fact it's the very end of *The House at Pooh Corner*:

So they went off together. But wherever they go, and whatever happens to them on the way, in that enchanted place on top of the Forest a little boy and his Bear will always be playing.

And then, last of all, a (Pooh's) 'Hum' which Joe Buffalo wrote himself, and which I think is strikingly beautiful:

> *Tiddley pom*
> *I like TV*
> *Tiddley pom*
> *I like Calpol*
> *Tiddley pom*
> *I like light*
> *Tiddley pom*
> *I like having a bath*
> *Tiddley pom*
> *I like having a soggy*
> *Tiddley pom*

> *I like staying awake at*
> *night to sing to the stars*
> *Tiddley pom*
> *I like staying awake at*
> *night to tell stories to*
> *the stars*

Joe Buffalo was my best friend in the world. Now he's the best seagull in the world, and Mummy and Daddy are seagulls with him – we're here now and we're there with him too.

We love him.

The jacket of *Henry and the Sea*, illustrated by Teri Gower, published in July 1989 by Hamish Hamilton Children's Books

*A*NN For the few days between Joe's death and his funeral we felt fairly calm, we had to tidy up the house, think about getting refreshments for people attending the funeral, and just wind down. The physical effort of looking after Joe had become enormous: the constant adjusting of his position and h pillows; the waking in the night to give him a hug or make him comfortable; not sleeping properly anyway, because of anxiety.

When Joe died we were both exhausted, and the shock of his death was like a body-blow, completely debilitating. The first day, I didn't dare go out alone. I didn't think my legs would carry me, and my concentration was so poor that I wasn't sure I could cross the road safely. When I did go out, I found it was an enormous effort to walk down the road, and a surprise to see people getting on with their lives, as if nothing had happened; I felt isolated, part of another existence.

It seemed incongruous to hear people telling us that we were looking better, but it was probably true. The months of uncertainty had shown in our faces, we had looked drawn and tired all the time. But the tension had been in anticipation of what had now happened; there was nothing left to fear, so it had faded away. Later we had to deal with the prospect of life without Joe, which would bring new problems, but now we just felt empty, applying ourselves to the practicalities of Joe's death – a calm period before the grieving really began.

ALEX Sleeping with Ann on the night Joe died was both an extraordinary experience and quite numbing. We were back together in our own bed for the first time in over a month. We were sleeping together as a couple who had no child for the first time in five and a half years (more, if you count Ann's pregnancy, when we already felt like parents). We were also utterly exhausted, exhausted in a way I cannot explain. Maybe just tired of life.

I felt like an ex-parent. There was no one to call me 'Daddy' any more. I did not yet feel as bad as I had expected, but Joe Buffalo was still so close, and his death had had a kind of calm and beauty I had not expected. I say that, but I don't know how much I am trying to convince myself of that fact. It was also horrible, the worst experience imaginable. Perhaps I would have felt terrible if I had been dying and Joe had been in the room to say goodbye, but I would have preferred it that way round. A father or mother should not have to see their child die.

*

In the days after Joe's death, I dealt with my feelings in m
normal manner: by writing. I wrote compulsively. On the eve (
Joe's funeral, I sat down and wrote the words I would speak th
following day. At other times, I wrote anything and everything
could remember about Joe. I wanted to capture his remarkabl
character, but knew how impossible that was.

I started shaping an article about Joe, writing not simply fo
myself but for some imagined audience – perhaps *Granta*, th
literary magazine, which had recently run several pieces abou
cancer and death which I had found honest and helpful. I wante
the world to know about Joe Buffalo, and at the same time fel
guiltily that I was using the experience of Joe's death, trying t
fit it into the pattern of my life and work, as if it were somethin
I could absorb and control.

A week or so after his death, attempting to capture for thi
article the looming silence of the house and our sense of empt
ness, I wrote:

> I cannot hear his voice, so I write this. I can hear it in my
> head or on tape, but not in the house, where I want to hear
> it, not in the actuality of my life now, whatever that is. The
> house is awfully quiet: life is no longer punctuated by the
> endless stream of cartoon voices from the video, the more
> recent mantra of video games music and effects, the constant
> chatter of Joe Buffalo himself.
>
> . . . A favourite expression was 'Oh, boy!' Or he would look
> at us sternly and ask, 'Are you playing a joke on me?' One of
> the last things he said to his mother while I was writing
> upstairs, the night before he started to die, was, 'Tell Daddy
> I sure miss him.' I sure miss Joe; I miss his point of view, his
> company, his unique commentary on life.
>
> . . . Joe's life seems a full one in many respects; certainly it
> was full of love. I can listen to a tape of his voice and know
> that nothing I write comes close to capturing his spirit, his
> charm, his spontaneity, the immense gifts he gave to Ann
> and me during his life.
>
> We will always be with him, and him with us, but I wish I
> could hold his hand, feel responsible for his life, for attempt-
> ing to interpret the world to him, once more. He was just a

small animal who died. Which is all, in the end, any of us
can be.

finished the article and sent it to Charles. At the beginning of
'ebruary, Ann and I went away for a week to Morocco, for our
irst holiday in two years and the first trip we had taken without
Ioe in a lifetime – his lifetime. When we came back and opened
our mail, there was a letter from Charles's associate, Pat Kava-
nagh, telling me that the *Observer* wished to publish the article.
was thrilled. I did not know when the *Observer* would run the
piece, but hoped it would be soon. In fact, they held it until July
and the publication of Joe's children's book, *Henry and the Sea*,
when they gave it a full page in a section of the *Observer Review*
ronically titled *Living*.

A NN We cried so much in Marrakesh. It was an unfamiliar
place with no memories, deliberately chosen for its foreign-
ness, its distance from our normal life, as well as its cheapness.
But everything we did made us think of Joe. Every time we did
something new: rode in a horse-drawn cab, or saw a camel, or
watched the story-tellers in the square, we would think about
how Joe would have responded. It seemd as if we always had the
same thoughts. If I felt the tears coming I would look at Alexander and see that he was crying too.

One day we went to visit a village called Setti Fatma at the
foot of the Atlas mountains. It was cold there, and it was rain-
ing. A local guide, Ali, offered to take us on what we expected to
be an innocuous walk to see a waterfall, but we found ourselves
climbing rocks, making what was, for ill-prepared city-dwellers,
a quite hazardous climb. I was terrified. My fear of heights and
poor co-ordination were barely equal to the climb, and it was
only the fact that my fear of going back alone was as great as my
fear of going forward, that kept me moving. But when it was
over, there was that rush of euphoria that comes after crossing a
fear barrier. I had done something that scared me and survived.

I really felt as if something important had happened to me on
that trip to Setti Fatma. Maybe it was discovering that I hadn't,
after all, used up all my reserves of courage and energy. Going

back to the city I felt very calm, almost happy. Alex asked me if
was thinking of Joe. I was – some nebulous thought, just th
fact of him. I wondered how Alex had known, and he said, 'I jus
do.'

It seems as if we were very close then. I had been afraid of wha
would happen to us when Joe died. Though we had been throug
an intense period together, and been so united, a part of ou
emotional life had been on hold, the part that involves jus
being a couple. I was afraid that we wouldn't have a relationshi
any more, but it seemed that we could still talk to each othe
and find each other interesting.

I was afraid, too, about having more children. Our life didn
seem complete without a child, but I didn't feel ready to launch int
having a baby; physically and mentally I needed a rest. Ideall
another child would come much later, when our life had settle
and there was a new context for it. Now it might seem like a hurrie
replacement, second best to the son we'd lost. But at my age I ha
no time to waste, nor even the right to take it for granted that
could have a child. And that was the thing that frightened me mos

I wanted to think that there would be another child in my life
and I was sure Alex did too. The implications of not having on
were awful. Not only the emptiness of the future, the deprivatio
of the joy and love I'd experienced once before, but the fact tha
even if I couldn't have a child, Alex could, if he found a younge
partner. If that happened, how could I blame him? If he wante
children as much as I did, it would be the logical course. Th
generous thing would be to let him go. But how could I bea
losing him, or seeing him with a child that wasn't mine?

When you love an adult, it is rarely without some reservatior
however minor or unimportant. But when you love your child, i
is totally unqualified. I don't think any other love can touch th
power of that adoring, protective emotion. I miss loving Joe, an
I miss the love he gave me.

To lose an only child must be the most difficult thing in th
world. It isn't that I think the pain is any less if you have othe
children, but large families retain the shape of their lives. I
your only child dies, the whole structure of your life collapses.

When you have young children, you fantasize about having time to yourself: time to write, or think, or read, or work. When Joe died, we had nothing left but time, and it was worthless without him – if he wasn't there to interrupt us, or go home to, it had no value. For a long time I couldn't get used to the freedom, the fact that I didn't have to plan with Alex which of us would be out when, so that one of us was always with Joe. One afternoon when he was going out, a couple of weeks after Joe's death, I found myself reminding him that I had to leave at 5.00 p.m. Realizing that there was no need for him to be back before I left the house made me feel empty, not liberated.

There was nothing to get up for, and I had no energy anyway. The first few weeks I lay in bed reading all morning; probably I needed to rest and unwind, but mostly I couldn't face doing anything. When I went out, I still looked at toys and children's clothes. Gradually that stopped, it became less interesting and more painful. I feared I would end up as some mad old woman haunting children's departments. When I was in a strange place I would be checking for danger, the way a mother would: were the stairs safe, was the window secure, what was there to fall over, or hurt?

When I looked at the clock, I would think about what we would be doing if Joe were alive. Was it time for Linda to come, or would we be playing? I noticed when his favourite television programmes were on. Now I have stopped thinking in terms of his illness and try to imagine what we would be doing if Joe had stayed healthy. Getting ready for school, going to the beach or to play with friends. I miss the constant activity, being needed, having a focus to my life.

It is hard to think about him walking into a room, hard to think about him on his feet. When friends bring their children round now, children who had known Joe, I marvel at them walking downstairs, doing things for themselves, it is so long since I've had an able-bodied child. So I don't expect Joe to walk into a room, but I do wonder what it would have been like to have continued to have him in my life, my friend, my companion. Those wonderful conversations, his unique intelligence, walking down the road together, rushing to school at the last minute, watching the clock till it's time to collect him. If Joe had stayed healthy, I would have treasured the hours when he was at school. I would have been racing around trying to pack shopping or working or an exercise class into that time, but when it is infinite there's no pressure to do anything.

Before Joe died, I was worried about how I would react to other children when it happened. Would I resent my friends who still had healthy families, especially those with more than one child? I'm glad to find that I don't. I enjoy seeing Joe's friends, and I love the way they still talk about him. It will be strange to watch them grow up, and wonder how Joe would have kept pace with them, especially James Kerry and Vanessa, who were born in the same month. Ever since his birthday in August, we have been thinking of Joe as a six-year-old. At the moment it's still easy to imagine him growing, it's been such a short time; in a year or two, it will be more difficult.

ALEX I knew when Joe died that there were various things to look forward to which would, if not help me feel better, then at least distract me from the emptiness left by his death. In particular, there was the publication of *Henry and the Sea* in July, which I hoped would give Ann and me some sense of Joe continuing; and before that, in late March/early April, there was the publication both here and in America of *The War Zone*, which greatly excited me.

These were simply distractions, though, and I knew that they would not help me rebuild my life – our lives, Ann's and mine. They were certainly better than facing the total uncertainty and financial disaster of our lives in the period before Joe's cancer was diagnosed, but I would have happily traded the new sense of direction in my work for the life of my son.

In this period, the two or three months after Joe's death, I worried a little – though perhaps not as much as I had before Joe died – about what might happen to Ann and me as a couple. It was like starting all over again, and yet at the same time it wasn't. It was like going back to how life was before Joe was born, but with all the experiences and memories, the love and fun and arguments, of the intervening five and a half years.

In the weeks immediately after Joe's death, I felt an intense love towards Ann – a sense that we had been through something unique together, something outside the bounds of ordinary life, something that could never be shared with anyone. Our week's holiday in Marrakesh, which we had felt apprehensive about, was one of the most intimate and enjoyable we had ever had. We cried a great deal and our thoughts constantly returned to the last time we had travelled abroad with Joe – the weekend in Rome at the end of 1986 – but we also felt relaxed and happy and adventurous. Morocco was suitably alien, the city was beautiful, the mountains even more so, and we felt hopeful for the future.

Perhaps what worried me as much as our relationship was who I was now as an individual. I had lost my identity as a father, and I did not feel satisfied with anything else. I felt that I loved Ann, and that the years we had spent together had a depth and a power that I had only just begun to realize, but I was scared by the fact that we might not be able to have another child, and almost certainly could not have more than one.

I had more confidence in myself as a writer than ever before (though that did absolutely nothing to banish the fear each time I sat down to write that nothing would come), but writing was not enough.

Just before Joe was born, I had vowed to myself that I would never again let my career be the centre of my life. Since I had left school, I had felt that every moment of every day was directed in some way towards exploring what I was capable of creating in terms of work and finding ways of achieving those ends. I was about to become a father, and I determined that Ann and Joe would be the centre of my life – everything else would be secondary.

Now, without Joe, I felt lost. I had Ann, but it was as if I had to learn how to love her again – we had directed our tenderness so much towards Joe throughout his illness and before, that we had lost any identity as a couple. We had been a family, a threesome. Being two people together again somehow did not feel right.

*A*NN When this book was suggested to us about three months after Joe died, I said yes immediately. It was something to do, something I could write without doing any research. I thought most of it would be easy, I thought it would be cathartic, a good way to work through the worst parts, and a way to record it all while it was still fresh in my mind.

That was true at first, but it feels as if it has got harder and harder to write, to remember. When a chapter was finished, I would feel elated, but there was always another one to begin. I would hate the idea of sitting at my typewriter, having to get started again. I would prevaricate, want days off, I resented having a deadline, I wanted to write it at my own pace, but that would probably have meant never finishing, always flinching from the final part.

At the beginning, I was almost looking forward to writing about Joe's death. I thought I remembered it so clearly, that it would be easy, a relief, to write it all out. Now, nearly six months later, I have finally written it, trying to relive the emotions, completely failing to do them justice. It has been very difficult, and not very successful.

When Joe died, Alex advised me to write down my feelings, just to get them out of my system, because I might want to revisit them one day. But while he sat at his keyboard, writing and writing for days, I just sat downstairs, numb and completely unable to confront what I'd just been through. When Alex was writing he had no thought of publication, that came later, but now he has the advantage of drawing on that record, the freshness. I should have written about Joe's death as soon as we decided to do the book, it was very vivid then, but even though I knew I was going to have to do it, I couldn't face it right away, I had to work up to it, do it all in chronological order, that was the only way.

I thought that writing the book would be a way of working through my emotions. The first chapters did help. I had talked over my feelings of responsibility that Joe wasn't diagnosed earlier several times, with different people, and each time I had felt better for a while, but each time the sense of guilt had returned. Writing about it was more effective, I felt less burdened by it, and I felt at the beginning that maybe the whole book would be as cleansing.

But as it progressed, I began to feel myself being distanced from the entire experience. Every time I wrote Joe's name, I felt as if I were operating in the third person, on the outside, writing about some event I knew very well. Instead of being part of the mourning process, I began to feel the book carrying me away: the need to be objective, to think about construction, and worry about using the same adjectives over and over again; the necessity of trying to be readable when a really personal account would probably be repetitive and incoherent, unpublishable, a scream in print.

ALEX I felt enormously grateful to Charles when he first suggested writing this book in March 1989. I had made a fresh start on *Tribes* since Joe's death, feeling that I could not simply continue with it as though I were the same person as before; but it was proving difficult. I sat and thought about Joe so much; I wanted to write about him all the time. I tried to filter my emotions – my anger, the energy I felt, but also the despair – into the novel, but they did not fit. The thought of working through the whole experience of Joe's illness and death seemed like an excellent way of recovering some kind of clarity.

I also liked the idea of working with Ann. I felt we could create something unique together – we had shared the experience so completely, we both could write; perhaps we might produce something that in some way might help other families, especially those going through any similar kind of trauma.

I was especially keen to try and write about death; there are so few books that deal with the subject in any helpful way, and several friends had told me that when someone they loved had died and they had tried to find books which might help them understand what they were feeling, they had been directed to the 'occult' or 'religious books' sections of bookshops. Perhaps this book will end up similarly classified.

Above all, though, I wanted to write about Joe. The idea of a book which would communicate at least some small part of what a wonderful, funny, idiosyncratic, loving person he was appealed enormously. It would be a kind of immortality for him – though, in a sense, *Henry and the Sea* serves that purpose best.

Writing this book has been a different matter. Initially, Ann and I threw ourselves into it, finding a working pattern, a way of deciding what each would write about, when we would overlap, how to try and balance the medical detail with a picture of our life with Joe.

Soon, the strain began to show. We had started work at the beginning of May, but by June I was feeling increasingly anxious and hostile. With every day, I felt worse about Joe's death. Whereas initially I had floated on a sort of adrenalin high, convincing myself that I could cope with the loss, I realized as Joe's memory grew more distant that he wasn't coming back.

I kept telling myself that writing this book was therapeutic, which originally we had thought it would be, but forcing ourselves to confront the detail of Joe's cancer every day began to take its toll. Ann now not only had to cope with the book (and she had never written a book before), but with me, and I was becoming almost deliberately difficult to live with.

I resented everything. Perhaps I resented her strength; perhaps I simply resented Joe's death. I realized how much I wanted to change my life – how I hated the way that life seemed to go on without Joe almost exactly as it had before. One day, I washed up some cutlery and found myself staring at it, hating it, thinking: 'I was washing this fucking cutlery before Joe was born, and here it is, still in one piece, and he's been born and lived and died.'

I found that, with a few exceptions, I did not want to see our old friends. I wanted to escape from my old life – not yet from the memory of Joe himself, but from the world that had surrounded him. I had made some new friends among the students in Brighton, and what I wanted more than anything was to start a completely new life, which I began to realize did not include Ann. If I could have gone into the fire, phoenix-like, and emerged reborn, I would have done so.

A*NN* Even though we had survived so far, in the summer I still had the nagging feeling that I was on trial. Not in any judgemental way, but simply because, in a year or two, if it was obvious that I couldn't have a child, Alex might decide that he could not continue. I pictured us as a lonely couple, with a house full of photographs and mementoes, dwelling in the past because we didn't have an adequate present or future.

True, there was a lot happening in our lives professionally. I could try to pick up my writing career. Maybe I would finally have the time and impetus to write a novel. And Alex had so much going for him, two novels commissioned, and the satisfaction of seeing *The War Zone* and *Henry and the Sea* published.

When you don't have children, professional achievements are very important. When you have a family, they are still important, but they take on a different perspective: you want them to enrich your child's life somehow, add to your identity as a parent. For us, any accomplishment is going to seem hollow now, because indirectly everything we did had been for Joe, to support him, because he was there waiting for us. They had a value because we had something – Joe – even more valuable in our lives.

ALEX When we first outlined this book, Ann and I wanted an ending that would be honest and yet not too depressing. Obviously, we would deal with Joe's death, but we wanted to suggest a continuity, perhaps even some thought of happiness.

When Joe died, even as I lay still holding his hand, I thought about holding some sort of memorial on the Palace Pier, which was pretty much his favourite place in the world. Initially, I thought about organizing something that week, but lacked the energy and decided it would be more appropriate to hold some sort of party to commemorate Joe and celebrate the publication of *Henry and the Sea* when it came out in July.

Ann and I hoped that this might provide a suitably positive conclusion to this book. With help from Hamish Hamilton, and with the co-operation of the management of the Palace Pier and their publicist, Pamela Robinson, we held a party for family, friends and the press, to mark the publication of *Henry*.

It took place on Thursday, 13 July 1989. Ann's mother, Alice, and my parents came, as did friends from Brighton and London, many bringing their children – Joe's friends – with them. The *Observer* sent a photographer, having finally scheduled the piece I had written after Joe's death, to run the following Sunday. The afternoon was gloriously hot and sunny, the sea sparkled, seagulls flew overhead – it could not have been better.

Except that my relationship with Ann was suddenly under enormous pressure, imposed by me. It was as if I was cutting off from what should have been a moment of great intimacy, of great sorrow, but also of love. I seemed afraid to share my feelings with Ann and unwilling really to give space to hers.

You cannot control life, and while it would be nice to present the party on the pier as the end of this book, it does not feel right. It is now October 1989, and our lives have gone on. The past two months of writing this have been unbelievably painful and, it seems to us, destructive.

Perhaps we should not have started it, but perhaps what we have been through has been no more than a forced period of grieving. We have had to confront thoughts and feelings head-long, when we might have preferred to tackle them more gently and over a longer period of time, but I do not believe we could have avoided them indefinitely.

Any parent who goes through the experience of losing a child faces some of the most difficult and painful adjustments life can demand. The natural order is turned on its head. Your child is your future; from the moment your child is born, unless you are totally delinquent as a parent, you cannot help but take it into account when you think about what lies ahead.

If your child dies, you lose the future. You certainly lose the future you might have shared; and you may feel that you have lost everything – which is how we have felt for much of the time since Joe died.

I look at pictures of him and imagine how he might have grown. He would be six now, and I find I think of him as being six; perhaps he will grow up in my thoughts as he would have in real life? One photograph of him in particular makes me feel very sad: it hangs on my workroom wall and shows him, aged three, clutching a football in Hyde Park. It is such a corny thought, but I so wanted to be a father playing football with my son as he grew up. I am not even very good at football.

He used to come everywhere with me, and I miss that so badly. I loved driving with him in the car, just the two of us together, chatting. When he was first ill, I missed swimming with him worst of all. Now I have almost forgotten what it was like, and that frightens me. Worst of all, I miss being able to hug him. If I had had a bad day or was simply feeling low, if I had had an argument with someone or was anxious about our lack of income, one hug from Joe would put everything in perspective. One hug from Joe made me feel alive.

I am scared of forgetting him, and yet know that I won't. I have to let go of him, and I know I have started that process, but it hurts. I don't want to live in the past, I want to discover a future that is alive for me, but at the moment I feel caught in-between.

Back in June, I asked Jane Roderic-Evans if she would help me find a psychotherapist. I was feeling worse about Joe's death, not better, with every day, and I thought it would help. I was very fortunate and was referred to a therapist, Dr Philip Dodgson, who has helped me cope both with myself and with writing this book, and who has shown enormous friendship and sympathy.

He has helped me confront the loss of meaning that Joe's death has created for me. Joe's life was the happiest, most fulfilled period of my life, and in a sense this applies most of all to the two years of Joe's illness. I had never before experienced such a clear sense of purpose – that I was here to help Joe be happy, to love him and Ann, and to care for him. Now I miss that purpose almost as much as I miss Joe.

At the moment, the only identity I want for myself is as a father. I cannot wait to be a father again, and yet I feel so confused over my feelings towards Ann. The desire to turn my back on the past – our past – and start clean is strong, though I recognize that this may be a stage of grieving in itself. I am frightened by the thought of our having another child together, because I am frightened by the thought of all the echoes it would produce.

I loved every part of Ann's pregnancy and Joe's birth and life, but find myself disturbed by the idea of repeating it in any way. It is not that I believe we would try to turn another child into a replacement of Joe – if anything, we would probably try too hard not to – but that I fear the experience would somehow be second best. The thought of having a child at some point in the future with someone else does not, at the moment, create such fears, though obviously I would always have echoes of Joe even if another partner would not.

I feel uncomfortable about exposing such private thoughts in public, and hope that my only motive for doing so is the wish to share my understanding of why so many couples break up during the serious illness of their child or following their child's death. Ann's and my future is unresolved and of importance only to us; the emotions we have been experiencing, however, are a part of what we have been through together and have tried to deal with in this book.

ANN Though I had anticipated problems for us originally, I was not prepared for them when they came. I had considered them, but I thought I had more time.

I still don't really understand what made Alex change. One day we were cautiously happy, the next it had fallen apart. I have a desire to retreat into our relationship, to lean on what we have left, the love and the memories, and try to enjoy whatever positive might come of the future.

Losing Joe doesn't make me love Alex less, but now I have got to try to understand that he doesn't feel the same. That for him our life together is intolerable without Joe, and that even if we did have another child it would seem like a grotesque re-enactment of our time with him, that it would seem like memories come to life, a charade, that it would all be unreal and unbearable. I don't especially want to live in the past, but I do want to know that it's there, and that we can share it and remember it, in a way we couldn't with anybody else. But Alex doesn't feel like that, he wants to cut it off, throw it away, to be on his own, or start again with someone else. He doesn't want me, not because I'm getting older, although I am, but because I'm just a reminder now, a relic, the way Melissa would have been if she'd been left behind.

I wish I could get more angry about it. I am angry at fate for taking away my child, and then taking away the little bit I still had left, the part I might have rebuilt on. But I don't see how I can stop Alex needing to run away from the past. I think if he

knew how to escape these feelings, he would. I can even understand how he feels. I understand it, but I don't like it, and I don't
share it.

*A*LEX The biggest question that can never be answered
in terms of our care of Joe is whether we prepared him
adequately for death. I tried, at various times, to tell him –
particularly when we thought he might be starting school – that
other people might have different attitudes to his cancer, that
they might tell him he would die. He seemed to want to change
the subject, just as he wanted to change the subject when he was
first paralysed and we asked him if he was worried about not
being able to use his legs. He always seemed comfortable talking
about dying in terms of becoming a seagull or a dolphin, and
when he started to die, we felt comfortable using that language.

I cannot be sure now that we should not have said to him
bluntly, 'Joe, you may die quite soon. This illness may kill you.' I
could never find those words, and I doubt that if I had to repeat
the experience, I would find them then. Ann and I always
followed our instincts, and would follow them again.

This applies also to our behaviour in the last months of Joe's life:
we became increasingly angry and demanding parents, but I feel
our anger and insistence on our wishes being heeded were totally
justifiable. I know that as Joe's condition declined in November
and December 1988, I vowed that if we had to experience the pain
of Joe's death, it would be on our terms and not surrounded by
people we didn't wish to be with. We did not plan for Joe's death to
happen at home, but we are very glad that it did. We particularly
did not want it to happen at the Royal Alexandra, where we no
longer felt comfortable. The death of a child, if it has to happen,
should be as beautiful and magical as it can be – and it should take
place wherever the child and parents feel most comfortable.

*A*NN Everything I have written in this book is as true to
chronology, the facts and my emotions as possible. I have
tried to give some idea of what it is like to be a mother in this
situation. Before we began, we thought we might produce a

book that was some kind of handbook on how parents might cope with hospitals in the case of a long illness. In the end, there is no overt advice, though there are conclusions to be drawn.

I have only ever had one child, and that does not make me any kind of an expert on child-rearing. But it did make me an expert on what was emotionally right for my son. If it seems that Alex and I were difficult or demanding or unreasonable, it was always in pursuit of what we believed was best for him. Doctors talk about the management of a patient's illness, an unfortunate word more reminiscent of the factory floor than human life. Let them manage the sickness by all means, but parents must be allowed to manage the quality of their own children's lives.

I feel as if writing the book has suspended my grief. Instead of being able to let my feelings evolve naturally, I have been constantly looking back – not at the things I want to remember, but at what is relevant to the chapter I have been working on. I don't want to reject the miserable times, but I would like to choose when I have to think about them. I feel as if I am losing the lovely little details of Joe's life, the things he used to say and do, in trying to retain the broader generalities of his illness.

It is hateful to write about the periods when Joe was in pain and remember the fear and desperation we felt. Some of the worst times have been writing about the people we criticized. We haven't mentioned every little pinprick or irritation – very few considering how many people we have had to deal with – but it would be misleading to pretend that all our encounters were easy; they have been part of the experience. And having to recall those incidents, trying to separate my emotions from what actually happened, trying to be fair, has been distressing.

But now I can go back to just drifting, maybe that's what I should have done all along. I can let my memories free again, and see what comes to mind, let my instincts decide how to grieve.

And maybe finishing the book will help lessen the tension with Alex. Though it started harmoniously and helpfully, our individual reactions to writing it have contributed to the friction between us. His inability to be generous with me during the writing of the second half of this book has made it doubly difficult: his constant mode of criticizing my presentation, or my punctuation, or finding practical faults with my work, and not bothering to tell me until days later that he liked what I had written; the way he frequently sabotaged my will to work by disappearing without explanation for many hours, so that my insecurity and mistrust and misery built to the point where I couldn't write. These are the emotions that I produced, it is true, but it's the suspicion that he knows how to exploit them that nags.

It hasn't just been the writing of the book that has stopped my grieving process, it has been Alex's treatment of me too. Having to deal with the disruption of my life, when it has already fallen apart with Joe's death, has made me concentrate on the present too much – on thinking about what mood Alex is in today, if he's going to be civil to me, or show affection, or be hostile and critical. There have been periods when we've been almost happy and relaxed together, accepting that we are going to part, as if we've reached a new understanding. But they have always been followed by a backlash of aggression from Alex, in case I got too confident.

Alex's feelings may moderate now the book is finished, though ironically it was only the impossibility of writing it unless we were living together that has kept him from leaving so far. He may not feel so intensely now it is done, but I think he will still go soon. He needs to be alone to work out his feelings. Maybe he will decide to come back eventually, although I doubt it. I have to decide if I would want him back. Joe's death hasn't made me reject Alex, but I think his behaviour towards me finally has. And it's all part of the same process in the end.

All the time we have been finishing this book, I have been hoping that things will work out for us eventually, though I think it may take a very long time. But trying to sum up some thoughts for this final chapter, I see the hopelessness of it. Just as writing about the hopes we had for Joe's recovery exposes them as desperate and unfounded, even pathetic sometimes, so I see myself approaching Alex and his changing feelings in the same way. A couple of weeks ago, we finally removed all Joe's remaining toys from the basement, and painted over the Snoopy birthday mural. We had at last managed that part of saying goodbye. Now I think it is just a question of finding the right moment with Alex, the moment when I cannot only face it but accept it.

I don't know where we will be this time next year. Probably not together, but probably friends. This time now is the worst part, I think, and the next few months. It's just a question of assimilation, like everything else, just a matter of being given time.

ALEX I will not explore here fully the anger I still feel at Joe's death, because I do not think it can be explained away – only experienced. I know that it is common to bereaved parents, and imagine that it may be very disturbing to some, but I also know that it is too easy to attribute everything to one cause, when my anger may have other roots as well. Joe's death has undoubtedly exposed inadequacies and frustrations and a huge degree of selfishness in my life; it has made me want to reassess myself.

If this book suggests an ability on our part to impose a shape to our emotions or exercise some control, it is just that: an illusion. Our feelings are still chaotic and painful, though not always tempestuous – sorrow can be very quiet, almost peaceful, at times.

But there are also times when I would like a padded room in which to throw myself against the walls, in which I could scream unselfconsciously. I feel a need to exorcise the pain physically, to work it out of me in a sweat. Elisabeth Kübler-Ross, an American psychiatrist who has spent much of her life working with dying children and their families, and who has written excellent, uniquely helpful books such as *On Death and Dying* and *On Children and Death*, believes that every hospital should have such a padded room where not only parents but also the medical staff could go to deal with their feelings about death.

And it is certainly death that is behind my anger. Not simply Joe's death – though that is enough – but the fact that there is no way of thinking about his without thinking also of my own.

I thought I was comfortable with death. Before Joe was born, I had always been interested in it in a way that I now recognize was rather abstract – it seemed sufficiently distant to contemplate without distress, rather like a beautiful but fiery star in the night sky. Shortly before Joe's birth, while I was in Maine, I had my first physical premonition of it, as I have mentioned, swimming in a lake one evening. I felt it was something I could accept when it came, but was in no hurry to do so.

I am in no hurry now, but I realize that Joe's death has exposed both my fear and my fascination with death. My anger is that I cannot control it, just as I cannot control life. I wanted Joe to live so much, that at times I elevated my part in a natural process to a god-like role: I felt it was almost a personal battle between death and me.

Now I find that I am far too conscious of death. I have become obsessed with age and with ageing; I look at people – even teenagers – and see a shadow of what time will do to them. In my darkest moments, I feel as if I am just waiting to tick people off as they die – an unhealthy state of mind at thirty-four, or at any other age. My parents are still alive, but I know that will not always be so, and that thought terrifies me. At the moment, though, I seem to show my love for them, and for Ann and the people I am closest to, only as hostility and resentment. I feel angry with the world for taking Joe Buffalo, and yet the people I punish are the ones I love the most.

I am afraid of dying, and intrigued by it. At my worst, I am a scared little boy. I try to hide it with a sort of bravado – a sense that I can look death in the eye and not flinch. Joe's death was peaceful and beautiful and horrible; it took away some of my fear of the physical act of dying – I had never been in the presence of a dead person before, let alone seen someone die – but it could not immediately diminish my fear of ceasing to exist.

I am afraid of pain and of not-being, but somehow I feel that Joe's death will ultimately help me grow stronger. I cannot believe, having held his hand as he died, that his life had no meaning. This book is part of Ann's and my attempt to give it meaning, but the meaning Joe truly had was personal and unique to him: he enriched everyone he came in contact with, as we all do, even at our most negative. He taught me to love; I may temporarily not be very good at it, but I hope that I will be again.

*

Two days ago, listening to a tape of Joe and me playing a video game called *Ice Climber* on Christmas Day 1988, two weeks before his death, I came across a brief exchange of dialogue which seemed, somehow, both significant and reassuring. During Joe's illness, Ann and I were always finding meaning in the smallest details of life with him, and particularly in the video games – which so often involved reaching a higher level, or even, in the case of *The Legend of Zelda*, gaining extra life-force.

I would like this to stand as the ending of the book because, in its own small way, it is like our parting from Joe. I feel guilty that he had to go into death alone; I wish we could have accompanied him, to protect him in the way any parent would. But perhaps also I hope that he has gone somewhere more wonderful, more extraordinary, ahead of me; perhaps there is some small element of envy.

Joe was happy; his character in *Ice Climber* had just reached one of the highest points possible of the ice mountain it had to climb. We each had independent control of a character. As mine tried to follow Joe's, it fell off the screen. Joe was up there alone.

JOE: [excited] I never thought we would make it all the way up
       here, Dad!
ALEX: [as his video game character falls off the screen] Aah! Oh
       well, you're on your own, kid!

Acknowledgements

We would like to thank the many people who helped and supported us while Joe was ill:

Charles Walker, whose idea this book was – our agent but, more importantly, our friend throughout Joe's illness. Christopher Sinclair-Stephenson, who agreed to publish the book, and Peter Straus, our editor at Hamish Hamilton, who continued to encourage us when Christopher left.

Thanks to our parents and all our family, who lived through this experience too. Especially Lynne Hayes, for showing us that the human spirit can overcome the worst setbacks, and her husband, Peter, for proving that love and moral support are as valuable as medical expertise. Their example strengthened our hope that sheer will-power might effect a cure.

We can never adequately thank the two people who were closest to us as Joe's death approached: Linda Williams, Joe's best friend, who helped him achieve the miracle of walking again, and shared our irrational hopes; and Beryl Ruston, for her presence and protection, and for making it possible for Joe to die at home. Their love and friendship exceeded all professional demands.

We owe an enormous debt to the many doctors and nurses who cared for Joe. Sometimes we knew only their surnames or their first names; we hope they recognize themselves and remember the many ways in which they helped.

At St Stephen's:
Dr Leonard Sinclair, Dr Bob Phillips, Professor Wastell, Mr Peter Cox, Dr Harris, Dr Lilias Lamont.

Also all the house officers who showed an interest in Joe, especially Dr Lucy Moore, for her swift diagnosis of cancer; Dr Mary Judge, for her unfailing sympathy and honesty, and her interpretations of medical jargon; and Dr Simon Horsely, the only one who wouldn't take any shit from our son.

The other house officers: Leon, Kathy, Anna, Henry, Mike, and Lindsey Corrie. All the X-ray and ultrasound staff, for their patience with an apprehensive child. The many nurses and student nurses, too many to name, but including: Sharon Doughty, Linda Martin, Toni Raji, Nisha Shah, Sharon Bell, Carole Middleton, Angie Isaacs, Karen Addison, Fiona Gray (who also knitted a most wonderful buffalo sweater), Jane, and Sister Young. Equal thanks to the play-workers, Anna Whitsun and Grahame, who made being in hospital as much fun as possible; and to the domestics, porters and ambulancemen, for their kindness.

At Charing Cross:
Mr Peter Richards and Mr Howard; Mrs Beevis and Lorraine, the physio-therapists; and Hannah, the playworker.

In Brighton:
Dr Chris Reid, Dr Rodriguez, Staff Nurse Karen Bravery. Sister Sharp, Judy the physiotherapist, Anne Little, the community paediatric nurse, and Geoff Dubeau and Derek Vidler, the porters who wheeled Joe's bed through the streets. Also our GP, Dr Jane Roderic-Evans, for her unfailing support and encouragement and her colleague Dr Paul Gayton, for his concern. And Dr Philip Dodgson, for the sympathy and guidance he has given Alexander since Joe's death,

At Hammersmith and Queen Charlotte's Hospital:
Mr Christopher Wood, for letting us continue to hope; and his secretary, Carol Wilson.

We are grateful to our many friends. Some of the following have helped in tangible ways with favours, or presents for Joe; some have made a difference, possibly without even knowing, by some well-timed word or action, or just by keeping in touch. The prayers of others have been appreciated, even by two unbelievers, as a gesture of positive thought:

Teri Gower, for her constant presence and the love she put into her drawings for *Henry and the Sea*; Annette Motley, for her optimism, and for giving Joe his friends Melissa and Leglin; Christine Hampson and Betty Logan, for their advice and concern, and for discovering the Magic Potion; Harry Hampson; Mary Norman, who once found the time to send us flowers even though she was in labour; Spike Denton and Neville, for morale-boosting: Gloria Satta, in Rome, for asking the Pope to write to Joe; Nigel Andrews, for his loyalty; Harlan Kennedy; the Hoyt family, Gus, Vi, Cherie and Bonnie; the Gervais family, Dini, Jerry, Jessie, Beth and Johanna; Susan Ruskin, Tom Ramirez and Hall who helped us relax and reflect in the midst of writing this book; Karen Eisenstadt, who showed such friendship and hospitality soon after Joe's death; Yasmin de Sousa, Lindy and Bob Storer, Sarah Radclyffe, Lynda Myles, Doe Czernay, Rosemary Reid and Philip Pope, Nicolas and Theresa Roeg, Clayton Beerman, Frances Lynne, Michael and Claire Ryan, Mozafar Aminian, Sevilla Delofski, Bob and Anna Scott, David and Montserat Joy, Liz and Francesco Camisa, Sue Blackmore, Denise and Yves Barre; Rosemary Davies at the BBC, for making sure Joe saw the last episode of a favourite cartoon series; Father Stephen of Our Lady of Dolours, Fulham; Suzanne, Pamela Robinson, and all the staff at the Palace Pier, Brighton; Mr Alex Wishart; Dr Jacobs; Matthew Manning and Phil Edwardes, for always being hopeful, but never misleading us; Alan Wright and Natalie Nortcliffe, Joe's Father Christmas and his helper; Gray Jolliffe, for permission to reproduce Joe's birth announcement card; Kim and Phil Ryan, for making us so welcome when we moved to Brighton; Jenny and Hugh Clench, Rosemary Machin, Stevie and Denny, Louise Bartlett, Hugo Martin; the staff of the Hard Rock Café, London; and all the taxi drivers who refused to charge a fare while Joe was ill.

Thanks, too, to Anthony Burgess, for the incredible boost his letter gave us, and for permission to reproduce it here; and to Professor Stephen W. Hawking, whose book *A Brief History Of Time* was strangely comforting in its account of a physicist's search for understanding, and whose own battle against motor neuron disease was inspiring.

And, especially, we thank the children who were Joe's friends, who kept in touch and always made him feel he was one of the gang – and who still talk about him: Daniel Machin, James Kerry, Alice Norman and Sam Murphy, Statten and Max Roeg, Katy and Tom Storer, James Ryan, Sebastian Barre, Vanessa Austin-Locke, Christopher Excell, Sandy Armour Ryan, Benjamin and Naomi Clench.

Most of all, we thank our son, Joe Buffalo Stuart, whose courage and good spirits were the source of our strength throughout his illness. We miss him every day. The best part of our lives was over much too soon.

Ann Totterdell and Alexander Stuart
Brighton, November 1989